God Never Meant for Us to Die

God Never Meant for Us to Die

The Emergence of Evil in the Light of the Genesis Creation Account

PIERRE GILBERT

WIPF & STOCK · Eugene, Oregon

GOD NEVER MEANT FOR US TO DIE
The Emergence of Evil in the Light of the Genesis Creation Account

Copyright © 2020 Pierre Gilbert. All rights reserved. Except for brief quotations in critical publications or reviews, no part of this book may be reproduced in any manner without prior written permission from the publisher. Write: Permissions, Wipf and Stock Publishers, 199 W. 8th Ave., Suite 3, Eugene, OR 97401.

Wipf & Stock
An Imprint of Wipf and Stock Publishers
199 W. 8th Ave., Suite 3
Eugene, OR 97401

www.wipfandstock.com

PAPERBACK ISBN: 978-1-5326-9962-7
HARDCOVER ISBN: 978-1-5326-9963-4
EBOOK ISBN: 978-1-5326-9964-1

Manufactured in the U.S.A.　04/15/20

To my children, Rachel, Stephen, Pierre James, and his wife, Myra, and to my grand children, Valerie and Matthew. May they always live in the radiance of the love and the power of the living God and his Son.

Contents

Acknowledgments		ix
Abbreviations		xi
Introduction		xiii
1	Making Sense of Pain, Death, and Evil	1
2	The Creation Story: Myth or History?	28
3	God's Purpose: A Special Kind of Creature	47
4	Life and Death: The World as We Experience It	79
5	A New Equation to Resolve	110
6	Parsing Out a Biblical Theology of Evil	130
Conclusion		162
Epilogue: Hope		184
Bibliography		197

Acknowledgments

THERE ARE SO MANY books being published these days that we forget how much work is required just to produce one. Books do not just fall out of the sky. They often require years of research to complete. But that's not all. The publication of a major work requires the encouragement and support of family, friends, and colleagues.

In this respect, I must first thank my wife, Monika. Her keen and resolute interest in being a dialogue partner over the years played no little role in helping me hone many of the ideas I develop in this book.

I wish to acknowledge the contribution of Pastor Travis Reimer for reading the early version of this book. His assistance, detailed suggestions, and thoughtful critiques were invaluable.

I owe a great debt of gratitude to my old friend, Glenn Smith, who, on short notice, volunteered to read the near-final version of the manuscript. His judicious and insightful observations were most beneficial.

I am particularly thankful for all the students who, over the years, took my course on the problem of evil. Their willingness to engage this most significant human dilemma was inspiring, stimulating, and challenging.

I am deeply grateful to Canadian Mennonite University and MB Seminary for granting me two six-month sabbatical leaves to focus on this project. Without the support of these institutions, it is doubtful this book would have ever seen the light of day.

To God be the glory.

Abbreviations

ABD	*The Anchor Bible Dictionary.* 6 vols. Edited by David Noel Freedman. New York: Doubleday, 1992.
ANET	*Ancient Near Eastern Texts Relating to the Old Testament.* 3rd ed. Edited by James B. Pritchard. Princeton: Princeton University Press, 1969.
BDB	Francis Brown, S. R. Driver, and Charles A. Briggs. *Hebrew and English Lexicon of the Old Testament.* Oxford: Clarendon, 1909.
CGR	*Conrad Grebel Review*
EQ	*The Evangelical Quarterly*
ET	*Expository Times*
GDT	*Global Dictionary of Theology.* Edited by William A. Dyrness and Veli-Matti Kärkkäinen. Downers Grove: IVP Academic, 2008.
GKC	*Gesenius' Hebrew Grammar.* Edited by E. Kautzsch. Translated by A. E. Cowley. 2nd ed. Oxford, 1910.
JBL	*Journal of Biblical Literature*
JNES	*Journal of Near Eastern Studies*
JSOTS	*Journal for the Study of the Old Testament, Supplement Series*
NIDOTTE	*New International Dictionary of Old Testament Theology and Exegesis.* 5 vols. Edited by Willem A. VanGemeren. Grand Rapids: Zondervan, 1996.
NTS	*New Testament Studies*

STJ	*Stulos Theological Journal*
TB	*Tyndale Bulletin*
TDNT	*Theological Dictionary of the New Testament*. 10 vols. Edited by Gerhard Kittle and Gerhard Friedrich. Translated by Geoffrey W. Bromiley. Grand Rapids: Eerdmans, 1964–76.
TWOT	*Theological Wordbook of the Old Testament*. 2 vols. Edited by R. Laird Harris, Gleason L. Archer, and Bruce K. Waltke. Chicago: Moody, 1980.
TSF	*Theological Students Fellowship Bulletin*
VT	*Vetus Testamentum*
WTJ	*Westminster Theological Journal*

Introduction

As anyone who has ever written a substantive paper, a thesis, or a book knows, the last step in the completion of the project often turns out to be the introduction. No exception here. One would think that the introduction to a book on such an ominous topic would be characterized by a special kind of somberness and a keen sense of the tragic character of life. And for good reason. Evil, pain, and suffering are as intrinsic to human experience as cream in coffee. There is literally no end to the list of tragedies men and women experience. If illness, aging, and natural disasters were not enough to make our lives miserable, we also must take into account the phenomenal capacity some people have to turn the manageable vagaries of life into tragedies. Not a pretty picture all around. Even when life is relatively good and uneventful, the internet has now given us the terrible gift of ubiquity: there isn't a disaster or a mass murder that goes unreported within five minutes of it occurring.

Some people might counter that the cyberspace ubiquity with which we have been blessed or cursed, depending on how one looks at it, needs to be put in perspective by a longer view of history. Sometimes, there is nothing like a little history to put everything into a better perspective. In this case, I'm afraid history is not going to be of much help. In preparation for another book, I spent several months reading in the field of military history. At the end of this journey, I arrived at the tragic and inescapable conclusion that to study human history is to study the history of war. War and violence percolate through the centuries like lava in an active volcano.

To be human is to be condemned to live with the constant threat of suffering, misery, and death. At this point, I could, as is customary in books that deal with this topic, include two or three tragic stories to illustrate the depth of human suffering. But to be honest, I hesitate to adopt this well-worn path. First, I'm not convinced that to begin with a litany of such stories will add to most readers' awareness of the human condition. Second, as pervasive as suffering might be, it is not the whole story.

After investing so much time and energy in this project, I was surprised to rediscover a wonderful truth about human existence. That there is a problem of evil is unquestionable. But perhaps the real question is not why there is so much evil, but why there is any good at all. I'm not talking about minuscule samples of good peppered here and there like rare specks of gold in an abandoned mine. Human experience is full of good, joy, and happiness. As C. S. Lewis observes, "The settled happiness and security which we all desire, God withholds from us by the very nature of the world: but joy, pleasure, and merriment, He has scattered broadcast. We are never safe, but we have plenty of fun, and some ecstasy."[1] Take little children. Unless they are abused or mired in dire circumstances, children everywhere are happy and delight in life. Little boys and girls laugh at the merest pretext: the sight of a wiener dog, an unusual sound, a funny word, a hiccup, even a facial contortion can send a toddler reeling with delight and uncontrollable laughter. As G. K. Chesterton notes, to a three-year-old, mere life is an endless cascade of wonders:

> This is proved by the fact that when we are very young children we do not need fairy tales: we only need tales. Mere life is interesting enough. A child of seven is excited by being told that Tommy opened a door and saw a dragon. But a child of three is excited by being told that Tommy opened a door.[2]

Those who spend too much time reading and writing about evil may, through sheer overexposure, become convinced that suffering encompasses all of life. If no one can deny the tragic character of human life, neither can we deny the reality of so much joy that unexpectedly comes our way as we journey through life. That there should be so much joy and happiness despite the ever-looming presence of evil is perhaps the real question that should be addressed. But unless we are prodded to focus on that enigma, we will not, for it is the presence of evil that stops us in our tracks.

The reality of evil trips us up for two reasons. First, as Lewis explains so clearly in *The Problem of Pain*, evil ultimately manifests itself as pain. There is nothing theoretical about embodied evil; it is abrasively and oppressively real. To be caught in the jaws of evil is to be caught in a vice-grip

---

1. Lewis, *Problem of Pain*, 116.
2. Chesterton, *Orthodoxy*, 51.

that urgently and intensely commands our attention. Second, if we are powerless to avoid staring at evil, it is because we intuitively sense that there is something unnatural about it.

We may not be able to formulate a universal definition of evil, but we can all agree on one thing: evil exists, and it *ought* not to. We feel and know that something is not as it should. If evil were only something we observed in the universe, surely, we could deal with it. But this feeling that something is not right. This brokenness that imposes itself to every man and woman is not just out there; it's inside our very self. It is something we cannot escape and are powerless to fix. If this wrongness was entirely normal, the natural outcome of a long evolutionary process, we would not spend one instant pondering it. I don't think we would notice it. But something deep within us is amiss. It's as if we are no longer what we once were. Christian tradition refers to this sense of loss as the fall. Chesterton's description of this aberration is as insightful as anything ever written about it:

> And to the question, "What is meant by the Fall?" I could answer with complete sincerity, "That whatever I am, I am not myself. This is the prime paradox of our religion; something that we have never in any full sense known, is not only better than ourselves, but even more natural to us than ourselves.[3]

If evil is not congenial to who we are, where does it come from and why do we find it in the deepest recesses of the human soul, as if fused to our very DNA? While our society has become exceedingly proficient at depicting evil, it has also become proportionately inept at explaining why the world is as it is. Why does evil, in all its perverse "glory," rise up, like some ghoulish phoenix, in every new generation? Is this a learned behavior that is somehow transmitted through an intractable socialization process we are not fully aware of? If that is the case, why can't we identify these mechanisms and use our formidable scientific knowledge to eliminate evil from human history once and for all?

But deep down we know better. Evil is not some alien entity that surreptitiously emerges out of thin air to invade our souls. It's much more serious and terrifying than that. Jesus aptly said it in Matthew 15:19, "For out of the heart come evil intentions, murder, adultery, fornication, theft, false witness, slander."[4] This may well be the clearest assessment of evil ever uttered. In our most lucid moments, we have no choice but to admit, even if reluctantly so, that Jesus was right. Evil nests in our innermost being!

---

3. Chesterton, *Orthodoxy*, 167.

4 Unless otherwise noted, all Scripture quotations are taken from the New Revised Standard Version © 1989.

For believers, this reality represents the most ferocious assault on the Christian faith and gives rise to a seemingly inextricable dilemma: how can a good, loving, and omnipotent God allow evil and suffering to plague the lives of his creatures. This is the question I will relentlessly pursue in the pages of this book.

At this point, a brief orientation may be helpful. American philosopher Susan Neiman has rightly observed that the emergence of evil is the most important philosophical problem humans face. And yet, despite the tsunami of attention the issue has received throughout history, the explanations offered to account for human suffering fall into two major camps. In the one instance, evil is viewed as eternal and necessary, rooted in the very person of God (or the gods) or the very fabric of reality. The other way to frame evil is to negate its intrinsic reality, as witnessed, for instance, in pantheistic systems, where the distinction between good and evil essentially collapses.

There is almost a universal resignation (a capitulation?) to the idea that evil is an unavoidable and necessary component of human existence. Somewhat surprisingly, Christian tradition has also failed to offer a truly distinct perspective on evil. Augustine, a giant whose footprint looms large on the theological landscape, postulated that all instances of evil have purpose and will eventually be woven into a greater whole that will attribute significance to everything, even the most revolting acts of human cruelty. For his part, the second-century bishop Irenaeus of Lyons posited that God designed the world as we know it as a "sphere of soul-making."[5] Most theologians, philosophers, pastors, and ordinary Christians comfortably live between these two poles.

If these views are correct, then evil must ultimately be defined as a good, an indispensable element of reality. This position may not at first sight seem problematic to some, but it entails two inescapable difficulties, the first theological and the other pastoral. Theologically, such an outlook effectively limits the goodness and power of God, for any pronouncement in that respect is qualified and undermined by the notion that God could not bring about the completion of his project for humanity without the introduction of evil in the creation process. On the human side, Christians who experience tragedy will either face a crisis of faith fueled by a lack of confidence in God's power and goodness, or they will frantically search for the key that unlocks the mystery of divine purpose as it pertains to their specific circumstances.

---

5. Hick, *Evil and the God of Love*, 372.

This book represents a response to the problem of evil that affirms the absolute goodness and power of God, as well as evil's irredeemable nature. The originality of my approach lies in framing the reality of evil in the light of God's original design for humanity, as formulated in Genesis 1:26–28, and a more precise assessment of the purpose and the implications of the injunction against eating of the "tree of the knowledge of good and evil" in Genesis 2:15–17.

At the core of my thesis is the conviction that God never intended for humans to experience suffering and death, and that evil never was an inevitable component of God's original plan for humanity. I begin with the assumption that the Genesis creation account was intended to function as a theodicy, i.e., a text expressly written to exonerate God from all responsibility for the presence of moral evil. I demonstrate that the narrative argues against any form of divine determinism and strictly ascribes the emergence of evil to human agency.

The major benefits of this study are twofold. First, it creates a credible scenario in which God bears no moral responsibility for the deployment of evil in the world, thus removing one of the major stumbling blocks to belief and trust in God. Second, it serves to rehabilitate the credibility of the creation narrative as the most coherent explanation for the emergence of evil in human history.

The book ends with a reflection on the profound and overwhelming hope that the Christian faith offers to those who commit their lives to Jesus Christ. The hope of the resurrection encompasses all dimensions of human life: the need for justice, the human yearning for a permanent home, psychological healing without the loss of personal identity, and eternal life as perfect and free creatures living forever in joyful fellowship with the living God and the myriads of men and women who will populate the New World.

Before embarking on this exploration of what is undoubtedly the most difficult question all men and women face, the reader may do well to consider G. K. Chesterton's most judicious reminder of what Christianity declares to be most fundamental about human experience.

> The mass of men have been forced to be gay about the little things, but sad about the big ones. Nevertheless (I offer my last dogma defiantly) it is not native to man to be so. Man is more himself, man is more manlike, when joy is the fundamental thing in him, and grief the superficial. Melancholy should be an innocent interlude, a tender and fugitive frame of mind; praise should be the permanent pulsation of the soul. Pessimism is at best an emotional half-holiday; joy is the uproarious labour by which all things live.... Joy, which was the small publicity of the

pagan, is the gigantic secret of the Christian. And as I close this chaotic volume, I open again the strange small book from which all Christianity came; and I am again haunted by a kind of confirmation. The tremendous figure which fills the Gospels towers in this respect, as in every other, above all the thinkers who ever thought themselves tall. His pathos was natural, almost casual. The Stoics, ancient and modern, were proud of concealing their tears. He never concealed His tears; He showed them plainly on His open face at any daily sight, such as the far sight of His native city. Yet He concealed something. Solemn supermen and imperial diplomatists are proud of restraining their anger. He never restrained His anger. He flung furniture down the front steps of the Temple, and asked men how they expected to escape the damnation of Hell. Yet He restrained something. I say it with reverence; there was in that shattering personality a thread that must be called shyness. There was something that He hid from all men when He went up a mountain to pray. There was something that He covered constantly by abrupt silence or impetuous isolation. There was some one thing that was too great for God to show us when He walked upon our earth; and I have sometimes fancied that it was His mirth.[6]

---

6. Chesterton, *Orthodoxy*, 169–70.

1

Making Sense of Pain, Death, and Evil

PAIN IS INTRINSIC TO human existence. It is universal. It often appears with no warning and strikes indiscriminately. For all our romantic notions about Mother Nature as the great giver of life, she is equally at ease in her role as purveyor of death and destruction. Tsunamis and tornadoes roll over cities and towns as carelessly as a riding lawn mower over an anthill. For those who should manage to avoid natural disasters, there is ultimately no escape. Like an ominous predator, silent, calculating, and implacable: Death awaits.

As "natural" as pain may be, men and women continue to anticipate and experience it with as much anguish, despair, and puzzlement today as they ever did in the past. Suffering and death may be natural, but they do not *feel* natural. Unless we are facing a debilitating illness that sucks out our will to live, we never quite shake off the feeling that we were never meant to die.

One of the fundamental attributes of the human mind is its relentless drive to make sense of reality. History is one long and uninterrupted attempt at making sense of the human condition.

Before we examine what the Bible says about this issue, it is essential to explore, even if briefly, some of the major answers that have been articulated in the past in order to get a sense of where the edges are, whether there are elements common to some of them, and whether any of these responses provide a comprehensive response to the presence of evil in our world. Such a survey is an important step as it may in fact provide critical insights into the nature of evil and our perception of it.

In a pluralistic society, pastors, counselors, and chaplains increasingly interact with men and women of other faiths, atheists, New Age spiritualists, as well as nominal and committed Christians. While it may not be necessary to have an in-depth knowledge of every religious and philosophical perspective on evil, it is helpful to have at least some sense of where a person may be coming from in terms of providing adequate pastoral care and proclaiming the Christian hope. Sharing the gospel and addressing the human condition are intrinsically linked. Sharing the good news requires bridges, and building bridges requires some familiarity with the most basic elements of a person's beliefs. In this respect, some sense of how various religious and philosophical systems view evil may prove to be particularly useful.

Before we get into this brief tour, it is imperative we understand that the presence of suffering in the world is fundamentally a Christian problem. The notion of evil as a "problem" is unique to Christianity and remains, for that reason, a formidable objection to the intrinsic goodness of the Christian God and the validity of the Christian faith. But we will get back to this a little later.

Doing such a survey entails two major difficulties. First, no such exercise can completely do justice to the complexity of the concepts involved. The purpose of this chapter, however, is not to parse all the subtleties of each possible position but to provide a map that shows the broad outlines of how evil is framed in various traditions. The second difficulty relates mainly to the "instability" or ambiguity of evil as a concept. Whereas we all seem to recognize evil when we see it, providing a universal definition is a much more slippery task than it may seem at first. This fluidity in how evil is defined needs to be acknowledged and taken into account in any overview of the problem.

Surveys dealing with the problem of evil customarily organize the material according to religious or philosophical categories. Because similar understandings of evil often overlap religious and philosophical lines, I chose to organize the material in a manner that more clearly highlights substantive distinctions in how evil is defined and managed.

EVIL AS INTRINSIC TO THE FABRIC OF REALITY

The Gods Are Evil

In some traditions, evil is viewed less as a problem than as a fundamental part of reality. In such a perspective, while evil may be viewed as *real*, it is not perceived as an intractable theoretical problem. It is merely perceived as an intrinsic part of the fabric of the universe. Evil is not so much a problem as it is an unfortunate characteristic of the world in which we live. Such a view of evil is found, for instance, in ancient Mesopotamia.

For ancient Mesopotamians, evil is real. No attempt is made to deny or put a positive spin on it. It is not, strictly speaking, an intellectual riddle to resolve as much as a disturbing fact of human existence that needs to be addressed and managed. Much of ancient Mesopotamian mythology and wisdom writings are profoundly preoccupied by the reality of pain and evil.[1] In ancient Mesopotamia, the origin of human suffering is directly linked to the gods themselves. Its presence can be accounted for in terms of functional and ontological causes.

According to ancient Mesopotamian myths such as the *Enuma Elish* or the *Atrahasis*,[2] human beings were created to relieve the lower gods, the *igigi*, from the task of serving and feeding the higher gods, the *annunaki*. In Mesopotamian thought, human beings play a utilitarian role. Humans are slaves who are at the mercy of deities who have nothing but contempt for them.[3]

In ancient Mesopotamia, suffering is rooted in a strict cause-and-effect mechanism. Human hardship is always the result of an offence committed against the gods. In some sense, pain is always deserved. But as anyone who is familiar with ancient Near Eastern literature knows but too well, the problem is that the rules governing this presumed cause-and-effect mechanism are not transparent. Because ancient Mesopotamian religions are essentially empirical systems in which nature serves as the ultimate barometer of the will of the gods, divine will always remains fluid and without a solid baseline.

Mesopotamians believed they could gain the favor of the gods through the sacrificial system. Unfortunately, there could never be a perfect correspondence between ritual and divine satisfaction, as the two major areas of concern, climactic conditions and international relations, which were believed to be under the control of the gods, were in a constant state of flux. Despite all their efforts to discover the will of the gods and to gain their approval, experience taught them that the gods lived on a plane that was ultimately beyond any human standards of justice.

Evil did not, however, simply reside in what the Mesopotamians experienced at the hands of the gods. They viewed evil as an intrinsic part of who they were; a component of their very DNA. They believed the seeds of evil were intertwined with human nature itself.

1. See, for instance, Bottéro, *Religion*, 101–2; 114–15; 164; 166; 169; 186–202; 220.

2. A translation of these myths is found in *ANET*, 60–72 (Enuma Elish), 104–6 (Atrahasis). See also Matthews and Benjamin, *Old Testament Parallels*, 9–18 (Enuma Elish), 31–40 (Atrahasis), and Dalley, *Myths from Mesopotamia*, 228–77 (Enuma Elish) and 1–38 (Atrahasis).

3. For more details, see Bottéro, *Mesopotamia*, 210.

Ancient Mesopotamians were extremely lucid about their condition and its origin. The ultimate cause of this evil "DNA" was squarely lodged in the very nature of the gods themselves. Humans percolate evil, because they are made of the same stuff as the gods. In both the *Enuma Elish* and the *Atrahasis*, we read that humans are made out of a substance that combines clay and divine matter. The purpose of the clay was to insert the seeds of death into human nature, thus ensuring they would not live forever. In a sense, human DNA contains divine DNA. The implication is that whatever flaws the gods have, humans will reflect them as well.

In Mesopotamian thought, there is thus no "problem" of evil. It's all quite straightforward. There is evil in the world, because evil is inherent to the divine world. This view of evil is not unique to the Mesopotamians. The same could be said of the worldview that became prevalent during the Greco-Roman period.

The Way Things Are

While the belief that human beings derive their nature from some mythical gods may seem quaint to the average modern reader, I am not entirely convinced we have significantly moved much beyond the ancients' understanding of the world. According to the theory of evolution, which virtually functions as myth in Western culture, our environment and our very nature, for that matter, result from a process that has occurred over billions of years. While the existence of an infinitely wise and powerful divine engineer is most often excluded from the evolutionary equation, scientists and others will often refer to some kind of overarching guiding force such as "Nature" or "Mother Nature" to account for the evolutionary mechanisms that have given rise to the extraordinary "engineering" marvels that are an intrinsic and routine part of our daily lives.

Whether it is due to some careless anthropomorphism or an unconscious admission that time and chance will forever remain inadequate factors in explaining the billions of mind-numbing processes that make life possible, modern thought banks on two certainties. First, it assumes the notion of progress; there is a force or a law that pushes history along. Second, the way the world is, including the reality of pain and suffering, is as it should be. It cannot be otherwise, for if everything we see and experience is intrinsically the outcome of a mindless evolutionary process, then we cannot introduce the notion of moral evil to qualify any aspect of human experience.

If, for instance, the degenerative biological process that eventually leads to death is described purely in naturalistic terms, how can we then speak of illness, aging, and death as evil in any meaningful manner? In fact, we could push the theory to its logical conclusion and vociferously argue that moral evil is but an illusion. Why not? If all we see is the result of a natural process of selection, then there is really no foundation to characterize any of even the worst vicissitudes of human existence as intrinsically evil. We are left with esthetics: a terminal illness is considered bad simply because it happens to distress us. There can be no moral evil. There can only be natural evil, for if everything we experience is the outcome of an impersonal process, it cannot carry the burden of moral accountability.

God Is Incompetent, Impotent, Contingent, or Nonexistent

While ancient Mesopotamians were not the only ones to regard evil as something real, the conclusions others have arrived at with respect to the nature of God vary. For instance, in some cases the presence of evil is evidence of God's incompetence. The most striking articulation of this thesis was offered by Alfonso X who became king of Castile in 1252. After studying astronomy for several years, Alfonso came to the conclusion that God underperformed when he created the world. He wrote, "If I had been of God's counsel at the Creation, many things would have been ordered better."[4] While such a statement would not as much as raise an eyebrow today, this declaration drew the wrath of clergy and theologians as well as universal condemnation for nearly five hundred years!

As philosopher Susan Neiman, author of *Evil in Modern Thought*, points out, it was only when Alfonso's controversial and nearly blasphemous statement eventually landed on the seventeenth-century philosophical beach that the French philosopher Pierre Bayle came to Alfonso's defense. For Bayle, Alfonso's divine indictment was crucial, for it was the foot in the door for a repositioning of reason with respect to creation. "Alfonso stood for any claim that human reason contains in itself more sense and order than the world it faces."[5] If Alfonso implicitly accused God of incompetence, Bayle did not hesitate to raise the specter of criminal behavior or at least criminal negligence. "History, said Bayle, is the history of the crimes and misfortunes of the human race. A God who could have created a world

---

4. As quoted by Neiman, *Evil in Modern Thought*, 15.
5. Neiman, *Evil in Modern Thought*, 21.

that contained fewer crimes and misfortunes, and chose not to do so, seems nothing but a giant criminal Himself."[6]

The English philosopher David Hume (1711-1776) developed this idea further. Hume began with the assumption that God's purpose in creating the world was to produce a paradise for humanity's enjoyment. The argument is simple. If God intended this world to be a place where men and women would enjoy a maximum degree of pleasure and satisfaction and a minimum of discomfort, then the enterprise was a massive failure. Either God did not wish to make such a world, or he was unable to do so. However we look at it, we have a serious problem. At worst, God is either indifferent, fundamentally impotent, or a cruel overlord; at best, an underachiever.

Responding to the reality of evil by invoking divine incompetence, if not divine wickedness, has not been without its modern-day knights. More recently, Rabbi Kushner gave new life to this idea in his best-seller *When Bad Things Happen to Good People*.[7] While Kushner did not challenge God's goodness and sympathetic stance toward human suffering, he nevertheless maintained that the evidence points toward a God who is unable to effectively resist evil. While God offers strength and support to those who suffer unjustly, his ability to counteract evil is limited. God cares a great deal about human suffering and wishes he could do something about it, but much of it is beyond his control.

According to Gregory A. Boyd, Kushner's book represents one of the best-known expressions of the most basic tenets of process thought, a philosophy first articulated by the philosopher Alfred North Whitehead (1861-1947) and applied to the context of faith by his assistant Charles Hartshorne (1897-2001).[8] According to process philosophy, human beings experience and understand reality through a process that involves memory and perception, both creatively unified by experience. Thus, human beings are described as being in a continuous process of becoming. Process theology extends this principle to the entire universe. All of reality, including God, is in a process of becoming; God himself representing the "all-embracing experience that unifies the world."[9] Boyd writes:

> Hence the interplay of God experiencing the just-past world, and the world then experiencing God, constitutes a perpetually creative advancement. The cosmos, and God, are thus in the

---

6. Neiman, *Evil in Modern Thought*, 18.

7. Kushner, *When Bad Things*.

8. Whitehead, *Process and Reality*. Hartshorne, *Divine Relativity*, and *Natural Theology for Our Time*.

9. Boyd, *Satan*, 273.

process of becoming. God enriches the world, and the world enriches God. God influences the world, and the world influences God. According to Process thought, this process has gone on and must continue to go on forever. This is not the result of a choice God makes. It is the metaphysically necessary structure of existence itself.[10]

As Boyd further points out, this organic view of God and the universe implies that God only seeks to influence the universe; he does not impose his will. As such, the constitutive parts of the cosmos, including free agents, will not always cooperate with the divine "call." When this is the case, evil ensues.

While I cannot do justice to all the nuances of process thought, two major difficulties nevertheless emerge. First, there is little doubt in my mind that the system effectively collapses the distance Christianity has traditionally maintained between God and nature; process theology dangerously totters on the edge of the pantheistic black hole. Second, process theology essentially frames evil as an integral part of reality.[11]

In response to Alfonso's and Bayle's indictment, Gottfried Wilhelm Leibniz (1646–1716) produced a book-length treatise on the problem of evil known as *Théodicée*.[12] Leibniz challenged the idea that the presence of evil in the world is proof of God's underachiever status. Leibniz began with the assumption that since God is all-powerful, all-knowing, and good, there is nothing that can prevent God from creating the best of all possible worlds. If that is the case, we are compelled to conclude that this indeed is the best of all possible worlds. As Neiman reminds us, this does not constitute a qualitative claim about the goodness of this world; "it simply tells us that any other world would have been worse."[13]

Whether Leibniz's argument effectively answered Bayle's charge is open to discussion. On the one hand, some will undoubtedly remain unconvinced by the apparent circularity of it. On the other, even if we were to argue that Leibniz successfully challenges the assessment of God as an underachiever, the fact remains that if this is indeed the best of all possible worlds, it remains difficult, all things considered, to avoid the impression that God is essentially and ultimately limited. While God may have had lofty and noble designs for the human race, because of factors that are allegedly

---

10 Boyd, *Satan*, 273.
11. See Boyd, *Satan*, 273–74. Also Coleman, "Process Theology," 709–11.
12. Leibniz, *Essais de Théodicée*.
13. Neiman, *Evil in Modern Thought*, 22.

beyond his control, God could not avoid creating a world in which evil and suffering would be intrinsic to the very fabric of existence.

Finally, there are those who view the presence of evil in the world as proof that there is no God. Not only do they view the absurdity of human life as proof of God's inexistence, they in fact go so far as to believe that religious fanaticism is the major source of violence in the world. Before becoming a Christian, C. S. Lewis himself wrote that it was the presence of evil in the world that compelled him to reject the existence of God. More recently, such avowed atheists as Christopher Hitchens and Richard Dawkins breathed new life into this argument.[14]

EVIL AS AN ILLUSION

As I hinted at in the opening lines of this chapter, at first sight, it would seem counterintuitive to posit evil as anything other than a harsh reality of human existence. Most of us rarely take the time to ask whether the pain we witness or experience daily could really be just some trick of the mind. We may not always be intensely conscious of evil, but when we collide with it, it becomes undeniable and palpable. Anyone who has experienced a debilitating accident or has been diagnosed with a terminal illness will readily testify to the *reality* of evil. But as odd as it may seem, some religious systems do in fact challenge the intrinsic reality of evil and suffering.

According to Hinduism, for instance, what we commonly designate as evil may not necessarily be so. Hinduism is generally defined as monistic, a system that views everything as an aspect of "god." All of reality is part of the divine and the divine is part of everything.

In fact, the very idea that the world we experience is the only reality or may even be distinct from the divine is said to be an illusion (*maya*). Whether the Supreme Reality is identified as Siva or Brahman, depending on the traditions, the underlying idea remains roughly the same.[15] Everything is part and parcel of a unique reality, an aspect of an undivided unity of all that exists. In this kind of framework, concepts like good and evil are stripped of any significance; they become matters of perspective.[16] Crandall University professor of religious studies John Stackhouse writes:

---

14. See Hitchens, *God Is Not Great*, and Dawkins, *God Delusion*. See also Harris, *End of Faith*; Dennett, *Breaking the Spell*.

15. See Stackhouse, *Can God Be Trusted*, 16–18; Kaplan, "Three Levels of Evil in Advaita Vedanta," 116–29; Cenkner, "Hindu Understandings of Evil," 130–41.

16. See Cenkner, "Hindu Understandings of Evil," 139.

This ocean of being, into which individual beings (such as human souls) one day will enter like raindrops, is truly beyond personality. It is a kind of energy field, the original and final unity within and through which everything exists. Thus it makes no sense to speak of God having a moral nature, as being good or evil or both, for Ultimate Reality has no personality at all.[17]

Within the Christian tradition, it is impossible to ignore Augustine (AD 354–430), a giant whose footprint looms large on the theological landscape. His writings have and continue to influence and shape how we think about evil.[18]

When Augustine converted to Christianity, his view of good and evil also dramatically changed. Before his conversion, Augustine was a Manichaean who embraced the notion of evil as a force engaged in an eternal struggle with the good. Following his conversion, two major transformations occurred.

First, Augustine reaffirmed the absolute sovereignty of God. While the great Christian scholar did not go so far as to hold God responsible for evil, moral evil having emerged out of human free will, he nevertheless maintained the overarching notion of divine sovereignty.[19] In Augustinian thought, free will and moral accountability appear to be in opposition to God's sovereignty. While both concepts are held as equally true, ultimately, the precise basis for attributing moral responsibility to a creature that is described as fulfilling God's will is not entirely made explicit. Augustine writes, "For in the very fact that they acted in opposition to His will, His will concerning them was fulfilled."[20] This juxtaposition of concepts creates

17. Stackhouse, *Can God Be Trusted?*, 18.

18. My discussion of Augustine's view of evil focuses on the function Augustine attributed to evil rather than its nature. Augustine defined evil in terms of the corruption of something good rather than as an independent entity; as the "privation" of something that should otherwise be there. For an in depth treatment of Augustine's view of evil, see Evans, *Augustine on Evil*.

19. "And if we do not believe this, the very first sentence of our creed is endangered, wherein we profess to believe in God the Father Almighty. For He is not truly called Almighty if He cannot do whatsoever He pleases, or if the power of His almighty will is hindered by the will of any creature whatsoever." Augustine, *On the Holy Trinity* (*NPNF* 3:267).

20. I quote Augustine more extensively to provide the reader with a broader context for the above citation. "These are the great works of the Lord, sought out according to all His pleasure, and so wisely sought out, that when the intelligent creation, both angelic and human, sinned, doing not His will but their own, He used the very will of the creature which was working in opposition to the Creator's will as an instrument for carrying out His will, the supremely Good thus turning to good account even what is evil, to the condemnation of those whom in His justice He has predestined to punishment,

an apparent contradiction in terms: humans have free will and yet they are not free with regard to God.[21] Commenting on Augustine's explanation for a crime committed against an innocent person, Boyd writes:

> Though God ultimately controlled the event, however, Augustine believed that the perpetrator was nevertheless morally responsible for acting as he or she did. The free decision of the criminal functions as the *immediate* explanation and locus of responsibility for the misdeed, but God "who gives power to wills" and was thus ultimately in control of the crime functions as the *final* explanation of the event.[22]

Second, Augustine developed an understanding of evil that is integrated into what is called an "aesthetic" perspective, where evil is framed in the context of a larger picture in which everything, "even the misfortunes of life, has its rightful place in the order of creation."[23] Augustine proposes that all evil will eventually be woven into a greater whole, a beautiful tapestry, as it were, that will attribute significance to everything, even the most revolting acts of human cruelty. According to Augustine, our perception of what is evil may be distorted by our inability to see the whole picture.

Case in point, William Willimon notes that while what we call amoral or natural evil, i.e., the kind of pain that results from natural phenomena such as earthquakes, hurricanes, floods, etc., can properly be deemed "evil" only from a human standpoint. It is not necessarily so from an objective perspective.

> Likewise, the things that we call natural evil are usually the result of orderly processes of nature which come crashing down upon us. It is not necessarily "evil" that a rock falls from a cliff

---

and to the salvation of those whom in His mercy He has predestined to grace. For, as far as relates to their own consciousness, these creatures did what God wished not to be done: but in view of God's omnipotence, they could in no wise effect their purpose. For in the very fact that they acted in opposition to His will, His will concerning them was fulfilled. And hence it is that 'the works of the Lord are great, sought out according to all His pleasure,' because in a way unspeakably strange and wonderful, even what is done in opposition to His will does not defeat His will. For it would not be done did He not permit it (and of course His permission is not unwilling, but willing); nor would a Good Being permit evil to be done only that in His omnipotence He can turn evil into good." Augustine, *On the Holy Trinity* (NPNF 3:269).

21. Boyd explores the difficulties of such a view of human free will and God's sovereignty in *Satan*, 59–83.

22. Boyd, *Satan*, 58–59.

23. Willimon, *Sighing for Eden*, 44.

and rolls onto a highway. The rock is simply acting in accord with gravity, a law we rely upon and enjoy.[24]

In the same way occurrences of "natural" evil must be viewed in the context of a broader horizon to be accurately ascertained, it is imperative to view all manifestations of evil as part of a larger picture in order to assess them adequately. Willimon adds:

> That is, in the sight of God, many aspects of life which we consider repugnant, unfair, and unwarranted—even sin and its consequences—combine to form a beautiful harmony which is ultimately very good. If there were no bad, then we would not know what is good, just as we would not know light without darkness, health without illness, Augustine says.[25]

According to Boyd, Augustine's theodicy demands that all things, good or evil, must in the end be seen as ordained by God or allowed by him. He writes:

> When confronting tragedies such as cancer, crippling accidents or natural disasters, believers sometimes attempt to console themselves or others by uttering truisms such as "God has his reasons," "There's a purpose for everything," "Providence writes straight with crooked lines," and "His ways are not our ways."[26]

This viewpoint, which Boyd calls the "blueprint worldview,"[27] probably best represents the position most Christians fall back on when disaster strikes. This should come as no surprise. The human brain constantly seeks to establish cause-and-effect relationships for everything that happens. Men and women are compelled to infuse even the most unfortunate events with purpose. While appealing to God's sovereignty to explain a child's death or an aggressive cancer may provide much needed comfort, the reality, as Boyd aptly points out, is that such a view makes it nearly impossible to reconcile the presence of evil with the goodness of God. In fact, it virtually locates the ultimate source of moral evil in the person of God himself.[28]

Besides the conundrum this position creates, in a sense, it could also be said that Augustine's view challenges the very reality of evil. In a way that oddly echoes the understanding of evil in Hinduism, evil appears to have no

---

24. Willimon, *Sighing for Eden*, 43.
25. Willimon, *Sighing for Eden*, 43.
26. Boyd, *Satan*, 12.
27. Boyd, *Satan*, 13.
28. Boyd, *Satan*, 13–14.

real substance. Just as the darker shades contribute to the overall beauty of a woven carpet, evil will ultimately be integrated into the larger picture of God's reality. Augustine writes:

> All have their offices and limits laid down so as to ensure the beauty of the universe. That which we abhor in any part of it gives us the greatest pleasure when we consider the universe as a whole. . . . The very reason why some things are inferior is that though the parts may be imperfect the whole is perfect, whether its beauty is seen stationary or in movement. . . . The black colour in a picture may very well be beautiful if you take the picture as a whole.[29]

It would of course be a grave error to suggest that Augustine viewed evil merely as an illusion. As John Hick observes, "Augustine had no inclination to deny its presence and its virulent power."[30] Yet the articulation of his aesthetic view resulting from his profound desire to maintain and affirm God's sovereignty does seem to open an unintended path toward monism. Hick further notes:

> Evil tends to disappear, its terrible reality concealed within the larger pattern. For example, as Sertillanges expatiates on the organic and aesthetic perfection of the creation, evil seems to diminish in importance and we are invited to see the universe from a standpoint from which it is lost to view in the sublimity of the whole.[31]

EVIL AS TUTOR

We sometimes attribute a redeeming value to human pain because of its role in developing moral virtues. The Bible, for instance, contains numerous allusions to the positive role of suffering. In the book of James, trials are said to contribute to strengthening faith: "My brothers and sisters, whenever you face trials of any kind, consider it nothing but joy, because you know that the testing of your faith produces endurance; and let endurance have its full effect, so that you may be mature and complete, lacking in nothing" (1:2–4).[32]

---

29. Augustine, *Of True Religion*, 40.76.73–74.

30. Hick, *Evil and the God of Love*, 45.

31. Hick, *Evil and the God of Love*, 198. Hick also notes other examples of monistic thought in Spinoza and, more recently, Christian Science (*Evil & the God of Love*, 23–31).

32. This principle is echoed in Rom 5:3–5; 2 Cor 4:16–18; 12:7–10; 1 Pet 1:6–7.

Throughout Christian history, leaders have and still frequently extol the merits of suffering with respect to character development. Trials are to the human soul what vigorous exercise is to the body. Suffering tests and probes our faith, produces compassion for others, incites us to call on God and rely on him, forces us to draw on such human virtues as courage and resourcefulness, produces patience, etc.

As C. S. Lewis notes, the fact of pain is God's way of capturing our attention: "God whispers to us in our pleasures, speaks in our conscience, but shouts in our pain; it is His megaphone to rouse a deaf world."[33] Pain shatters the illusion that all is well and that what we have is sufficient for us.[34] Lewis observes that pain can also serve as a rough indicator of whether we follow the inclinations of our sinful nature or lean toward God's will. Lewis contends that the surrender of the self to God does and will entail some degree of pain.[35] Whether that is always or necessarily the case may be open to debate, but we cannot deny the fact that pain can play a corrective role in our lives.

But the real question is not whether evil can be used to nurture moral virtues, but whether it is, in principle, necessary for the development of moral qualities. According to the second-century bishop Irenaeus of Lyons, the world as we know and experience it, with all of its difficulties, including the reality of pain and suffering, is necessary to transform imperfect creatures into mature ones. Irenaeus came to this position as a result of his interpretation of the creation story found in Genesis 1–3. In contrast to Augustine, who viewed Adam and Eve as perfect individuals who inexplicably disobeyed God, for Irenaeus Adam and Eve were imperfect creatures who needed to be subjected to a maturing process in order to become the kind of creatures God intended for them to become. Willimon writes:

> Their sin is not damnable revolt and rebellion but rather the result of their weakness and immaturity. Accordingly, their sin calls forth God's compassion more than God's wrath. Adam and Eve are not driven away from God; rather, they are driven, as were all women and men who came after them, into countless new experiences and adventures with God."[36]

For Irenaeus, the presence of evil, pain, and suffering is not viewed so much as a disastrous anomaly as an indissoluble part of the process needed to enable Adam and Eve and all humans to mature. John Hick, one of the

33. Lewis, *Problem of Pain*, 91.
34. Lewis, *Problem of Pain*, 94.
35. Lewis, *Problem of Pain*, 97–98.
36. Willimon, *Sighing for Eden*, 50.

twentieth century's foremost specialists on the problem of evil, views Irenaeus's position as the key to articulating a plausible theodicy for today. Though we may not be in a position to explain how and to what extent every instance of suffering works itself out in terms of human development, Hick contends that this world is exactly the kind of world that was and is needed to produce mature human beings. He writes:

> My general conclusion, then, is that this world, with all its unjust and apparently wasted suffering, may nevertheless be what the Irenaean strand of Christian thought affirms that it is, namely a divinely created sphere of soul-making.[37]

The notion that pain is necessary to help men and women achieve maturity is partially paralleled in traditional Buddhist thought. This is not to suggest that Buddhism and Christianity agree on what constitutes evil. Whereas Christianity provides clear moral parameters to distinguish between good and evil, in Buddhism, all of human existence (*samsara*) with its endless cycle of suffering, decay, and death, is described as "unsatisfactory." To live is to suffer. Liberation from this life of misery can only come through the attainment of enlightenment (*nibbana*), i.e., the full and complete understanding of reality.[38] *Nibbana* represents a state that is beyond good and evil. It is chiefly characterized by an absence of craving and attachment. Stackhouse writes, "It is the dissolution of the self in the halting of desire. For the Buddha taught that desire breeds attachment and thus the fear of loss, and frustration over the goods one never gains."[39]

In Buddhism, evil is defined as that which is opposed to the attainment of enlightenment or *nibbana*, i.e., ultimate reality. In the Buddhist tradition, "evil" describes whatever distracts one from *nibbana*. It takes root in ignorance, particularly "in one's failure to see that the world is unsatisfactory."[40] The Buddhist definition of evil is much broader than in the Christian tradition. It is not simply characterized as moral deficiency or gratuitous pain. Since evil is whatever can distract humans from achieving *nibbana*, it therefore encompasses actions and attitudes that reach far beyond the Christian definition of moral evil.

The Buddhist's chief aim is to *recognize* that human existence (*samsara*) is fundamentally unsatisfactory. In this context, the purpose of evil and more particularly the reality of pain, is educative. By facilitating the

---

37. Hick, *Evil and the God of Love*, 372.
38. More commonly known as *nirvana*.
39. Stackhouse, *Can God Be Trusted?*, 22.
40. Vajiragnana, "Theoretical Explanation of Evil," 99.

realization that human existence is unsatisfactory, suffering compels one to forge ahead in the search for enlightenment.[41] Thus what we commonly perceive as evil plays a tutoring role in human life.

EVIL AS SPIRITUAL WARFARE SHRAPNEL

In his discussion of evil, Augustine provides a threefold categorization in order to maintain the notion of God's goodness. The first of these is moral evil, i.e., the kind of evil that is the result of the abuse of human free will. The second, metaphysical evil, refers to the intrinsic limitations of human existence. The third, natural or amoral evil, designates the kind of pain that results from phenomena that are not directly caused by human agents such as earthquakes, hurricanes, tsunamis, etc. While the categories of moral and metaphysical evil provide solid elements of response to the enigma that evil represents for Christians, natural evil remains, for the most part, an opaque reality and constitutes a kind of evil that is exceedingly difficult to integrate into a comprehensive system.

According to science, what we define as natural evil is merely the outworking of natural phenomena that ultimately make life on earth sustainable. When Mother Nature, as it were, unleashes floods and earthquakes, tragic events that often entail the loss of life and property, scientists are quick to remind the general public that it's nothing personal. According to science, such events in no way constitute expressions of divine retribution for moral failings . . . at least in theory. In reality, despite the clean break the scientific model creates between morality and natural calamities, some version or other of a moral law of retribution will tend to reassert itself in times of extreme adversity. Even in such a secular and post-Christian age as ours, people often waste no time dropping the why question at God's doorstep when disaster strikes.

As a case in point, the 2004 tsunami that devastated Southeast Asia and caused an estimated 230,000 deaths was not, at least initially, simply dismissed as a geological hiccup. Journalists, commentators, pundits of all stripes, and ordinary people were compelled to ask why a loving God would allow so many to die on that fateful day. Why would such a catastrophe strike such a poor and destitute population? A tsunami does not discriminate. It rolls over the virtuous and the immoral alike. It spares neither the infant nor the pregnant woman. It is blind to social status; the poor fare no better than the rich.

---

41. For more details, see Vajiragnana, "Theoretical Explanation of Evil," 99–108.

While no other natural catastrophe since then has elicited as much public theological despair,[42] the human instinct to seek some underlying moral law to rationalize the unthinkable always simmers below the surface. For instance, our obsessive reflex to see a cause-and-effect relationship between extreme weather events allegedly caused by global warming and human activity could potentially be viewed as another symptom of our propensity to look for some consistent and predictable moral order in the universe. In the same way Job's friends, who desperately needed to prove Job's guilt to maintain the integrity of a moral universe in which happiness and morality are inexorably linked, radical environmentalists cannot resist assimilating the alleged degradation of the planet into a moral construct. Environmentalism is not merely about "saving the planet." It is as much about an expression of our primal need to affirm the old law of retribution and in so doing preserve the most fundamental tenets or our moral universe intact, namely, that we always get what we deserve.

Gregory Boyd has endeavored to integrate natural evil into a coherent theological system. Unlike medieval theologians and, more recently, some fundamentalist Islamic and Christian clerics, who have sought to interpret natural disasters in terms of a cause-and-effect moral framework, and unlike those who view human devastation resulting from natural disasters as the simple outcome of random factors, Boyd suggests that such occurrences may be the visible outcomes of a spiritual war. Boyd contends that what we commonly refer to as "natural" evil (also known as amoral evil) is nothing but *natural*. Infants dying in an earthquake, a pregnant woman starving to death because of a drought, or the ravages of the bubonic plague throughout history do not simply seem evil; for Boyd, they constitute manifestations of moral evil. Boyd maintains that it is a misnomer to refer to the endless miseries nature inflicts on humans as *natural*. For Boyd, these phenomena result from the actions of supernatural agents known as demons. While such a view will seem foreign to modern thinkers, Boyd reminds the reader that this was in fact the predominant view in the early church. It was eventually cast aside as a result of Augustine's prominence and "the influence of Enlightenment naturalism, rationalism and biblical criticism."[43] Boyd writes:

> In short, Satan and his legions are directly or indirectly behind all forms of "natural" evil. Satan turns the neutral medium of the

---

42. Not even the deadly 2010 earthquake in Haiti or the 2011 tsunami that struck Japan appeared to cause as much mediatic theological hand-wringing.

43. Boyd, *Satan*, 295.

natural order into a weapon just as human agents sometimes use rocks, sticks or water as weapons when they choose to do so.[44]

EVIL AS OPAQUE REALITY: THE FAITH SOLUTION

No one ever escapes the impulse to find some kind of an answer to explain the reality of suffering in our world. Some people may be more passionate, organized, and articulate in their search. Others may be more intuitive about making sense of their existence. The reality is that we all look for an answer and eventually learn to live with whatever explanation we settle on.

As far as Christians are concerned, some will articulate very sophisticated responses; pastors and academics will or should belong to this category. Others, however, may settle for a simpler solution. As Barry L. Whitney points out, what he calls the "faith solution" has tended to have broad currency in conservative circles. "The faith solution appeals to faith as the ultimate (and only legitimate) solution to the theodicy issue: God has given or permits the evil and suffering we must endure for good reasons, it is held, reasons that are beyond complete human comprehension."[45]

There is no shortage of good reasons to yearn for a simple response to the problem of evil. When we consider why a good and loving God might allow a young boy to die from leukemia or why an all-powerful God should allow a little girl to drown in a tidal wave, it becomes very tempting to find some kind of comfort in an explanation that simply affirms the necessity to have faith and leave it at that. But to respond to seemingly meaningless tragedies like the death of children by appealing to some vague notion of "God must have his reasons" is simply not adequate in terms of the witness Christians are called to bear. Appealing to the mystery of God's will may be existentially satisfying to some in a time of intense grief, but this is not, as a matter of principle, a strategy in which we should find final refuge.

Whitney notes that the faith solution is now mostly associated with conservative Christianity:

> The premise upon which the faith solution is based (noted earlier) is no longer prevalent outside conservative circles—Thomism and evangelical Protestantism, and the general populace with its popular theology, largely untouched by academic theological discussions.[46]

---

44. Boyd, *Satan*, 318.
45. Whitney, *Theodicy*, 7.
46. Whitney, *Theodicy*, 8.

I do suppose that traditionally, Christians, particularly under the influence of Augustine, have indeed resorted to the faith solution to reconcile their faith in God to the seemingly absurd and meaningless manifestations of evil in our world. But I would hesitate to confine people who hold such a view to those who have been "largely untouched by academic theological discussions."

It would be inaccurate to view the faith solution as the exclusive domain of the theologically naïve. I can think of at least four contemporary theologians who have postulated positions that could be said to lean in the same direction. All four are highly respected scholars and could certainly not be described as having been "untouched" by academia.

Stanley Hauerwas, author of *Naming the Silences* (1990), states that it is not his intention to explain why a seemingly good and all-powerful God would allow some to suffer for no reason. In fact, not only does he express profound suspicion toward those who may attempt such a feat but adds, "I hope to show why this way of putting the question of suffering is a theological mistake."[47] For Hauerwas, there is no point in asking why we suffer; we must simply persevere in our faithfulness to God and in the conviction that he loves us.

The renowned New Testament scholar N. T. Wright, in *Evil and the Justice of God*, offers helpful insights into the significance of the cross as God's answer to evil and the nature of forgiveness. Wright does, however, also caution the reader against trying to "solve" evil. He writes, "If you offer an analysis of evil which leaves us saying, 'Well, that's all right then; we now see how it happens and what to do about it,' you have belittled the problem."[48] Wright wishes to ensure that any solution we articulate should not resort to either offering a caricature of God or soften the brutality of evil.[49]

Wright is particularly mindful of those theologians and philosophers who have "solved" the problem of evil by watering down some aspect or other of Christian orthodoxy. Wright reminds his readers that it is unwise to seek a simplistic solution to a very complex issue. It is best to "address it in a mature fashion, and in the middle of it come to a deeper and wiser faith in the creator and redeemer God whose all-conquering love will one day make a new creation in which the dark and threatening sea of chaos will be no more."[50] Wright points out that in the end, "we are not told—or not in

---

47. Hauerwas, *Naming the Silences*, ix.
48. Wright, *Evil and the Justice of God*, 40.
49. Wright, *Evil and the Justice of God*, 39–41.
50. Wright, *Evil and the Justice of God*, 41.

any way that satisfies our puzzled questioning—how and why there is radical evil within God's wonderful, beautiful and essentially good creation." For the moment, our responsibility is to believe in the promise of a renewed world and even now demonstrate the victory of the cross by anticipating its reality in our lives.[51] In all fairness, while Wright's caution is not quite as radical as Hauerwas's, he nonetheless remains very guarded with respect to articulating even a tentative explanation for the presence of evil in the world.

John Stackhouse adopts a similar approach. While he goes to great lengths in terms of establishing the basic framework in which evil must be discussed, he too asserts that our response to evil cannot simply be a matter of understanding. A "complete" theodicy, i.e., an exhaustive and integrated explanation as to the absolute origin of evil, its expressions, and its continued flowering in human experience despite our best efforts to contain it, is beyond reason. Stackhouse further states that the infinite intricacies of the dynamics inherent to the presence of evil in our lives and God's providence may forever remain beyond human comprehension.[52] The most appropriate response to the reality of evil in this world may not so much reside in a comprehensive answer but in learning to trust God as he is revealed in Jesus Christ, and let our resulting transformed lives become an answer to the problem of evil.[53]

The French reformed scholar Henri Blocher adopts an approach that is said to be commonly held in conservative circles, and one that also betrays a kind of theological agnosticism that, in my opinion, is not fully warranted. In *Evil and the Cross*, Blocher offers a characteristically enlightening survey of the various solutions to the problem of evil, as well as an incisive critique of each.[54] Unfortunately, when it comes to his own view, Blocher seems virtually paralyzed by the Calvinistic tenets that structure his theological framework. For instance, he discredits the free will explanation on the grounds that it undermines the notion of God's sovereignty. Blocher in fact creates a theological dilemma that cannot be resolved. While he maintains, on the one hand, the notion of God's absolute goodness and sovereignty,[55] and, on the other, the reality of evil and human responsibility,[56] he also states that nothing can escape God's will. No one acts of his own will. "The Creator is not content simply to determine times and allot places (Acts

---

51. Wright, *Evil and the Justice of God*, 164.
52. Stackhouse, *Can God Be Trusted?*, 90–91.
53. Stackhouse, *Can God Be Trusted?*, 168–76.
54. See particularly Blocher, *Evil and the Cross*.
55. Blocher, *Evil and the Cross*, 96, 90.
56. Blocher, *Evil and the Cross*, 85–90, 99.

17:26); everything that happens depends on his will."⁵⁷ So God is absolutely sovereign in the sense that nothing happens without his willing it, yet "evil is always the deed of one or of several created beings, *exclusively* [my emphasis]."⁵⁸ While Blocher is well aware of the contradiction these statements imply, he neglects to explore further the precise formulation of the apparently antinomic nature of the propositions he puts side by side or to examine more closely some of the biblical statements, such as 1 Sam 16:14–16 (see also 16:23; 18:10; 19:9), that appear to attribute "evil" to God.

> How can we reconcile God's perfect goodness, his love for us his creatures and his hatred of evil with the fact that he does not work in everyone the desire for good and the doing of good? What is the meaning of sovereignly permitting? The thorn of these questions is deeply and sharply embedded in the human mind, even the renewed mind of the believer; as the individual thinker clings to the "I" of Christian teaching, he feels his mind under fearful strain, almost to breaking-point.
>
> Scripture teaches us that we shall not find, at least in this life, the rational solution that so many have sought after. It does not give us the answer.⁵⁹

For Blocher, it is preferable to avoid attempting to understand the problems associated with the reality of evil in our world. As he writes, "Evil is not there to be understood, but to be *fought*."⁶⁰

Many of the issues raised by Blocher and others with respect to the presence of evil in our world are indeed beyond human reason. But Blocher makes two errors. First, he fails to adequately define his terms of reference. There is not necessarily a contradiction in terms between holding to God's sovereignty, on the one hand, and maintaining human responsibility, on the other. Much of the logical strain associated with such statements is often the result of inadequate definitions. Second, some of the apparent contradictions attested in Scripture are not as intractable as they may first appear. Some of the difficulties as are found, for instance, in 1 Sam 16:14, 15, 16, 23; 18:10, and 19:9, where an "evil" spirit is said to originate from God, can, more often than not, be resolved by a more careful exegesis of the text.⁶¹ While

---

57. Blocher, *Evil and the Cross*, 91. In this category, Blocher also inserts "evils, calamities and transgressions" (90).

58. Blocher, *Evil and the Cross*, 99.

59. Blocher, *Evil and the Cross*, 101.

60. Blocher, *Evil and the Cross*, 103.

61. For instance, it should be noted that the Hebrew word *ra'h*, which is translated by "evil," does not only denote moral evil as such. It is also used in certain contexts to

we may not be in a position to account for every aspect or manifestation of evil in our world, we must resist the temptation to find refuge in some form of theological agnosticism; this kind of escape pod is just too easy to take. While it is not possible to provide a comprehensive explanation for the presence of evil and every instance of gratuitous suffering, we should, at the very least, seek to reflect as much of the relevant biblical data as possible.

CONCLUSION

Not So Diverse After All

What I find particularly striking in terms of assessing the various responses we have examined is not so much the diversity of positions, as one might expect, but rather the scarcity of genuinely different options. The apparent multiplicity of perspectives that has been proposed to explain the problem of evil is deceiving.

When we look closely at the various attempts to decipher the reality of human suffering, the positions can basically be divided into two camps: those that lean toward monism and those edging toward dualism. Monistic explanations offered by Hinduism, Buddhism, and evolutionism emphasize the organic unity of the universe. Evil is a matter of perspective. Whether something is "evil" or not really depends on one's particular point of view. Dualistic explanations, on the other hand, emphasize the substantive and eternal nature of evil. Ancient Mesopotamian thought, Manichaeism, and atheism represent dualistic perspectives. While such uniformity may at first sight be somewhat surprising, what is even more disconcerting is to discover that either one or both of these views have had and continue to have a foothold in the Christian tradition.

Augustinian theology, with its emphasis on the "aesthetic" value of evil, has the potential to evolve a view of evil that is akin to what we find in monistic systems. On the one hand, the notion that God has a purpose for everything, including every kind of manifestations of evil, coupled with the notion that everything that happens will eventually contribute to the beauty of the great divine canvas representing God's work in human history, does nod in the direction of a universal framework that in the end integrates all things. On the other hand, as John Hick points out, the Neoplatonist

---

denote a disaster, a catastrophe, misery, or distress (see BDB, 949). In such instances where *ra'h* is said to originate from God, it appears to refer to God's judgment (see Judg 2:15; 2 Kgs 21:12, 16; Jer 4:6; see also Judg 20:34, 41). For a different interpretation, see Page, *Powers of Evil*, 75–78.

assimilation of evil framed within a hierarchy of being dangerously moves toward a form of dualism. Hypothesizing a hierarchy of being in which only God is perfect implies that any created thing will by nature be imperfect. Such a state of imperfection will be deemed to be inherently unstable. As Hick writes, "They have been made out of nothing and for that reason inherently mutable, lacking the eternal poise of the uncreated self-existent Being."[62] If creation, being "imperfect," is by definition and nature "fragile,"[63] then it follows that sooner or later, the creatures will eventually fail. It is inevitable that humans will sin. In this framework, evil becomes therefore an intrinsic and intractable component of human nature. Because evil is inherently linked to created matter, it follows that the creation of a world free of evil may in fact lie beyond God's power. This is not to say that the Augustinian view of evil is either monistic or dualistic as such, but it does have the potential to metastasize into one or the other.

This ever-present potential for Christian theology to lean into monism or dualism is, for instance, evident in process theology, a system that virtually assimilates evil into the very person of God, thus making it eternal as a necessary component of existence itself. Any attempt to resolve the problem of evil by imputing it to an ontological limitation in the person of God does not constitute, I would contend, an adequate response in terms of the data Scripture provides about the nature of God.

The critical question that emerges here is whether evil, including gratuitous pain and suffering, represents a necessary component of human existence. Is evil necessary in order to produce moral virtues? Must we be exposed to corruption in order to highlight the beauty of goodness? Was the emergence of evil indispensable to bring humanity into a higher level of existence? In my opinion, every time we lean in this direction, we come closer to embracing some form of monism or dualism, neither one of which is acceptable with respect to resolving the classical formulation of the problem of evil.

Any solution that pretends to resolve the problem of evil by weakening the goodness and power of God, or collapsing the irreducible and scandalous reality of evil, should be rejected. The challenge is to arrive at a solution, even if by necessity an incomplete one, that maintains all three elements of the Christian dilemma and what Scripture teaches about the nature of God and the reality of evil.

---

62. Hick, *Evil and the God of Love*, 196.

63. An expression used by Père Sertillanges to denote the ultimate inevitability of failure (as cited by Hick, *Evil and the God of Love*, 196).

"Natural" Evil?

Because men and women live in an environment that often proves to be hostile to human existence irrespective of the moral character of the victims, no treatment of the problem of evil can altogether ignore the suffering resulting from natural disasters.

Are such events and the suffering they unleash simply a matter of random forces or are they somehow governed by moral principles that are not accessible to reason? Are earthquakes and plagues directly caused by divine intervention or are they, as Boyd suggests, the outcome of a war between supernatural beings and God? While some may experience some discomfort at the notion of chance and randomness, to attribute the occurrence of a lethal mud slide to demonic beings is no less concerning.

As attractive as Boyd's thesis may be with respect to offering a reasonable solution for natural evil, there are two major difficulties. On the one hand, how do we reconcile a view that depicts the universe as structurally hostile with the notion of a "friendly" cosmos offered in the Genesis creation account? As I demonstrate in my book *Demons, Lies & Shadows*, the intent of the first two chapters of Genesis consists, in part, in offering an alternative to a mythical view of the physical universe. Rather than being expressions of divine beings, the elements of nature are portrayed as objects to be investigated rather than worshipped. In time, this unique perspective led to the development of a worldview that could support the articulation of the scientific method.[64] On the other hand, if natural catastrophes can be attributed to demonic activity, in what possible way can we maintain the integrity of the scientific method or even a clear separation between what we would qualify as "natural" and "supernatural" phenomena? In Boyd's worldview, we find ourselves catapulted back into the medieval ideological swamp that indiscriminately (con)fused spirit and matter.[65] Rather than being a sound expression of biblical theology, Boyd is unwittingly guilty of reproducing a set of ancient beliefs that the biblical creation account was intentionally designed to undermine.

Before we conclude this discussion on natural evil, we might want to explore whether, as John Hick suggests, suffering deriving from natural causes can simply be viewed as part of a system designed to tutor the human race into a higher level of existence. In some respect, the idea has merit. Adversity does contribute to producing character. The all-too-common

---

64 For more details, see Gilbert, *Demons, Lies & Shadows*, 54–64.

65. The Canadian sociologist Fernand Dumont examines this problem at length in a remarkable article in which he examines the relationship between the Christian faith and science. See "Après le système chrétien," 187–92.

abrasive self-centeredness and self-indulgent behavior of those individuals who are born with the proverbial silver spoon in their mouth is a testimony to the salutary effects of adversity on one's character.

We cannot deny the fact that this world provides a framework for "soul-making." We live in an environment in which actions have real consequences. As the book of Proverbs repeatedly observes, there is a structural and inescapable law of retribution that governs our lives. But that is not the real issue. The question is whether we can legitimately appeal to this principle as a comprehensive explanation for the world as it is.

What do we precisely mean when we say that this world is a "vale of soul-making?" In what sense does the human species benefit? Even if the world as we experience it was indeed designed to guide the human race into a higher plane of existence, how exactly was this moralistic "evolutionary" process supposed to work itself out for humanity as a whole? It seems somewhat fallacious to compare humanity to some kind of organic entity that will develop to its full potential given the right conditions.

Even if men and women live in community, they are also intensely unique individuals who have a personal destiny and enjoy a significant degree of moral autonomy. The human race is not a collective consciousness. While individual men and women can indeed become better or worse, it is meaningless to apply such categories to the human race as a whole. Moreover, what about those who choose to embrace evil in response to their circumstances? Are human beings any more altruistic today than they were two thousand years ago? If this world is indeed designed to be a "vale of soul-making," what about children who die before they can benefit from the soul-making attributes the world offers? A hypothesis that only applies to some abstract human collective will simply not do.

The Skeptical School

For some, the best course of action with respect to dealing with the problem of evil consists in refraining from offering any solution that could be viewed as a comprehensive answer. Stanley Hauerwas, who is probably one of the best known representatives of this school of thought, maintains that such a project is an offense to sound theology and an unfortunate leftover from Constantinianism. He writes:

> It would be foolhardy, however, to deny the desire many feel to seek an explanation for suffering and pain. Even if I am able to show that such explanations are theologically and philosophically wrongheaded, the fact remains that when most of us are

confronted with the illness or death of our child, we want an explanation. It is almost as if we have a primitive need to know that such an illness or death does not render our existence and God's existence absurd. I will try to show that this seemingly "primitive need" has a particular form today that is often based on destructive presuppositions about the nature of our existence. Moreover, if we are to rightly express our care for one another through the office of medicine, it is imperative that we understand those presuppositions and why they have such a hold on us.[66]

A little further he adds, "I cannot promise readers consolation, but only as honest an account as I can give of why we cannot afford to give ourselves explanations for evil when what is required is a community capable of absorbing our grief."[67]

Hauerwas repeatedly states that the need to "explain" the problem of evil is a recent phenomenon, a child of the "Enlightenment project of extending human power over all contingency."[68] He makes the somewhat puzzling observation that Old Testament believers were not looking for an answer and adds that for early Christians, pain and suffering were not to be explained. Allegedly, these believers were not looking for an explanation but simply for the "means to go on even if the evil could not be 'explained.'"[69] While I am sympathetic to those who, like N. T. Wright and John Stackhouse, remind us that there are limits to reason's ability to account for every instance of suffering, I do not find Hauerwas's argument compelling. To deny there that is in fact a "problem" of evil is odd. To assert that Old Testament believers and Christians, up to the seventeenth century, were not concerned about finding answers is inaccurate. The Old Testament offers a variety of answers to what is keenly perceived as an existential issue. This is particularly evident in the Wisdom tradition (see especially Psalms 37, 73, and the book of Ecclesiastes).[70] In addition, as I will develop later on, it can be argued that the Genesis creation account does indeed propose a *bona fide* theodicy.

Furthermore, there are at least two difficulties that mar Hauerwas's thesis. First, I note his avowed quasi-allergic reaction to "Enlightenment presuppositions" or any treatment of the problem of evil that he perceives

66. Hauerwas, *Naming the Silences*, x.
67. Hauerwas, *Naming the Silences*, xi.
68. Hauerwas, *Naming the Silences*, 48.
69. Hauerwas, *Naming the Silences*, 49.
70. For an exploration of the argument that the book of Ecclesiastes represents a response to nihilism, see Gilbert, "Fighting Fire with Fire," 65–79.

is anchored in some ahistorical sphere disconnected from "a specific community of people."[71] This approach is very problematic, for if indeed any attempt to explain evil is merely a reflection of the "powers" and ultimately only serves to legitimize them, there is then no basis either for the articulation of a theodicy or even a debate.

Second, Hauerwas tends to create an opposition between a theoretical solution and the practical imperative to provide comfort and guidance in the face of suffering. Not only is such a dichotomy unnecessary, to propose that any attempt at articulating a theodicy is a mere extension of Enlightenment assumptions represents an oversimplification of the issues. This kind of distinction between "theoretical" (bad) and "practical" (good) is simply indefensible and in fact reminiscent of the kind of Christian fundamentalism that such authors denounce. My old systematic theology professor often used to say that "the heart cannot rejoice in what the mind does not believe." The ability to find comfort when tragedy strikes also entails a capacity to make sense of a world in which such tragedies can occur.

In any case, whether one is sympathetic to Hauerwas's quasi-agnostic stance or Wright's and Stackhouse's cautious positioning, as I will try to demonstrate, the biblical text does provide the outline of a comprehensive explanation for the presence of suffering and death in the world. And while we are not (and never will be!) in a position to offer a rationale for every instance of undeserved pain, it is our task and responsibility to carefully examine what the relevant biblical texts do affirm and to push the limits of our understanding of the mystery of evil where it is warranted and reasonable to do so. The desire and the task of articulating a theodicy for our times is not just the poisoned fruit of the "Enlightenment project." Undertaking such a venture in fact stands in continuity with the Old Testament and the New. Within an apologetics and evangelistic perspective, it is but one aspect of articulating the rational foundation of the Christian faith (1 Pet 3:15).

Whether the Old Testament offers a comprehensive explanation for the presence of evil is certainly open to debate. There is plenty of evidence to show that the inescapable reality of gratuitous pain, illness, old age, and death were profoundly unsettling to the average Israelite. That some of the authors wished to shed some significant light on the issue is beyond doubt. The Genesis creation account constitutes the most explicit discussion of the origin of evil in the Bible. Throughout Christian history, it has been viewed as the definitive explanation of the human condition.

More recently, however, many scholars have seriously questioned the relevance of the creation narrative as a comprehensive explanation for the

---

71. Hauerwas, *Naming the Silences*, 53.

presence of evil. In the next chapter, we will examine some of the major reasons that have led to the abandonment of the creation text and will seek to demonstrate why it should still command our full attention as the best explanation for why human existence fails to meet our most profound expectations.

2

The Creation Story: Myth or History?

THE CENTRAL PREMISE OF this book lies in the notion that the Genesis creation account contains critical information for understanding why there is evil in the world. Such an approach is by no means new. Throughout Christian history, theologians have recruited various elements of the creation narrative to provide a reasonable explanation for this most vexing problem. They have most notably focused their efforts on Adam and Eve's misuse of their free will as the original trigger of the induction of evil into history.[1]

FORSAKEN AND ABANDONED

Who Needs a Comprehensive Answer Anyway?

More recently, a number of philosophers and theologians have sharply veered away from the free will defense and a historical fall to account for the presence of evil in the world.[2] The French philosopher and phenomenologist

---

1. One of the most noted of such endeavors has recently been offered by Alvin Plantinga, *Nature of Necessity*. See also the updated version of his argument in *God, Freedom, and Evil*.

2. See, for instance, Ricoeur, *Symbolism of Evil*, 235. The renowned Old Testament specialist Walter Brueggemann is representative of a significant number of Old Testament scholars when he states that the narrative dealing with the creation of Adam and Eve has no historical significance with respect to explaining the origin of evil (*Genesis*,

Paul Ricoeur contends that the significance of the creation story can be understood only if "we completely renounce projecting the Adamic figure into history."[3] The renowned Old Testament scholar Walter Brueggemann agrees. He writes:

> Frequently, this text is treated as though it were an explanation of *how evil came into the world*. But the Old Testament is never interested in such an abstract issue. In fact, the narrative gives no explanation for evil. There is no hint that the serpent is the embodiment of principle of evil. The Old Testament characteristically is more existential. It is not concerned with origins but with faithful responses and effective coping.[4]

In fact, with the exception of a few conservative scholars such as the French Reformed theologian Henri Blocher and the Old Testament specialist Gordon Wenham,[5] the creation story seems to have altogether been put on the back burner. Several factors have contributed to this situation.

In the wake of such scholars as Walter Brueggemann and Stanley Hauerwas, there has been an increasing resistance to articulating a comprehensive explanation for the presence of evil in the world. Such an explanation is not nearly as important, so it is argued, as devising ways to cope as a community. To seek to understand is for Hauerwas akin to idolatry.[6]

Give It a Rest

For others, there is what I like to call creation narrative "fatigue." The appeal to human free will, the fall, and original sin seem for many to have gone as far as it can while remaining still profoundly unsatisfactory.[7] For instance,

---

41–44). Bruce Vawter similarly states, "The story of the 'fall' is a paradigm of human conduct in the face of temptation, not a lesson in biology" (*On Genesis*, 90). In the same vein, John Hick writes, "Let us instead simply say without equivocation that the fall is a mythic conception which does not describe an actual event in man's history or prehistory" (*Evil and the God of Love*, 181). In a recent book on the problem of evil, Dinesh D'Souza, a conservative intellectual and Christian apologist, essentially dismisses the fall narrative simply because he cannot imagine how guilt can be inherited (*God Forsaken*, 41–43). I should note, however, that if we were to reject any new scientific discovery simply because we could not *imagine* how it could possibly be, we would still be offering sacrifices to the gods to ensure good harvests.

3. Ricoeur, "Original Sin," 284.
4. Brueggemann, *Genesis*, 41.
5. For more details, see Blocher, *Original Sin*, 37–62, and Wenham, *Genesis 1–15*, 91.
6. Hauerwas, *Naming the Silences*, 48.
7. See for instance Hick, *Evil and the God of Love*, 262–76. For a detailed critique of

the notion of a fallen humanity and a structurally fractured world severely conflicts with a radical environmentalist ideology that views the world as we have it, to echo Leibniz, as the best of all possible worlds. To suggest that humanity is the depository of some exceptional status, and that what we experience now is not what should be represents an intolerable offense. Radical environmentalists generally view the image of God and its corollary notion of a world under human dominion as the root cause of the environmental degradation that is allegedly occurring.

Another reason for the near-total neglect of the creation story derives from a misconceived perception of the literary character of the text. Theologians and philosophers generally define the creation narrative as myth, i.e., a story focusing on the gods and intended to explain the origin of humanity and the universe. While such stories may contain profound insights into the human condition,[8] they do not exhibit any historical facticity. The notion, therefore, that any aspect of the Genesis creation story may have any grounding in history is viewed as the height of fundamentalist naïveté. It is widely assumed that Genesis 1–3 was written late, sometime in the postexilic period (fifth century BC), displays the characteristics of myth, and offers itself as such to the reader. This is not to suggest that the text is of no use whatsoever, but its significance is symbolic or, perhaps more precisely, archetypal. As Blocher states, "At the reflective level, the claim is put forward that the meaning, the *intentio*, of the passage is better preserved, better promoted, indeed liberated, if we break it loose from a contingent, local accident."[9]

And perhaps most importantly, current scientific opinion strenuously argues against the representation of humanity as a species that has "fallen" from a previously better position. To speak of the *devolution* of the human race rather than its *evolution* is an assault on some of the most preciously held scientific assumptions regarding humanity's appearance and development.

In that respect, however, we need to remember the importance of approaching the conclusions advanced by paleoanthropology and Darwinism with utmost care and prudence. Notwithstanding the near-unanimous, indeed quasi-religious, assent the theory of evolution enjoys, it is in the end just that: a theory, and maybe more accurately a hypothesis. I don't wish to sound overly Neanderthal about all this, but I find it disconcerting that one hundred and fifty some years after the publication of Darwin's *On the Origin of Species*, the fossil evidence supporting the notion of interspecies

---

the notion of original sin from an exegetical perspective, see Biddle, *Missing the Mark*.

8. See Eliade, *Myth and Reality*, 8.
9. Blocher, *Original Sin*, 38.

evolution is still rather embarrassingly underwhelming.[10] This may explain why proponents of evolutionism so often vociferously denounce even mildly hesitant skeptics as irrational obscurantist fundamentalists. While I personally have a profound sense of admiration for the idea of progress that is presupposed by Darwinism,[11] I have to admit that I'm somewhat taken aback by the hostility so many harbor toward any challenge to the theory of evolution. Stanley L. Jaki, Distinguished Professor of Physics at Seton Hall University, writes:

> Darwin's own admission, that the failure of geological research to yield the infinitely many fine gradations between past and present species as required by the theory . . . remains as relevant as ever. What most effectively gives away Darwinism is the almost mystical faith voiced by its supporters in facing up to the absence of evidence and even to the contrary evidence.[12]

Besides the fact that Darwin himself stated that he would expect that further exploration into the fossil record would confirm his theory, the objections to the theory of evolution remain daunting. For a start, after 150 years, there is still virtually no evidence to support the development of living organisms from simple forms into more complex ones. There was no evidence when Darwin postulated his theory, and there is still precious little hard evidence even now.

It wasn't backward religious people who challenged Darwin; this honor goes to world-renowned paleontologists such as Louis Agassiz, Roderick Impey Murchinson, and Adam Sedgwick.[13] If Darwin's theory provided an entirely accurate picture of the process that gave birth to the wealth of species that populate the world, the fossil record should be chock-full of fossils showing the various incremental stages of development the theory postulates. I am well aware of the fact that we cannot expect, the fossil record being incomplete, the perfect preservation of every incremental development of an animal's evolutionary trail, but there should be countless examples of transitional forms. For all practical purposes, such examples are essentially

---

10. Philosopher of science and author of *Signature of the Cell*, Stephen C. Meyer, offers a very insightful and carefully researched investigation of one of the greatest challenges to neo-Darwinism, i.e., the rapid emergence during the Cambrian period of numerous animal forms without evolutionary precursors. For more details, see *Darwin's Doubt*. See also Behe, *Darwin's Black Box*.

11. C. S. Lewis discusses at length the relationship between the myth of evolutionism and the theory of evolution in "The Funeral of a Great Myth," 82–93.

12. Jaki, *Cosmos and Creator*, 120.

13. Meyer, *Darwin's Doubt*, 7–14.

absent from the record. Where are the extinct transitional mammals with only one eye or three, or an eye on their forehead and the other under their chin? Every species of dinosaur that has been found has two eyes strategically located to provide three-dimensional vision. Even if we admit, as we should, the incompleteness of the fossil record, by what occult magic has it only preserved the two-eye specimens and lost the earlier, nonviable forms? I want to remain open to any possibility; Darwin's theory will perhaps turn out to be undeniably true, but the fossil record offers little concrete evidence to support it.

Even if we could prove the notion of interspecies evolution by random and small incremental changes, how do we explain the appearance of such engineering marvels as the hydrogen atom, which cannot have been produced by natural selection? What are we to make of Lehigh University biochemist Michael Behe, who produces example after example of biochemical mechanisms that are so complex, "irreducibly complex," to borrow his expression, that they could not possibly be the result of a mindless evolutionary process or natural selection?

Take, for instance, the flagellum, a hair-like appendage that protrudes from certain cells and is used for locomotion. This organelle is a relatively simple biological motor that requires thirty to forty protein parts to function; the absence of even one essentially disables it. The engineering exhibited by this organism is simply stupendous. Not only does the flagellum enable the cell to move forward, but it also possesses a clutch that enables it to shift into neutral or reverse![14] While it is not my intent here to address the scientific legitimacy of the theory of evolution, I do believe there is sufficient evidence to question its quasi-religious status as infallible dogma.

While I do not side with those who believe the earth to be six thousand years old, who is saner? The person who fervently believes that all the marvels that stare us in the face, from the exquisite sophistication of a simple atom to the near-infinite complexity of the nanotechnology that animates every single organism on earth, are the outcome of a mere twelve billion years of mindless cosmic accidents and random mutations, or the person who thinks that an infinitely complex and powerful being engineered it all in six literal days? With all due respect, if reason, probability, and science are to be of any concern to us at all, I am afraid we have no choice but to side with the latter.

The main objective of this book is to explore the creation account's response to the presence of gratuitous pain and evil in the world. While I believe the story is anchored in real history, it is not my goal to demonstrate

---

14. Behe, *Darwin's Black Box*, 69–73.

its historicity or disprove the theory of evolution. My first concern is to provide an opportunity to at least hear the story.

I am not, however, simply indulging in an abstract academic exercise. The real significance of the narrative ultimately lies in whether there is any justification in tying it to history. In other words, if Adam and Eve are simply archetypal figures devised by the author to teach us about how we must relate to God, then it is indeed, as Brueggemann so confidently asserts, irrelevant in terms of providing a historical explanation of the human condition. If Brueggemann is right, then the story is indeed little more than a fable to be decoded for its insights into the human experience. While there is certainly great value in better capturing the meaning of the text and parsing its implications for our lives, if there is indeed a historical dimension to this account, then the story takes an entirely new significance in terms of the insights it provides into the root cause of evil, God's moral character, as well as his agenda for humanity. I believe there are sufficient reasons both to question Darwinism as a comprehensive explanation for human life and to crack open the possibility of a historical dimension in the creation story. While some readers may not be willing to accept such a possibility, I would, at the very least, plead for giving serious consideration to the message of the text.

The awkward fact remains there is no overwhelming or compelling evidence arguing against the existence of a primordial set of parents, nor is it intrinsically impossible to attempt some sort of reconciliation between scientific theory and the Genesis record. Blocher carefully reviews several such proposals and candidly recognizes the inherent difficulties of each.[15] The least unsatisfactory hypothesis, as Blocher puts it, is one offered by John J. Davis, which postulates, for instance, a nonliteral reading of Genesis ch. 4:

> With the story spanning tens of millennia and the genealogical links being understood as they would be in the following "digest" of European history: "Caesar begat Charlemagne, who begat Napoleon." The account starts with the emergence of *homo* type being identified as "Adamic." This ensures continuity with present humankind, which is likely to have proceeded from a unique center. It leads to the typical Neolithic situation, about thirty millennia later; as a popular summary of Neolithic culture, Genesis 4 could hardly be bettered.[16]

Blocher adds:

---

15. Blocher, *In the Beginning*, 213–31.
16. Blocher, *Original Sin*, 40.

Though we may feel uncomfortable with all the uncertainties when we try to correlate scientific data and the results of a sensible interpretation of Genesis 1–4, therefore, we may maintain as plausible the hypothesis that the biblical Adam and Eve were the first parents of our race, some 40,000 years ago; and we may posit an initial period of fellowship with God in their lives before they apostatized.[17]

Give It a Chance

In spite of the bad press the creation account receives these days, I maintain that Genesis 1–3 is essential to provide, if not a comprehensive answer to the problem of evil, at the very least, the basic elements of a coherent response that neither negates the reality of evil nor radically alters the orthodox view of God as perfect, absolutely good, and all-powerful. I would even go so far as to suggest that without a close and careful examination of the creation story, we are condemned to slide toward some form of monism or dualism. But before we get to the study of the text itself, three observations are in order.

First, as the German philosopher Hans-Georg Gadamer contends in his seminal book on philosophical hermeneutics, *Wahreit und Methode* (1960), the act of reading consists in the fusion of two horizons: that of the text and that of the reader.[18] On the one hand, the reader always occupies a cultural-historical standpoint, which, in a sense, necessarily limits what the reader can see. As Kevin J. Vanhoozer explains, "One's horizon is linked to one's prejudices, to one's habits of looking at the world in particular ways. Readers, in other words, always come to texts with a certain 'preunderstanding.'"[19] On the other hand, a text also has its particular horizon. For Gadamer, "Interpretation, then, is like a dialogue in which the reader exposes himself or herself to the effects of the text, while the text is exposed to the reader's interests and prejudices."[20] If understanding a text consists in a "fusion of horizons," this implies that the reader must at the very least be aware of his or her own inherent prejudices and limitations and be open to have them challenged by the text itself. The reader must be willing to give the text the benefit of the doubt.

Second, I would contend that to really appreciate the message of the text, it is imperative that we be willing to approach it with the presuppositions

17. Blocher, *Original Sin*, 42.
18. Gadamer, *Truth and Method*.
19. Vanhoozer, *Meaning*, 106.
20. Vanhoozer, *Meaning*, 106.

of the author. This doesn't mean that we uncritically accept such presuppositions, but that we temporarily suspend our own in order to facilitate our interface with the text.[21]

Third, as Vanhoozer further clarifies, it is indeed necessary to acknowledge "the right of the text to have its own say first."[22] The primary task of the interpreter consists in judging the act of communication the text represents on the basis of its own agenda and interest. This, as C. S. Lewis points out, represents an act of "surrender."[23] Lewis writes, "The first qualification for judging any piece of workmanship from a corkscrew to a cathedral is to know what it is—what it was intended to do and how it is meant to be used."[24]

With respect to Genesis 1–3, I would encourage the reader to enter into the internal logic of the text itself. It's the only way, I believe, to get at what the creation account is attempting to communicate about the genesis of the human condition. At this point, it is important to clarify that I do not, as some might naturally assume, simply intend to rehearse the major elements of the Augustinian theodicy. My objective is to give new attention to some of the elements of an orphaned story that, in my opinion, have too long been neglected.

MYTH OR HISTORY?

In order to assess the potential significance of the creation account, we need to more precisely identify its literary genre. In other words, what kind of text are we dealing with? As I pointed out earlier, Genesis 1–3 is commonly labeled as myth. While scholars know well what such a label may or may not imply, to qualify the creation story as a "myth," may be confusing for some readers. Creation myths are not unique to Hebrew literature. Archeologists have uncovered several examples in ancient Egypt, Mesopotamia, and throughout the world. In popular culture, the word "myth" generally denotes something that is false or not based on fact. When someone says, "That's a myth," the person usually means that the story is bunk. This is not

---

21 According to Giuseppina D'Oro and James Conelly, Robin G. Collingwood, a British philosopher and archeologist, held a similar attitude with respect to the study of history. They write, "Collingwood believes that in order to understand the thoughts of historical agents the historian must suspend his own beliefs and temporarily adopt those of the agents, even if they are deemed to be false" (see D'Oro and Connelly, "Robin George Collingwood").

22. Vanhoozer, *Meaning*, 374.

23. Lewis, *Experiment in Criticism*, 19; as cited by Vanhoozer, *Meaning*, 374.

24. Lewis, *Preface to Paradise Lost*, 1; as cited by Vanhoozer, *Meaning*, 374.

what I mean by myth. While there is no unanimous definition of myth,[25] for the purposes of this discussion, I will simply define it as an account that seeks to explain the world.[26] Creation myths fundamentally seek to provide as comprehensive a view of the world as possible. They endeavor to explain the nature of the divine, and the origin, role, and destiny of humanity.[27] Ancient myths are extremely valuable, for they provide an insight into the very heart of a culture's worldview.[28]

To refer to a text as myth has no direct implications for whether or not it represents an accurate picture of ultimate reality. All we can really say about such documents is that they reflect what people believed about the origin and the nature of the cosmos. Whether these claims are true is another issue. And this is exactly where the problem arises with respect to the biblical creation account. Scholars generally assume that these ancient myths reflect a primitive worldview. Though they may contain important insights about the human condition, their main value is that of a historical artifact.

While such an approach may be legitimate for Egyptian or Mesopotamian myths, it will not do for Genesis 1–3. First, not only did the creation story provide an authoritative and comprehensive portrait of the worldview the ancient Israelites *were* to embrace, the text is also framed within a broader canonical framework that offers it as inspired and authoritative for the community of faith. This gives it a significance that far exceeds whatever value it may have as an ancient document. As part of the canon of Scripture, this text is much more than just a description of what a particular people believed about the nature of the world; it in fact purports to provide a comprehensive worldview that accurately reflects reality.

If the creation account has been neglected in recent discussions on the problem of evil, it is in great part because of the failure to appreciate its true nature. The creation narrative belongs to a type of ancient literature that, according to Kenneth Kitchen, most likely emerged in the first half of the second millennium.[29] The *Myth of Atrahasis* and the Babylonian myth

---

25. See for instance, the insightful discussion of the meaning of myth in the context of biblical studies by Oden, "Myth and Mythology," and "Myth in the OT," 945–56, 956–60.

26. See Ricoeur, *Le conflit des interprétations*, 418.

27. See Bottéro, *Religion*, 77–81.

28 See Bottéro, *Religion*, 3–4. For more details on what is sometimes referred to as the intellectualist view of myth, see Tylor, Frazer, Horton, *Primitive Culture*; Frazer, *Golden Bough*; Horton, "African Traditional Thought," 50–71, 155–87.

29. See Kitchen, *Reliability*, 423.

known as the *Enuma Elish* are the best known examples of such accounts in ancient Mesopotamia.[30]

Genesis 1–3 can be technically categorized as a creation myth. As such, it shares a purpose common to ancient myths. As a creation story, Genesis 1–3 provides the broad outline of a worldview whose object was to compete against the religious ideology the Hebrews had acquired in four hundred years of slavery in Egypt. As a freed people about to begin a new phase of their existence in service to a God who was fundamentally different from every other god, distinct and unique, the Hebrews were also to adopt a new understanding of the world. The creation account was expressly written to provide such an alternative worldview.[31] As such, it parsed a new understanding of God, humanity, and the physical universe.[32]

In terms of our discussion of the problem of evil, this text is important, for it provides critical information about the nature of God's character, human suffering, and the less than ideal conditions that prevail in this world. Because it is, by virtue of its literary genre, a text that is designed to provide the building blocks of a worldview, we have no choice but to give it careful consideration. It is my contention that Genesis 1–3 contains invaluable

---

30. The *Myth of Atrahasis* is the most ancient mythological writing we have at our disposal. The great poem is written in Akkadian and dated prior to the oldest fragments recovered from King Ammisaduqa's reign (1646–1626 BC), fourth successor of Hammurabi of Babylon. The title is derived from the name of the hero that plays the role of the king of the country, *Atrahasîs*, which means "the exceptional wise" (see Bottéro, *La plus vieille religion*, 199). The *Enuma Elish* was compiled around 1100 BC from various Sumerian and Amorite traditions.

31. For more details on the polemic character of the creation story, see Kaufmann, *Religion of Israel*, 60–63; Bottéro, "Le Dieu de la bible," and *Naissance de Dieu*. See also Hasel, "Polemic Nature," 81–102.

32. Many biblical scholars do not agree with a dating of this text that locates it in the Mosaic period. Most critical scholars, in fact, attribute a final redactional date for Genesis 1–3 sometime in the postexilic era. Be that as it may, it is important to note that there is in fact little evidence to suggest any date for this text, let alone such a late one. Up until a few decades ago, critical scholars held to what's known as the documentary hypothesis (JEDP) as the best explanation for the development of the Pentateuch. According to this hypothesis, the Pentateuch can be divided into sections indicating various sources originating from different eras and regions. Although no new hypothesis has received the general assent of the scholarly community, the documentary hypothesis no longer receives unanimous endorsement. Following Wenham (*Genesis 1–15*, xlii–xlv), I think there is sufficient ground to support the existence of a creation story that would have encompassed the most important ideas now attested in the canonical narrative. The existence of such a story would be entirely compatible with Moses's mandate to create a distinct political entity. For a more detailed assessment of the documentary theory, see Cassuto, *Documentary Hypothesis*; Alter, *Biblical Narrative*; Garrett, *Rethinking Genesis*; Maier, "How Did Moses Compose the Pentateuch?," 157–61; Campbell and O'Brien, *Sources of the Pentateuch*, 10–15.

clues for uncovering the root causes behind the reality of evil and gratuitous suffering, and for resolving the apparent contradiction inherent to the classical formulation of the problem of evil.

I have much sympathy for those who have serious difficulties with respect to using the creation account to shed light on the reality of evil. Not only have such attempts proven to be, for many, less than satisfactory, the reality is that because of its perplexing literary characteristics, the text presents a number of serious interpretive challenges. In order to benefit the most from the interpretation of this text, it is crucial we keep several principles in mind.

First, I am working on the assumption that the text is divinely inspired and authoritative. If, as I suggested earlier, it is imperative that the reader give serious consideration to the presuppositions undergirding any text, then it follows that the reader should, at the very least, read the creation narrative as it was first intended to be read, namely, as inspired and authoritative.

Second, in order to benefit the most from reading this text, we need to remain focused on its primary objective, which consists in offering the basic outline of a worldview that reflects the true nature of things. While there is nothing to prevent us from asking any question of a text, the benefits of our investigation will be directly proportional to the degree to which these questions are consistent with its original intent. Readers may not be in unanimous agreement on what constitutes the precise character of a text's "intent," but we must nevertheless seek to lean in that direction. Questions that touch on worldview issues will find rich answers; those that are, in this respect, off-center, will not tend to be as significant. No one is immune from committing errors of interpretation. Distortions are part and parcel of the reading process. While I cannot pretend to avoid all such distortions, I will attempt to distinguish between reasonably reliable conclusions and those that may be considered more tentative and speculative.

Third, myth is by its very nature infused with symbolic and archetypal elements. In other words, it also speaks to the universality of human existence. Mythology is not about a particular individual or a specific incident; that would more properly be the object of legends and historical narratives. Myth is about the gods and their interactions with humanity. The interpretation of myth requires, therefore, that we pay special attention to these elements that may have universal implications. It goes without saying that for some scholars, the investigation of this text will be limited to searching for its symbolic and archetypal significance. I would contend, however, that it is not that simple. When it comes to Genesis 1–3, there are other considerations that must be integrated into the interpretive process.

HISTORICAL OR PARADIGMATIC/ SYMBOLIC/ARCHETYPAL?

In addition to the inspired character of the text, which should influence how we ought to receive the creation narrative, the other question that needs to be raised is that of the precise character of its literary genre.[33] Like other creation stories, Genesis 1–3 contains poetic, symbolic, and archetypal elements. But unlike other myths, there is also an unmistakable historical component; the author portrays Adam and Eve as concrete historical characters who are, for example, explicitly linked to patriarchal history. The precise question that is before us is whether Genesis 1–3 can simply be categorized as myth, or whether we need to broaden our literary categories in order to adequately accommodate the literary specificity of the text.

That Genesis chs. 1 to 3 contain poetic elements is beyond debate. As L. M. Pasinya demonstrates, the first chapter exhibits elements that are poetic and symbolic.[34] With respect to chs. 2 and 3, Gordon Wenham notes:

> The symbolic dimensions of the story linking the garden with the later sanctuaries support a paradigmatic reading. Water, gold, jewels, cherubim and so on link the Garden of Eden with the tabernacle and temples described later. The curses pronounced on the guilty anticipate those curses pronounced on those who violate the law. These elements give the story a universalistic flavor, or at least a pan-Israelite setting. "Adam" is every man in Israel.[35]

It goes without saying that the creation account cannot simply be categorized as a historical narrative in the way, for example, the patriarchal narratives or 1 Kings might. On the other hand, because of the unmistakable poetic and symbolic elements in the account, scholars have had a tendency to dismiss any link whatsoever between the story and history.[36]

---

33. For more details on the difficulties inherent to determining the literary genre of the creation account, see Thompson, "Genesis 1," 12–23; Blocher, *In the Beginning*, 36–38; Gibert, *Bible, mythes et récits*.

34. Pasinya offers a remarkable analysis of the opening chapter of Genesis in "Le cadre littéraire de Genèse 1," 225–42.

35. See Wenham, *Genesis 1–15*, 91. In a similar vein, John Milton contends that Genesis 1 is in fact a temple text, "It is describing the creation of the cosmic temple with all of its functions and with God dwelling in its midst" (*Lost World of Genesis One*, 84).

36. On that account, it should be noted that, for the most part, critical scholars also tend to dismiss much of the historical value of the patriarchal narratives. See for instance Thompson, *Patriarchal Narratives*; Van Seters, *Abraham in History and Tradition* and *Prologue to History*.

Notwithstanding the scholarly impulse to dissociate poetry from history, it should be noted that there is no inherent and necessary contradiction between the two genres. Such distinctions are entirely artificial and merely reflect modern literary canons. Ancient Hebrew texts do not neatly fall into simple literary silos.

Historical narratives can and do include poetic elements,[37] and poems can allude to historical events.[38] In principle then, a historical event can be expressed as poetry and articulated in such a way as to support symbolic and archetypical indicators. In terms of Old Testament literary conventions, the presence of poetic and symbolic elements in the creation account does not, in and of itself, exclude a historical perspective. While the creation account is similar to myth in terms of its function, and while it also exhibits the characteristics of poetry, the evidence at hand does not suggest a radical disconnection from history such as might be the case, for example, with many of the psalms or wisdom texts like the books of Proverbs or Ecclesiastes.

In the broadest sense of the term, the creation account is set within a historical framework. The expression "In the beginning" signals a move away from the cyclical view of history that was predominant at that time. The account sets the creation of the world within a historical framework; it alludes to an absolute beginning.[39]

As Wenham notes, there are indicators that suggest the author intended the text to be read as part of a greater historical framework. It represents one of the ways in which this narrative distinguishes itself from myth. For instance, the expression "These are the generations of,"[40] heading the detailed account of Adam and Eve in Gen 2:4, expressly links this story to the rest of biblical history, particularly the patriarchal narratives of

---

37. In a noted doctoral dissertation, Aldina da Silva observes that the dreams of Joseph narrative found in Genesis 37–43 are organized as an elaborate chiastic construction that highlights the movement from death to life characterizing Joseph's life (see *Une lecture de la théologie de genèse*, 37–50). As is the case with other Old Testament historical narratives, the significance of these texts goes beyond the specific actors and their historical circumstances; they are also infused with paradigmatic, symbolic, and archetypal significance in that they reflect universal human needs and concerns and contain definite elements of contextualization relative to faith.

38. A case in point is the Song of Deborah (Judg 5:1–31). While the text uses literary devices usually associated with poetry, such as metaphors, projections, repetition, hyperboles, etc., the poem is based on and evokes a historical event (see Judg 4:23). See also the Song of Moses in Exod 15:1–21.

39. The renowned Assyriologist Jean Bottéro suggests there is nothing comparable in Mesopotamia. See *Mesopotamia*, 82.

40. Hebrew *toledoth* sometimes rendered as "account."

Noah, Abraham, Jacob, etc.[41] The repetition of this expression signals that the events contained in the creation account should not simply be read as symbolic abstractions. As Wenham further observes, "The ensuing story of Cain and Abel and especially the genealogy of chap. 5, linking Adam with Noah shows that the author understood the earliest stories to be about real people."[42]

The creation account exhibits both the characteristics of myth (poetry, symbol, and archetype) and history. It is historical and archetypal. It speaks of a real Adam and Eve and circumstances that were unique to them, but it also contains elements that are intended to be read as archetypal and figurative, i.e., as applying to every human being. While the creation story belongs to the category of myth by virtue of its function, the reality is that it does not fully display the characteristics of mythology in terms of style and content.[43] Unlike myth, the creation account does not depict a universe in which there is a multiplicity of deities whose essence is mediated through the elements of nature. The text states that there is only one God, and that this God created the world. The expression "the heavens and the earth" encompasses the entire known universe. By the standards of its time, this is a most remarkable and surprising declaration. This simple statement contains the seeds of the eventual demise and destruction of the entire Mesopotamian mythical universe. In one swipe, this text fatally undermines the world of the gods and their powers. It truly was the toll bell that marked the end of the age of the gods and the beginning of the age of men. Genesis 1:1 affirms the absolute sovereignty of God over creation and distinguishes the person of God from the created order. At this juncture of history, it was a vision that departed radically from everything humans believed about the nature of the gods and their relationship to the physical universe.

Throughout history, humans have consistently believed that the divine was intrinsically entwined with the physical world. This is a view known as pantheism. In *Mere Christianity*, C. S. Lewis points out that in pantheism, the divine and the physical universe are believed to be almost one and the same. The divine is beyond good and evil. It is indistinguishable from the universe; so that if one could conceive of the universe disappearing, God or the gods would also be extinguished. The first verse of Genesis 1 is diametrically opposed to such a perception of the divine. The text conjures up the picture of a God who imagines and makes the universe in the same way

---

41. See Gen 5:1; 6:9; 10:1; 11:10, 27; 25:12, 19; 36:1, 9; 37:2.

42. Wenham, *Genesis 1–15*, 91.

43. See Gibert's critique of the use of the term "myth" to denote the creation account in *Bible, mythes et récits*.

an artist creates a work of art. To borrow from Lewis: "A painter is not a picture, and he does not die if his picture is destroyed."[44]

The author does not attempt to communicate to the Hebrews that Elohim is one god among many. Genesis 1 could not be any clearer: Elohim is the only God and sole creator of the universe. The notion of an only God, who is distinct from the physical realm, did not naturally emerge in Israel. The idea was as foreign for the Hebrews as it was for their neighbors. The inherent foreignness of the account explains perhaps why Israel repeatedly turned to foreign gods or sought to transform Yahweh into a mutation of Baal. Though the people of Israel struggled with idolatry, as the prophetic literature points out all too clearly, Genesis 1 leaves no doubt as to what the great theologian was trying to convey. Elohim is the God from whom everything proceeds. End of the story! This statement, further supported by the multiple declarations that follow in Gen 1:2–25, in which the author disconnects the phenomena of nature from the direct intervention of the various nature deities of the Mesopotamian pantheon, contrasts sharply with the world of myth.

In fact, some scholars have expressed serious reservation about classifying the Genesis creation account as myth. In terms of style, Genesis 1–3 contrasts with myth particularly by virtue of a sobriety that is more akin to historical narrative than to myth. The renowned Old Testament scholar Gerhard von Rad writes:

> The narrator does not reply to many impertinent questions because his own standpoint, of course, is not within Paradise but outside it, and he refrains from all fantasy and speculation about what existed before the Fall. In this respect the reticence, indeed soberness and calm of the Biblical story is especially noticeable in contrast to the arrogant and harsh colors in the myths of other peoples.[45]

The narrative, he adds, "has very little in common with a real myth."[46] Blocher writes, "The whole atmosphere differs profoundly from that of myth."[47] The Roman Catholic Old Testament specialist Pierre Gibert, following Jean-Pierre Vernant, notes that great methodological care must be exercised when applying the category of myth to the Genesis creation account.[48]

---

44. Lewis, *Mere Christianity*, 40.
45. Rad, *Genesis*, 97.
46. Rad, *Genesis*, 95.
47. Blocher, *Original Sin*, 49.
48. See Gibert, *Bible, mythes et récits*, 97.

In summary, there are at least three reasons for resisting the impulse to characterize Genesis 1–3 as solely myth. First, as von Rad reminds us, the text exhibits a stylistic soberness that contrasts sharply with myth. Second, the entire mythological divine infrastructure is evacuated. Third, the text itself creates a link between the events outlined in Genesis 1–3 and patriarchal history. This "organic" connection is confirmed by the Genesis narrative in the lineage found in 5:1–32 and later continued in the Table of Nations in 10:1–32, with an explicit articulation between Shem and Abraham in 10:1, 21 and 11:10, 26–32, and 12:1.

THE WITNESS OF THE NEW TESTAMENT

The historical anchoring of Genesis 1–3, especially as it relates to Adam and Eve, is also echoed in the New Testament. Most prominent in this regard is Paul's own assessment of Adam as a historical character. In Rom 5:12–21, Paul unreservedly recognizes the historicity of Adam. In 5:12, the apostle associates the emergence of sin to one man's act of disobedience.[49] Furthermore, Paul clarifies the fact that sin is not just some abstract principle that has always been part and parcel of human existence. Sin is something that has a definite and distinct point of origin: "Therefore, just as sin came into the world through one man . . ."

In v. 13, Paul confirms the emergence of sin as resulting from a historical incident in two ways. First, he positions Adam's sin and the emergence of the Mosaic law on a similar historical horizon: "sin was indeed in the world before the law." Second, he states that the principle of sin as transgression existed before the promulgation of the law. In other words, sin predates the law and finds its source in a space/time violation of God's command just as it is described in Genesis 3.

In Rom 5:14, Paul states that "death exercised dominion from Adam to Moses." By mentioning Adam and Moses side by side, he places them both on the same historical plane. In vv. 15 and 16, Paul reiterates the organic connection between Adam's sin and human death: "For if the many died through the one man's trespass . . ." In this verse, Paul underlines the historical character of Adam's transgression by comparing it with the free gift of grace brought about by "another man, Christ." Verse 16 contrasts the nature of the free gift obtained through Christ with the effect of Adam's sin. The latter resulted in God's condemnation, which is an allusion to the

---

49. For a detailed discussion of this issue, see Dunn, *Romans 1–8*, 271–72; Fitzmyer, *Romans*, 405–7; Bruce, *Romans*, 118–23; Stott, *Romans*, 148–54; Moo, *Epistle to the Romans*, 314–29; Mounce, *Romans*, 139–43.

divine judgment in Genesis 3. The former, brought about through Christ's agency, resulted in justification.[50] Verse 17 associates death's universal dominion with a historical act: "the one man's trespass." Note the parallel between Adam and the person of Christ; both are portrayed as historical characters. The same idea is reiterated in v. 19 where "one man's disobedience," described here as a historical event, is contrasted to another "man's obedience." In vv. 20–21, Paul creates a correspondence between the sin of Adam and the saving act of Christ.

Paul does not simply describe Adam and his sin as an archetype. While I believe Adam's sin can be interpreted as a symbol of humanity's rebellion against God, in this case Paul refers to Adam as a historical person. Incidentally, Paul is not averse to attributing symbolic significance to Adam. In v. 14, he identifies him as "a type of the one who was to come." This thought is echoed in 1 Cor 15:45–49 where "the first man," Adam, is contrasted to the "last Adam." In this passage, Paul attributes archetypal significance to Adam who stands here for all of humanity.

> Thus it is written, "The first man, Adam, became a living being"; the last Adam became a life-giving spirit. But it is not the spiritual that is first, but the physical, and then the spiritual. The first man was from the earth, a man of dust; the second man is from heaven. As was the man of dust, so are those who are of the dust; and as is the man of heaven, so are those who are of heaven. Just as we have borne the image of the man of dust, we will also bear the image of the man of heaven.

Finally, Paul puts Adam on the same historical plane as a number of other Old Testament characters such as Abraham (9:7), Isaac (9:7, 10), Rebekah (9:10), Jacob and Esau (9:11–13), Moses (9:14), Pharaoh (9:17), and Elijah (11:2).[51] Adam's historical character is further highlighted in 1 Tim 2:13, where Paul appeals to the creation of Adam and Eve, and then Eve's transgression, to justify his exhortation to the women of that community.

Paul's view of Adam as a historical figure is crucial for his argument. In the first four chapters of Romans, his main objective is to demonstrate that all human beings, Jews and non-Jews alike, are guilty before God. But human guilt is not, of course, the end of the story. In ch. 4, Paul proclaims the principle of justification by faith. And in ch. 5, the apostle identifies

---

50. Compare with 1 Cor 15:22: "for as all die in Adam, so all will be made alive in Christ."

51. See also Jude 1:14, where Adam is included in Enoch's ancestry: "It was also about these that Enoch, in the seventh generation from Adam . . ."

the precise object of that faith, i.e., Jesus Christ (5:8–11). The question, of course, is why are we all in a position of radical enmity with respect to God? Is this just part and parcel of human nature? If so, then the ultimate cause of evil must lie at the creator's feet.

For Paul, the root cause of the human condition is no mystery. He explicitly ties it to a historical event, i.e., Adam's transgression as stated in Rom 5:12: "Therefore, just as sin came into the world through one man, and death came through sin . . . " As I wrote earlier, while there are symbolic, archetypal, or figurative dimensions to the Genesis account of the fall, Adam and Eve's act of disobedience is also presented as a historical event. If the fall is simply figurative of every person's sinful impulse, then Paul's entire argument is no better than a house of cards in an earthquake; in fact, it is much worse. Without a historical fall, Paul has no case whatsoever, and the epistle's argument collapses.

My own thesis with respect to the problem of evil is entirely contingent on the notion of a historical fall. Without such an event to anchor the intrusion of sin into human history, I don't think it is possible to provide a coherent response to the presence of evil in the world. If most contemporary solutions to the problem of evil involve either a challenge to God's omnipotence or goodness, or, alternatively, a banalization of evil, it is most likely because of a general unwillingness to take into account the possibility of a historical act of disobedience at the pinpoint origin of human history.

CONCLUSION

The creation text does not easily fit into a neat literary box. On the one hand, while it evokes mythology in terms of its function, the author inserts the story within a historical framework. The critical events surrounding the creation of Adam and Eve, their divine mandate, and their disobedience relate historical events pertaining specifically and uniquely to these two individuals. If we are to fully assess the possible implications of this text for our discussion, we must carefully consider the implications of the historical dimensions of the text.

On the other hand, the creation account is not merely a historical narrative. In line with the great creation myths that emerged in the first half of the second millennium, it is also designed to provide a basic conceptual framework with respect to the nature of God, humanity, and the universe. If the historical aspects of the account draw attention to the specificity of Adam and Eve, the mythical dimensions of the text draw attention to the universal character of the story. The first links the act of creation and Adam and Eve to the rest of history, thus indicating the narrator's intent for the reader to view it within a historical framework. The second ensures that this story will not be read as a simple historical account, but as a narrative that has universal implications. The archetypal dimension reminds the reader that there is more here than meets the eye. If I may be permitted to use a digital analogy, the creation account is a little like a "compressed file." The narrative's mythical or paradigmatic character points to a "high density" of meaning, a symbolic dimension that requires special care to access more of the text's hermeneutical potential as well as the various levels of meaning embedded in it. This will be the focus of the next chapter.

3
God's Purpose: A Special Kind of Creature

THE PROBLEM

IN ORDER TO ACCOUNT for the presence of evil in the world, we must begin with the correct starting point. To attempt to make sense of our existence by looking at the present condition of the world is as futile as trying to make sense of the design of a cannibalized car abandoned in a field. No amount of philosophical speculation could ever account for the presumed incompetence of engineers for designing a contraption that has no wheels and is lacking an engine and a transmission.

To look at the world as it is today without inquiring about God's primordial motivation in creating it is to forever condemn ourselves to go in circles and arrive at the only conclusion the present state of affairs permits, which is to repeat the familiar chorus that so many have sung throughout the centuries: "If I had been at God's counsel at the Creation, many things would have been ordered better."[1] We have no choice but to proclaim God's glaring incompetence if we insist on maintaining his benevolence, or should we want to maintain our belief in his infinite power, sadly acquiesce to his cruelty.

---

1. This sentiment, formally expressed by Alfonso X, who became king of Castile in 1252, is reported by Susan Neiman as part of her discussion of Leibniz's theodicy (*Evil in Modern Thought*, 14–18).

Most philosophers and theologians tend to approach the problem of evil from this side of history. Like those who might follow a trail of bread crumbs to find their way back home, they are convinced they can arrive at a solution for the reality of evil in our world by observing the present and working backward. While such an approach may in some instances reflect good deductive reasoning, it will always prove to be inadequate with respect to articulating a comprehensive explanation for the human condition. At best, we will realize the futility of the approach and find refuge in some form of agnosticism. At worst, we will find refuge in a sad but not uncommon tautology: this is the way it is because it is the way it is.

Regardless of our religious or philosophical convictions, as we saw in chapter 1, attempting to make sense of evil through a deductive process only leads to a dead-end. Like the confused man who vainly attempts to explain to the tourist how to get to his destination, in the end, he is forced to concede that "you can't get there from here."

While I would not necessarily agree with their conclusions, as Irenaeus, Friedrich Schleiermacher,[2] and more recently John Hick[3] have hinted at, in order to gain an adequate perspective on why the world is as it is, it is imperative we ascertain what God's original intent may have been. For instance, for Hick, the world was designed to serve as a "vale of soul-making." If this is true, then the world as we have it is entirely consistent with God's original intent in that it represents the kind of environment needed to allow for the moral development of the human species. The beauty of this position is that it appears to entirely remove any sense that there is something fundamentally wrong with the world. It is indeed the best of all worlds.

In some respect, I suspect that on a most basic level, Hick's intuition is correct. We need to start the discussion by ascertaining as best we can God's original intent for his creation. But could it be that simple? Was the world, with all its violence, suffering, and the universal reality of death, originally willed by God to serve as some sort of moral boot camp? I am not challenging the notion that the world as we know it can indeed serve as a "vale of soul-making." The reality is that it can and does represent a place where character is formed, and moral virtues are developed.

Two questions must, however, be raised. First, does the world in its present shape really reflect God's original design? Is this the kind of world God had originally envisioned for humanity? In other words, is the present world best designed to fulfill God's intent for the human race? Or, to frame it more narrowly as conservative commentator and author Dinesh D'Souza

---

2. Schleiermacher, *Christian Faith*.
3. See Hick, *Evil & the God of Love*.

argues in his book *God Forsaken*, is this in fact the *only*, not the best, but the only possible world God could create? He writes, "Given God's objective to make humans, God constructed the universe not in the best possible way, but in the only way that it could be constructed. In other words, God chose the sole option available to produce the result that he wanted."[4] D'Souza claims, based on a new assessment of recent advances in "physics, astronomy, brain science, and biology,"[5] and as he puts it, the discovery of the fine-tuned universe, sometimes called the Anthropic Principle, that the universe God needed to create in order to bring about his purpose for the human race had to be the universe in which we live . . . evil, pain, death, and all. I should point out here that what D'Souza describes as a radically new solution to the presence of evil doesn't, on closer examination, seem all that innovative.

The other objection relates to a more pragmatic issue. If indeed the world was originally designed by God to serve as a "vale of soul-making," making it the best if not the only possible world God could conceive of with respect to his hopes for the human race, then how exactly does our experience of the world accomplish this objective? What are the precise mechanisms that should lead to the improvement of the human species as a whole? Is humanity irrevocably moving toward the ultimate fulfillment of God's original intent for humanity? Are we collectively more mature now than twelve thousand years ago? I doubt it. How deluded would we need to be to believe something like this? If history teaches us anything, it's that war, violence, cruelty, and man-induced chaos are the norm, not the exception, as many naïve Westerners have come to believe. The will to destroy is still as inextricably dissolved in our genetic makeup as sugar in a Coke bottle. The human race is no worse or better than it has ever been.

If the moral evolutionary process the world is allegedly designed to produce is not collective, is it then just individual? If so, what is the end product supposed to look like? Are there individual men and women out there who reflect the ideal outcome of what the world is presumed to be designed to deliver? Let's be honest. Only hopelessly delusional people would even claim to embody the lofty ideals such a process presumes. While adversity can indeed produce certain moral virtues, judging by the lawlessness and violence of our inner cities, that doesn't seem to be working out all that well for a lot of people who often have more than their share of trouble. As for the rest of us, we can only sigh along with Pierre Jougnelet who, remembering the great French poet Charles Péguy (1873–1914), writes:

---

4. D'Souza, *God Forsaken*, 30.
5. D'Souza, *God Forsaken*, 14.

> Remember what Péguy called the forty year old man's secret. One needs all the illusions of youth, fed by many merchants, to be satisfied with one self. In time, because of his failures and his shortcomings, even more so because of his successes and the erosion of one's happiness, man discovers that he is not lovable. This "I" who is inside him, he endures it . . . barely, sometimes he hates it, more often, he tries not to think about it and finds refuge in mediocrity. . . . We understand then what salvation entails. In as much as my defects and my limitations are real, that I recognize them and hope no more, I discover, one day, that I am loved. I am seen. The one who looks upon me doesn't ignore my misery; in fact, his gaze makes it that much more real, but it transforms into repentance my vague despair. . . . Thus in a turnaround we could call a second birth, the man who is loved discovers he can love. The object of infinite attention, he becomes a source of attention that he bestows on himself, to all things, and even more so to the Savior who has given him life.[6]

If this world is indeed supposed to be a "vale of soul-making," there is precious little evidence that it is fulfilling or ever will fulfill its purpose. If the efficacy of this "vale" might be deemed a possibility given enough time, then what about children who die before they reach the age of reason? In what possible way is this world a vale of soul-making for them?

While I think Hick makes a valid observation about the opportunities the world offers for the development of moral virtues, its glaring inadequacy in terms of actually producing perfectly mature individuals points to a profound discontinuity between what is and what ought to have been. Everything leads me to believe that this is not the world God intended to create. Something catastrophic occurred somewhere along the way. In this respect, G. K. Chesterton eloquently notes:

---

6. "Rappelez-vous ce que Péguy appelait le secret de l'homme de quarante ans. Il faut toutes les illusions de la jeunesse, et encore entretenues par beaucoup de marchands, pour se plaire à soi-même. Avec le temps, à travers ses échecs et ses défaillances, plus encore à travers ses réussites et l'usure du bonheur, l'homme apprend qu'il n'est pas aimable. Ce moi qui est en lui, il le supporte en maugréant, parfois il le hait, plus souvent il essaie de n'y pas penser et se réfugie dans la médiocrité. . . . On comprend alors ce que signifie le salut. Alors que mes tares et mes limites sont bien réelles, que je les vois en vérité et n'espère rien, je découvre un jour que je suis aimé. Un regard est posé sur moi. Certes il ne méconnaît pas ma misère, il aiguise plutôt la conscience que j'en ai et change en repentir mon vague désespoir. . . . Ainsi dans un retournement qui est une seconde naissance, l'homme aimé se découvre capable d'aimer. Objet d'une attention infinie, il devient source d'une attention émerveillée qu'il accorde à soi, à toutes choses, et plus encore au Sauveur qui lui a rendu la vie." As cited by Dumont, "Après le système chrétien," 191.

But the important matter was this, that it entirely reversed the reason for optimism. And the instant the reversal was made it felt like the abrupt ease when a bone is put back in the socket. I had often called myself an optimist, to avoid the too evident blasphemy of pessimism. But all the optimism of the age had been false and disheartening for this reason, that it had always been trying to prove that we fit in to the world. The Christian optimism is based on the fact that we do NOT fit in to the world. I had tried to be happy by telling myself that man is an animal, like any other which sought its meat from God. But now I really was happy, for I had learnt that man is a monstrosity. I had been right in feeling all things as odd, for I myself was at once worse and better than all things. The optimist's pleasure was prosaic, for it dwelt on the naturalness of everything; the Christian pleasure was poetic, for it dwelt on the unnaturalness of everything in the light of the supernatural. The modern philosopher had told me again and again that I was in the right place, and I had still felt depressed even in acquiescence. But I had heard that I was in the WRONG place, and my soul sang for joy, like a bird in spring. The knowledge found out and illuminated forgotten chambers in the dark house of infancy. I knew now why grass had always seemed to me as queer as the green beard of a giant, and why I could feel homesick at home.[7]

This painful discrepancy we feel between what is and what ought to be is not simply the result of our overactive imagination. Unless we resign ourselves to believing in a world that accidentally emerged out of some mindless chaos, we are compelled to peer into the fantastic chasm that separates what is from what should be and despair. But if the world is indeed the outcome of divine purpose and reason, there has to be some explanation to account for the world as it is and more specifically for the suffering, so much of it gratuitous, that men and women experience or inflict on others. The ultimate explanation must be found in God's original intent. But as I intimated earlier, there appears to be no bridge spanning our present condition to a discovery of God's original purpose. Any hope there may be in breaking out of the circle in which the human mind is trapped resides in obtaining a new kind of data. My proposal is that such data is indeed accessible and can be gleaned from the biblical creation story found in Genesis 1–3.

---

7. Chesterton, *Orthodoxy*, 146–47.

IN THE IMAGE OF GOD

In order to get a more accurate picture of God's original plan for humanity, we need to examine more closely the notion of the image of God in Gen 1:27: "So God created humankind in his image, in the image of God he created them; male and female he created them."

Much has been written about the image of God. It has variously been associated with the human soul, free will, human conscience, the ability to think, love, create, etc.[8] While the notion of the image of God surely implies some or all of these elements, this is not where the primary emphasis lies. It is more likely that the "image of God" primarily denotes a kingly function. As Wenham points out, in Egyptian and Assyrian texts, the divine image is often attributed to the king in his role as divine *representative*. In Gen 1:28 and Ps 8:5–8, the image of God explicitly alludes to the mandate to rule creation, a definite royal function.[9] The text uses the concept of divine image to highlight humanity's status as God's vice-regent.

While I do not wish to downplay the profound theological implications the expression entails, it is important to keep in mind that the image of God first and foremost draws attention to humanity's role as God's representative on earth. The expression does not primarily allude to divine attributes individual men and women may or may not have; the image qualifies humanity as a whole. It is the human species that is created in God's image. The exceptional status and protection that the "image" confers to all human beings (Gen 9:6) is not contingent on whether any particular individual displays those moral characteristics that have traditionally been associated with the image of God. Individual men and women benefit from this special status simply by virtue of belonging to the human race.

That being said, the allusion to the image of God does not, *per se*, communicate a whole lot of information about God's original intent for humanity. The focus of the text is relatively narrow. Verse 28 seems to primarily attribute a functional definition to the image. Men and women are mandated to act as God's vice-regents on the earth. To be created in God's image is to be entrusted with ruling the world.

While the text doesn't expand on what this role entails, the nature of this vice-regency is not left entirely undefined. The assumption is that

---

8. For a summary of the various meanings attributed to the image of God, see Wenham, *Genesis 1–15*, 29–32.

9. See Wenham, *Genesis 1–15*, 30–31. For more details, see also Clines, "Image of God in Man," 53–103; Curtis, "Image of God (OT)," 389–92.

humanity will reign in a way that is consistent with God's righteous rule.[10] Wenham writes:

> Because man is created in God's image, he is king over nature. He rules the world on God's behalf. This is of course no license for the unbridled exploitation and subjugation of nature. Ancient oriental kings were expected to be devoted to the welfare of their subjects, especially the poorest and weakest members of society (Ps 72:12–14). By upholding divine principles of law and justice, rulers promoted peace and prosperity for all their subjects. Similarly, mankind is here commissioned to rule nature as a benevolent king, acting as God's representative over them and therefore treating them in the same way as God who created them.[11]

Some of the implications of this status are expanded in Gen 2:15–17, where God invites Adam to take care of the garden of Eden (v. 15), subsequently gives him the authority to make use of all the resources of the earth to do so (v. 16), and provides strict parameters to respect. The creature is not ultimately self-determining; if Adam is given a high degree of autonomy, God nevertheless expects him to work within a given framework, something I will explore more at length later.

The role attributed to the human race implies a special status for humanity. Human beings are not simply given the mandate to rule, but to rule like God would; showing love, concern, fairness, and justice. Only a special kind of creature can actually follow through on such a mandate. The creature must at the very least be similar to God in critical ways. If the creature is to love its fellow beings, show kindness to all of creation, and be loyal to the divine king, then it needs to be endowed with the capacity to perform these functions. The attribute needed to do so is what we commonly call free will. Without free will, there can be no love and no significant ability to show genuine loyalty to anything or anyone, let alone God.

Genesis 1:27 and 2:15–17 draw attention to several important ideas. First, at the center of creation, there is humanity; the universe is created for its benefit. Second, humans are created to be in fellowship with God in a way that is unique from the rest of creation. Third, the texts hint at God's primordial purpose behind the act of creation. God's original purpose, it appears, was to create a creature that would be endowed with free will and would live in perfect fellowship with him forever.

---

10. Cf. Deut 17:14–20; Isa 11:1–14; Jer 33:15; 1 Sam 10:25; 1 Kgs 9:4–9; 3:28; 2 Kgs 23:2.

11. Wenham, *Genesis 1–15*, 33.

That God wished to create a creature that would be most fundamentally defined by its ability to act freely is confirmed throughout Scripture. The Torah contains repeated exhortations to choose God and to reject idols.[12] The prophets call on the Israelites to abandon idolatry and to turn to Yahweh.[13] The wisdom writers invite an audience that is convinced meaning and truth can be found outside of biblical faith to consider trusting in God.[14] The gospels present Christ to men and women who are expected to make a decision with respect to whether they will follow him or not. The epistles contain countless exhortations for Christians to remain faithful to Jesus Christ.

What most clearly emerges from these traditions is the implicit recognition of a creature that is endowed with free will with respect to God. The biblical text describes a God who will go to extraordinary lengths to persuade men and women to turn to him without ever going over the line where persuasion becomes coercion, a point where free will can no longer endure.

To go back to our discussion of God's original plan, it appears God intended to create a creature that would be like him in one critical respect: it would be endowed with free will. This attribute would effectively empower the creature to enter into a relationship with God, extend love to others, and care for all of creation.

To resort to free will to describe human beings or to explain the presence of evil in the world is a commonly accepted axiom. The notion that Adam and Eve were free, and that sin emerged out of that freedom would be obvious to most readers. There is, however, another issue that needs to be addressed and which, I believe, is at the very core of the presence of evil in the world. The real question is not whether Adam and Eve were free. As important as that question might be, we need to position ourselves one step back and inquire about the process required to produce such a creature.

The query is not as trivial as it may appear at first, and that may be where most of the work done by philosophers and theologians shipwreck. When it comes to the creation of a creature that would be endowed with free will, most people would generally assume that God could generate such a creature by a simple act of creation or by fiat. There is often an underlying assumption that the creation of a being endowed with free will was, as with the rest of creation, simply a matter of God saying so. The commonly held

---

12. Cf. Exod 20:2–5; Lev 26:1–46; Num 14:9–10; Deut 4:1–40; 5:1–11; 6:1–25; 7:11; 27:15–26; 28:1–68; etc.

13. See Gilbert, "Function of Imprecation," 44–58.

14. See for instance Prov 1:1–33; Eccl 12:1.

assumption is that when God created Adam and Eve, the process and the end product were essentially complete.

There are at least two reasons to challenge this assumption. From a logical point of view, the creation of a creature that would be free with respect to God and would be compelled to always choose to do God's will is a contradiction in terms. As C. S. Lewis convincingly demonstrates in *The Problem of Pain*, either the creature is free or it is not. To speak of a creature designed in such a way that it is said to be "free" in regard to God and yet compelled to obey God is a statement that is in the same category as asking God to create a square circle.[15] Lewis points out that this is essentially a nonsensical statement; no more than a meaningless string of words. In a related discussion of divine omnipotence, Lewis writes:

> His [God's] Omnipotence means power to do all that is intrinsically possible, not to do the intrinsically impossible. You may attribute miracles to Him, but not nonsense. This is no limit to His power. If you choose to say "God can give a creature free will and at the same time withhold free will from it," you have not succeeded in saying *anything* about God: meaningless combinations of words do not suddenly acquire meaning simply because we prefix to them the two other words "God can." It remains true that all *things* are possible with God: the intrinsic impossibilities are not things but nonentities. It is no more possible for God than for the weakest of His creatures to carry out both of two mutually exclusive alternatives; not because His power meets an obstacle, but because nonsense remains nonsense even when we talk it about God.[16]

As many have pointed out, producing such a creature would be tantamount to creating an android that would have the appearance of self-determination but without the substance of it. It would be an illusion that could no doubt fool an outside observer and perhaps even the subject itself, but not God. And isn't that the critical question? While a creature might be made to be entirely content with the illusion of free will, such a situation would be intolerable to a God who is free and delights in granting freedom and some degree of self-determination even, it would appear, to such simple

---

15. Whether free will is compatible with divine omniscience and omnipotence has been the object of considerable debate. Compatibilists such as John Mackie and Anthony Flew believe that human freedom is compatible with divine determinism, whereas incompatibilists such as Alvin Plantinga view the notion of free will and determinism as contradictory. For a detailed analysis of these issues, see Martin, *Moral Responsibility*.

16. Lewis, *Problem of Pain*, 18.

creatures as dogs and butterflies. The God of the Bible is into reality, absolute reality, not illusion and deception.

God could create a creature that would in every respect be complete and whole, with the *ability* to make choices. But the one thing he could not do, by definition, was to endow the creature with a full articulation of free will with regard to himself. The reason is surprisingly simple: in order to be free with respect to God, the creature would need, in addition to an innate ability to make moral choices, at least one significant opportunity to choose between God and some other alternative. In other words, there had to be a context or a process that would permit the full exercise or implementation of the creature's free will. Without such an opportunity, free will can only and forever remain an inscrutable shibboleth.

That an additional step or process was necessary in order to produce the kind of creature God had in mind is confirmed by the creation story itself. For instance, the narrative frames humanity's creation differently from the rest of creation. When it comes to the elements of the universe, the "heavens and the earth," vegetation, the sea creatures, the animals, etc., the description is succinct and to the point: it all comes into existence as a result of God speaking. What we are talking about is creation by fiat: God speaks and things come into existence. The situation is quite different with respect to humans. While the summary statement in 1:27–30 describes the fact of humanity's creation and its status in relation to God and the rest of creation, chs. 2 and 3 provide a more extensive description. The description of Adam and Eve's emergence goes beyond the simple fact of their creation; something else is involved.

That the formation of the human race represents a unique aspect of creation is strongly intimated by three texts which, taken together, point to the exceptional character of the human race and to the necessity of a process to bring about humanity's full emergence.

The injunction not to eat of the "tree of the knowledge of good and evil" (Gen 2:17) turns out to be more than a mere command to obey God's instructions. It represents, as Gen 3:1–7 uncovers, a test, presumably designed, as all tests are, either to verify the integrity of something or to produce a given outcome. I'll come back to this question later. The temptation narrative in 3:1–7 provides a critical insight into the precise intent of the injunction found in 2:15–17. And the judgment narrative in 3:8–22 highlights the exceptional moral status of the creature by underlining Adam and Eve's culpability.

These texts not only establish the special character of the relationship that prevails between God and humanity but point to the creature's exceptional and unique nature. It bears repeating that they also highlight the fact that a much more complex process was required to bring about the full completion of the creative process with respect to the human race. No such additional steps are even as much as hinted at with the rest of creation. While the creation of the man is portrayed as a simple act of creation by fiat, the transformation of this creature into one that would be capable of relating to God as a free being required an additional step whose outcome would not be determined by God, but would entirely reside in the creature's hands. This additional step requiring a decision originating from the creature itself was necessary to ensure that a truly free creature would emerge rather than a highly sophisticated android.

It is important to keep in mind that human free will is first and foremost and most effective with respect to God. God intended to produce a creature that would be free with regard to himself. Such an objective logically demands a space between God and humanity in which Adam and Eve would have the opportunity to make a meaningful decision with respect to their creator.

Whenever the issue of free will is raised, we must always hark back to the axiomatic question of God's original intent. If God's only objective consisted simply in producing an animal with high cognitive attributes and the skills to take care of the earth, to create such a creature with the appearance of free will would be perfectly fine. No one would know the difference. But God's objective was much more formidable than that. Infinitely so. He intended to create a being that would have the capability to enter into a loving relationship with him. This kind of objective reflects an entirely different order of things. A relationship based on love assumes absolute freedom. Without freedom, there can be no meaningful way to initiate and maintain love. It radically differs from the master-slave relationship, which is contingent on the servant's obedience.

The fact that the creation of the human species is, in our text, intricately linked to a multi-stage process suggests a degree of complexity that is vastly beyond the creation of an intelligent animal. This observation is entirely consistent with our day-to-day experience. The more elaborate a project is, the more intricate the process will be. It should not be lost on anyone that God was in fact intending to create a creature that would in one critical respect be like him. It would be a creature endowed with a genuine degree of free will with respect to him. This in fact represents the inevitable condition for the creation of a being with whom God could enter into the kind of relationship that is envisioned in the text.

This should not come as a surprise. The creation of a people that would voluntarily serve God and reflect his character did not result from a magical wave of the wand; it required a long and arduous progression, which incidentally was in no way linear! The process that would permit the redemption of the human race did not occur by fiat either. It required the articulation and implementation of a precise strategy. God's plan of salvation necessitated the birth, life, death, and the resurrection of the Son of God. I could expand further, but I think these examples are sufficient to show the necessity of a process to bring about certain outcomes, even as it pertains to the spiritual realm.

If the creation of a creature that would be free with respect to God did indeed require a process beyond the mere fact of creation, then it becomes necessary to inquire about the nature of the process itself. For some, the mere suggestion of the necessity of a process to complete the creation of the First Two will seem absurd. If Adam and Eve were created in the image of God, as Gen 1:28 states, doesn't that imply that they were, right from the moment of creation, perfect?

One of the main reasons for the confusion lies in the fact that to most readers, the proposition that man was created in the image of God entails "perfection." It implies the beginning and the end; the totality of the process leading to the outcome. While Adam and Eve may in fact have been perfect in every way with respect to what they were as human beings, mind and body, it is important to point out that the narrative does not equate being made in the image of God with the entirety of the creation process as it pertains to the first humans.

PERFECT OR IMMATURE?

The question as to whether Adam and Eve were created perfect or whether an ulterior or secondary process was needed to "complete" the creation of man immediately raises what represents one of the major issues for anyone who has ever pondered what the creation narrative states about human beings. The question has to do with the fundamental nature of Adam and Eve at the moment of creation.

Regardless of whether the story is believed to be historical or not, most readers would assume that Adam and Eve were initially created perfect. This position is one of two predominant views that have been proposed with respect to Adam and Eve's initial nature.

The notion that Adam and Eve were created perfect was most famously articulated by Augustine. The other position, originally formulated by the second-century church father Irenaeus of Lyons, and recently revived by the American philosopher John Hick in what he calls the "Irenaean theodicy," hypothesizes that Adam and Eve were like morally immature children who needed to face adversity in order to become the kind of creature God intended for humans to become.[17]

Neither of these two proposals is entirely satisfactory. First, if, as Augustine surmised, Adam and Eve were "perfect," the rationale for the injunction found in Gen 2:15-17 is bound to forever remain an impenetrable enigma. Why would a morally perfect creature have need of injunctions and commandments? Second, we still face the broader issue of the apparent contradiction inherent to God creating a creature that is theoretically free with respect to himself without, however, the benefit of an existential space needed for the man and the woman to freely choose whether they wish to be loyal to God. Third, why would perfect creatures be so easily deceived into believing the serpent's lies, as described in Gen 3:1-7? Fourth, to echo a question many have asked me over the years: if in spite of their perfect state, Adam and Eve still failed to resist temptation, what assurance is there that those who will be perfected in eternity will not one day disobey God and reintroduce sin in the world?

These are legitimate questions that must remain unanswered if Adam and Eve were perfect and complete in every way at the time of their creation. While I will examine this issue at greater length later, suffice it to say that there is nothing in the narrative that suggests that when Adam was formed, the process was complete. Just to state the obvious, the creation of the female required a separate process, and the presence of the injunction in 2:15-17 intimates that another step, not involving God's direct intervention, was also needed to achieve God's full intent for the human race.

As for Irenaeus's notion that humans were as children requiring adversity in order to grow into mature adults, the main difficulty lies in that it assumes that humanity required a "fall," followed by a long and painful process, in order for the human race to achieve moral perfection. This position implies that the sorry sum of human history, with its endless supply of violence, war, destruction, and misery, was in fact an inevitable requirement to produce the kind of creature God had envisioned.

However we look at it, both positions force us to posit one of two hypotheses: (1) evil inexplicably originates from creatures that are deemed to have been created perfect; (2) evil ultimately finds its source in the very person of God, is encoded into the very fabric of reality, and represents an absolute prerequisite for the unfolding of being and history. If either one of these alternatives is true, then we do face a mystery of such unimaginable proportions that only a certain kind of blind faith can accept. But those are not the only alternatives.

---

17. See Hick, *Evil and the God of Love*, 217-24; 279-400.

The biblical evidence opens a third possibility. If indeed the fundamental issue is the formation of a creature that has free will with respect to God, it may not be necessary to describe the newly created humans as either "perfect" or "immature." The key point is to remember that ultimately *God wished to create a creature that would be free with respect to himself.* This is the "bull's eye," so to speak, of God's project and human free will. My hunch is that the creation of such a creature signaled in fact a radically new level of complexity. An endeavor that could perhaps be compared to resolving a mathematical problem having an infinite number of variables. If producing a creature endowed with free will is the problem, then the question must be: what is needed to resolve the equation?

I have suggested earlier that the creation of a free creature could not be achieved through divine fiat, not because it represents a project of such complexity as to be beyond God's power, but because of something else altogether. That such an outcome could not be brought about by simple divine fiat is not an *a priori* judgment or a gratuitous affirmation on my part. The creation of Adam and Eve is not simply described as an instantaneous act, similar to the rest of the created universe, but as a multi-step process that includes the first act of creation (Gen 1:26; 2:7), an invitation to partner with God (Gen 2:15–16) within a framework entailing a fundamental injunction (Gen 2:17), followed by an account of a temptation and subsequent disobedience (Gen 3:1–7). The narrative itself hints at the necessity of a process to fully implement Adam and Eve's free will particularly and specifically with respect to God.

If in fact the completion of the human project required the implementation of a process, I submit that words like perfect or immature do not adequately describe what Adam and Eve were when they were first created. While no terminology will do justice to what the text is describing, a word like "neutral" could perhaps more accurately characterize Adam and Eve's original state. Adam and Eve were created with an innate ability for self-determination without, however, the experience of actually doing so.

The issue is not whether they were "perfect" or "immature." While they were indeed "perfect" in the sense that they showed no physical or mental flaw, they could not be created by fiat with a full apprehension of the notion of free will with respect to God. Such awareness could only derive from participating in an event that would provide a meaningful opportunity to exercise that freedom.

In their original state, the first two humans did not possess a full understanding of what it really meant to be free with respect to God. To borrow a metaphor from computer science, it is as if the man and the woman had received the appropriate hardware and most of the software they needed to be human except for a critical add-on that needed to be "downloaded" at a later time and at their initiative. Adam and Eve had to participate in an exercise that would enable them to "download" a secondary program that would complete their understanding of what it meant to be free with respect to their creator. Let's call this additional program "Free Will 2.0." Because of the inherently complex nature of the outcome, an explicit decision originating from the man and the woman was required in order to bring about the completion of the process.

Based on the evidence offered in Genesis 2 and 3 and the actual description of the temptation account in ch. 3, I propose that some kind of test, a primordial choice of infinite significance was needed to activate the final stage of the implementation of the free will program. It was in the actual *experience* of this primordial and critical choice that the process of creating a free creature would be completed. The critical dimension of this test is not strictly tied to the act of eating the forbidden fruit as such. By this I mean that the *insight* needed to execute the implementation of free will did not necessitate *eating* the fruit as such.[18] What was needed was the creation of a radical point of critical choice where the creature would intentionally decide to obey or disobey. It is in the moment of decision that human free will would become fully realized. Whether Adam and Eve ate of the fruit or not, the ultimate outcome would be the same. It was in the very act of making the critical decision to eat or not to eat the fruit that the free will equation would be resolved.

I cannot overemphasize the importance of this point: the resolution of the test was not intrinsically tied to consuming the fruit. The resolution of the test was structurally linked to the decision process itself. Adam and Eve's ultimate choice was ultimately irrelevant in terms of the *primary* objective of the test, which consisted in providing the opportunity to make a decision that would originate from the creature itself and not from God. The desired outcome was predicated on the participation in an infinite point of critical decision. It is when Adam and Eve reached a final point of decision that they effectively implemented their free will with respect to God. In this respect, the first two were at a completely unique stage of human history.

---

18. In contrast, John Baker proposes that the fall narrative be read as part of a larger "garden myth" that teaches that it is in the act of eating the forbidden fruit that man moves from a state of blissful innocence to full humanity. The choice of freedom that eating of the fruit represents cannot be considered "sin" as such and the resultant state as the "fall." Baker, "Myth of Man's 'Fall,'" 235–37. In a similar vein, Carol A. Newsom suggests that from a comparative religions perspective, Genesis 2–3 is more adequately described as a "birth story, one that describes the birth of humans and the birth of culture" ("Genesis 2–3," 10).

This is where it is important to bring back to mind the peculiar character of the literary genre the creation story represents. If, on the one hand, the narrative echoes some of the characteristics of myth, which suggests an archetypal significance for Adam and Eve, the historical elements of the story suggest, on the other hand, that something unique and exceptional occurred, something that only applied to Adam and Eve as historical characters. Therein lies the challenge of interpreting the creation account: while it does address the most fundamental aspects of the human condition as an archetypal text, it also portrays, even if it uses poetic language to do so, a specific and unique historical situation. These two registers must always be present in the reader's mind.

AN INFINITE POINT OF CRITICAL DECISION (GEN 2:15-17; 3:1-7; 3:22)

In this section, I will examine three texts that provide important insights into the nature of the precise process that was required to complete the creation of Adam and Eve: Gen 2:15–17, 3:1–7, and 3:22.

The presence of an invitation to partner with God accompanied by an explicit injunction to refrain from eating of the "tree of the knowledge of good and evil" (v. 17) is the unmistakable signal that there was something distinct about the creation of the human race. While God could indeed attend to the first step of the creation of this new species, a subsequent action was necessary to complete the project. As the narrative conveys, a test of obedience turns out to be the key to completing this endeavor.

There is a common but incorrect assumption that readers often make with regard to the divine injunction found in Gen 2:17. It is generally believed that as long as Adam and Eve avoided the tree of the knowledge of good and evil and did not eat of its fruit, that they were in fact in full compliance with the command. This impression is further supported by the observation that Adam and Eve felt no shame: "And the man and his wife were both naked, and were not ashamed" (2:25). In this perspective, as long as Adam and Eve did not eat the fruit, they were deemed to be fully benefitting from the promise associated with obeying God's command. But there is also an assumption that as long at the tree remained accessible, sooner or later, they or one of their descendants would transgress the command and, in so doing, doom the entire human race. If this is how this text must be read, then the fall was indeed inevitable.[19] Given enough time, someone was bound to give in to temptation.

19. It should be noted, however, that the notion of a probation time of obedience

If we did not have the temptation account in Genesis 3, it would be permissible to arrive at this conclusion. But there is good reason to believe that this is not what the story is communicating. I will attempt to demonstrate that the injunction to refrain from eating the fruit refers to an identifiable event, something I describe as an infinite point of critical choice.

The expression found in 2:15–17 is reminiscent of biblical wisdom literature and curse and blessing language:

> The LORD God took the man and put him in the garden of Eden to till it and keep it. And the LORD God commanded the man, "You may freely eat of every tree of the garden; but of the tree of the knowledge of good and evil you shall not eat, for in the day that you eat of it you shall die."[20]

In typical wisdom fashion, the alternatives are expressed in terms of obedience and disobedience, each path entailing clear and irremediable consequences.[21] Unlike the gods of the ancient Near East, who hid their designs from their human subjects, God clearly defines the parameters of the test. Nothing is hidden. Before we examine the consequences of the choice as such, let me first offer some clarification with respect to the literary genre of the formula used in vv. 16–17 and its terminology.

First, while it is rarely noted by commentators, this text can best be described as a curse and blessing formula. While the blessing is implicit, the

---

leading to an exalted position is not unknown. In ancient Syriac tradition, it is stated that at some point humanity would attain a more glorious condition than the one prevailing in the garden of Eden (Brock, "Clothing Metaphors," 13). William N. Wilder observes that a similar idea was also expressed by John Calvin, whose observation in his commentary on Genesis suggests that had Adam and Eve remained upright, they would have moved on "to a better life . . . there would have been no separation of the soul from the body, no corruption, no kind of destruction, and, in short, no violent change" ("Illumination and Investiture," 52).

20. Unless otherwise noted, all Scripture quotations are taken from the New Revised Standard Version © 1989.

21. In the creation narrative, the wisdom motif is most clearly signaled by the life and death thematic attested in Gen 2:15–17. In addition, we should note the reference to the "knowledge [from the root *yada*'] of good and evil" in Gen 2:17, the reference to Adam naming the animals (Gen 2:19), and the allusion to Eve discovering that the tree is to be "desired to make one wise" (from the root *sakal*, Gen 3:6). The entire creation account echoes the most fundamental object of Hebrew wisdom which is to fear God (Prov 9:10) (see Schökel, "Sapiential and Covenant Themes," 468–80). For a broader discussion of the relationship between wisdom and creation, see Murphy, "Wisdom and Creation," 3–11. The renowned Reformed theologian Henri Blocher writes, "Again, along with several specialists, we can recognize that the way the story is treated places it with Wisdom writings" (*In the Beginning*, 36).

curse is introduced by the injunction to refrain from eating of the fruit and explicitly signaled by the explicit death threat: "you shall die."

Such formulas were widely used throughout the ancient Near East from at least the second half of the third millennium BC. Their primary role was to warn against committing certain actions such as disfiguring a monument, moving a border stone (*kudurru*), or rebelling against a suzerain. While some of the inscriptions make an explicit reference to a blessing for those who obey the terms of the injunction, most simply declare the destruction of the violator. The death penalty, however it might be expressed, is the unequivocal outcome of transgression.

Similarly, in the Old Testament, the curse motif is used to deter Israel from violating the terms of the Sinai covenant and to announce the judgment Israel will suffer should she be unfaithful to God (see Deut 27–28). In contrast to the usage of the curse in the ancient Near East, however, in the Hebrew Bible the curse is also attributed a pedagogical function. This is, for instance, evident in Lev 26:14–46, where the text announces a list of increasingly severe judgments intended to incite Israel to repent. Whereas the ancient Near East curse seeks the utter and irrevocable destruction of the violator, in much of the Old Testament, its implementation aims at disciplining the people of God.[22]

This is not to suggest that the destructive function is absent from the Old Testament curse. As Amos 4:12 indicates, if the people will persist in their unfaithfulness, there will come a point at which the corrective function of the curse will cease: "Therefore thus I will do to you, O Israel; because I will do this to you, prepare to meet your God, O Israel!" If Gen 2:16–17 represents a curse and blessing formula proffered in the context of a relationship between a superior and an inferior party,[23] as the allusion

---

22. The reason for this fundamental modification of the curse motif in Israel is tied to the Sinai covenant (see Lev 26:44–46). God's purpose in establishing a covenant with Israel was linked to the creation of a distinct people. While the insertion of the curse formula as an intrinsic element of the covenant is consistent with its ancient Near Eastern usage in terms of deterring Israel from seeking other gods, and though the language used exhibits a definite finality to it, it is not the primary intent of the curse formula to announce the expeditious and irremediable destruction of those who violate the covenantal injunctions. In the Old Testament, the implementation of the curse is primarily pedagogical (cf. Am 4:6, 7–8, 9, 10, 11). For more details, see Gilbert, "Function of Imprecation," 44–58.

23. This observation holds even if, in this text, the formula does not reflect the usual form of the curse and blessing. Most often, the curse and blessing formula is expressed as a two-part sentence including first a protasis that is introduced by the conjunction "if," followed by the injunction, then the apodosis outlining the curse proper. What ultimately signals the presence of a curse and blessing formula is not so much the presence of a specific form or expression, but the presence of an injunction accompanied

to the image of God in 1:27–28 also indicates, it will entail some important implications for the interpretation of our text.

Another reason for reading this passage as a curse and blessing formula derives from the precise language that is used in the expression: "the tree of the knowledge of good and evil" (v. 17). Why this is not, at first sight, more evident is due to the way most translations have rendered this text. As it stands, the text leaves the impression that we have, as is often suggested, a reference to either some type of abstract knowledge, the discovery of conscience, or some ethical insight.[24]

The Hebrew noun *daat*, "knowledge," is derived from the verb *yada*, "to know." This word most frequently implies more than abstract knowledge. It denotes the intimate experience of the object.[25] When, for instance, the text says, "Now the man knew (*yada*) his wife Eve" (4:1), the implication is that Adam obtained more than just Eve's phone number! Adam gained a personal and intimate knowledge of Eve. In this context, the verb is used as a euphemism to denote sexual intercourse. The kind of knowledge the author has in mind in 2:17 is experiential knowledge. This is the tree of the *experience* of "good and evil."

The other matter that requires some attention is the allusion to "good and evil" (*tov ve ra*). In this context, "good and evil" should probably not be primarily interpreted as referring to an ethical abstraction, but as an expression of a curse and blessing formula. This is not to say that this important text cannot offer a platform for an ethical or epistemological reflection.[26] My point is that if this is a curse and blessing formula uttered in a context that evokes the life and death motif so characteristic of Hebrew wisdom, then the primary function of this expression must consist in offering Adam and Eve an opportunity to determine their destiny: life if they obey (implicit) and death if they disobey (explicit). In this context, "good" (*tov*) would properly allude to the blessing, the good, and life, which is entirely consistent with its repeated usage in ch. 1 (vv. 4, 10, 12, etc.), where the expression "and God saw that it was good" (*tov*) expresses a most comprehensive assessment of

---

by a threat and a blessing (implied or explicit). For more details, see Gilbert, "Function of Imprecation."

24. "The knowledge that comes from the fruit is, as many commentators have argued, not simply knowledge of moral good and evil but rather the knowledge that makes all kinds of judgments possible, the power to make reflective, discriminating choices between what seems good and what seems bad" (Newsom, "Genesis 2–3," 11). For a detailed discussion of the meaning of this expression, see Stern, "Good and Evil," 405–18.

25. Wenham, *Genesis 1–15*, 100–101; Westermann, *Genesis 1–11*, 288–89.

26. See, for instance, Ricoeur, *Symbolism of Evil*.

what God has created.²⁷ "Evil" (*ra'*), on the other hand, would denote the curse, the opposite of the good, and death.²⁸

That the author does not use some of the more usual expressions to denote the blessing (from the verb *barach*) or curse (most frequently derived from *qalal* or *arar*) is inconsequential for our discussion. As Deuteronomy 27–28, Leviticus 26, and the prophetic corpus show, the writers enjoyed a wide range of literary freedom with respect to the formulation of oracles of judgment or salvation.

Assuming then that *daat* more specifically refers to experiential knowledge and that *tov ve ra'* more accurately reflects a curse and blessing formula, then a better translation for the expression the "tree of the knowledge of good and evil" would be: "the tree of the experience of the blessing and the curse." Not only does this translation more accurately renders the key expressions attested in this sentence, but it also more explicitly highlights the precise function of the tree. Rather than being an allusion to some allegedly inappropriate knowledge Adam and Eve could gain access to by eating of the forbidden fruit, this translation more accurately focuses on the injunction as a critical test for Adam and Eve to demonstrate their loyalty to God and put into place the last piece of the free will puzzle.

What is set before Adam and Eve is a choice between blessing and curse, life and death.²⁹ To interpret this expression as a reference to the potential for gaining ethical knowledge is a misrepresentation of the text.³⁰

---

27. "This is the 'craftsman God' who, in the way of the human artificer, stands back to look at what he has made and declares his satisfaction with it (cf. Isa 41:7: 'He says of the welding, "it is good [*tôb*]." He nails down the idol so that it will not topple')." See Gordon, "טוב," 353.

28. While the expression *ra'* is most often translated as "evil," particularly when alluding to evil perpetrated by men, it is frequently used to refer to disaster, destruction, or judgment. It is important to clarify the range of meaning of this word, especially in passages where a careless translation appears to ascribe moral "evil" to God (see, for instance, 1 Sam 16:23; 18:10; 19:9; 1 Kgs 14:10; 2 Kgs 21:12; Job 42:11; Ps 140:11; Isa 47:11; Jer 4:6; 6:1; 16:10; 18:11; 21:10; 31:28; 39:16; Ezek 14:22; Mic 2:3).

29. Derek Kidner similarly suggests that the tree of the knowledge of good and evil symbolizes the consequences of obedience and disobedience. He writes, "The tree plays its part in the opportunity it offers, rather than the qualities it possesses; like a door whose name announces only what lies beyond it." For more details, see *Genesis*, 63.

30. The expressions "good" (*tov*) and "evil" (*ra'*) are used to denote a wide range of concepts (for more details on *tov*, see *TWOT*, 793c, and for *ra'*, *TWOT*, 2191c). While they often denote ethical categories or behavior (for *tov*, see for instance Gen 16:6; 12:28; 1 Chr 16:34; 2 Chr 31:20; Ps 14:3; Jer 6:16–19, etc.; and *ra'*, Gen 6:5; 8:21; Judg 13:1; Amos 5:15, etc.), both terms are also used to describe the notion of blessing and curse (*tov*: Deut 10:33; 19:13; Josh 21:45; 1 Kgs 22:8; 2 Chr 18:17; Ps 23:6; etc.; *ra'*: Deut 31:29; 1 Kgs 5:4; 22:18; Ps 78:49; 121:7; Isa 31:2; 45:7; Jer 26:3; Ezek 14:21; Mic 1:12, etc.). Whether these terms refer to ethical categories or the curse and blessing is

God is setting before Adam the path of obedience and the path of disobedience. The first leads to life and the second to death. As to the consequences of disobedience, God is unequivocal. The text uses an emphatic Hebrew form, a Qal infinitive absolute paired to a Qal imperfect, which should be translated, "You will surely die!" or "You will surely experience death!"[31] What is set before Adam and Eve is not a simple prohibition to eat of the tree of the knowledge of good and evil, but a solemn invitation to trust God and to obey his command.

There are, however, a number of issues that are not entirely transparent here. First, the text offers little information with respect to what constitutes compliance with the injunction. Verses 16 and 17 primarily focus on the gravity of the divine command and the consequence of disobedience. The text appears to refer to a simple injunction that can either be obeyed or disobeyed. In this respect, the equation is straightforward and unmitigated: disobedience will lead to death. The alternative is not even made explicit. The most natural interpretation is that of an injunction that is obeyed by default until such a time as it may not be. Read in isolation, this passage suggests that as long as Adam and Eve refrain from eating the fruit, they are deemed to be in compliance and, consequently, the beneficiaries of the blessing and the fullness of life, in perfect counterpart to the experience of death in case of disobedience. While this undoubtedly represents the most natural reading of this passage, I would contend that the rest of the narrative does not support such an interpretation.

As a case in point to show the necessity of reading 2:17 in the light of ch. 3, let's consider v. 17, which states that the punishment for disobeying the command would be death. The statement is categorical and unambiguous. If the narrative ended here, we would have to assume that the author was in fact referring to an immediate death sentence in case of disobedience, analogous to instant death by electrocution when grabbing a high voltage cable with bare hands.[32] But as things turn out, the first two do not die when they

---

contingent on context. In Deut 1:39; 7:16; 2 Sam 14:17; 1 Kgs 3:9, *tov* and *ra'* clearly denote ethical categories. In 2:17 and the other passages where *tov* and *ra'* are used similarly, such as Gen 2:9; 2:17; 3:5; and 3:22, the expressions refer to the blessing and the curse. This usage is confirmed by Deut 30:15, where the two expressions explicitly denote the people's destiny depending on whether they obey the injunctions of the covenant: "See, I have set before you today life [*tov*] and prosperity, death and adversity [*ra'*]." In this passage, *tov* is parallel to "prosperity" (life) and *ra'* is parallel to "death" (it should be noted that the same root is used here and in 2:17).

31. GKC, 342, §113n.

32 In fact, the temptation narrative in ch. 3 suggests that Eve was under the same impression. Her assumption was that the fruit was poisoned. This may explain why Gen 3:6 emphasizes the harmless character of the fruit. Eve assesses whether the fruit is

eat of the fruit. This leaves the reader with only two options. Either there is a major literary inconsistency between 2:17 and 3:8–24,[33] or we are to interpret the announcement of judgment in 2:17 in light of the actual implementation of the curse in ch. 3. Rather than questioning the integrity of the overall narrative, I think it is more appropriate to give the text the benefit of the doubt and inflect more precisely the significance of the death penalty in 2:17. I am proposing in other words that we carefully discern the internal logic of the entire narrative in its canonical form.

In this respect, there are three things to note. First, if we read 2:17 in the light of 3:8–24, it appears that the death sentence announced in ch. 2 encompasses a much broader and extensive definition of death than an immediate cessation of life. Second, while the judgment announced in 2:17 seems to be mitigated in the sense that Adam and Eve are not immediately terminated, ch. 3 leaves no doubt as to the immediacy of the consequences of disobedience. The moment ("in that day") Adam and Eve eat of the fruit, the curse is deployed, the principle of death, *as defined in ch. 3*, is introduced into the world, and physical death eventually catches up with Adam and, we presume, Eve as well in due time (cf. Gen 5:3). Third, the categorical and unmitigated character of the imprecatory formulation in 2:17 is entirely consistent with the normal use of the curse. The primary purpose of the curse formula resides in deterring the hearer or reader from engaging in a given course of action. While the announcement of judgment in 2:17 does get to the essence of the consequences of disobedience, i.e., death, without being so precise so as to contradict the description of its implementation, a formulation that would mitigate the sentence would be rhetorically counterproductive. In order to be effective as deterrent, the curse formula must leave no doubt as to the ultimate outcome of the transgression (see Deut 27–28).

Some might object to this view of the curse by pointing out the presence of a mitigating principle in Leviticus 26, where the curses are intended to bring about the repentance of the people and not its destruction ("And if in spite of this you will not obey me" [v. 18]). But even if Leviticus 26 introduces an element of moderation, the initial affliction is extremely severe,[34] and the text leaves no doubt as to the outcome of the imprecation: God's

---

indeed fit for human consumption and concludes that it is.

33. See, for example, Toews, *Original Sin*, 6–11.

34. "I in turn will do this to you: I will bring terror on you; consumption and fever that waste the eyes and cause life to pine away. You shall sow your seed in vain, for your enemies shall eat it. I will set my face against you, and you shall be struck down by your enemies; your foes shall rule over you, and you shall flee though no one pursues you" (Lev 26:16–17).

judgments will relentlessly strike Israel until she repents or is entirely destroyed (vv. 39-40).

To come back to our earlier question: Were Adam and Eve deemed to be in full compliance with God's command as long as they did not eat of the forbidden fruit? And if so, were they already experiencing to its full extent the implicit blessing that accompanies obedience? While at first sight we could be justified in answering in the affirmative, several elements argue against this option.

As indicated above, the entire narrative is deeply couched in Hebrew wisdom. The injunction is not simply about avoiding the consumption of a certain fruit, but about making a fundamental decision to embrace Yahweh and be faithful to him. In Hebrew wisdom, the exhortation to choose Yahweh is as intentional as deciding to worship idols. An act of the will is required one way or another. Religion, true faith by pure osmosis is entirely foreign to the Old Testament. If children will absorb culture as naturally as a sponge absorbs water, there is a dimension of faith that always lies outside of culture.

The use of a curse and blessing formula does not, in and of itself, argue in one direction or the other. Most of the ancient Near Eastern curses are simply intended to dissuade potential offenders. In such cases, as long as the reader refrains from violating the terms of the inscription, all is well. The curses are understood to become effective only when a transgression occurs. In other cases, the curse formula appears in contexts where the target audience is explicitly identified. In such cases, the texts address either a future situation that will test the loyalty of the hearer with the attendant consequences, or a situation that requires a concrete decision with respect to a precise injunction, including irreversible consequences in case of a transgression.[35]

While there are no exact ancient Near Eastern parallels for the curse and blessing formula found in Gen 2:17, there is, however, no question about its function: any violation of an injunction always results in an irreversible

---

35. Some are found, for instance, in international treaties such as between Ramesses II of Egypt and the Hittite king Hattusili III (thirteenth century BC), Ashur-Nirari V of Assyria and Matti'ilu of Arpad (eighth century BC), and the Esarhaddon's suzerainty treaties (seventh century BC). These conditional curses address every facet of the relationship between two states and presuppose an initial commitment to the terms of the agreement and continued loyalty. Curses attested in loyalty oaths function in a similar fashion. Curses that pertain to specific commitments made by individuals are also found in myths, epic poems, and legends (see Gilbert, *Le motif imprécatoire*, 38-41, 45-53). There are also unconditional curses uttered against an individual for committing a specific offense. These are mostly found in myths, epic poems, and legends (Gilbert, *Le motif imprécatoire*, 54-65).

judgment. Transgression is a one-way option. Ancient Near Eastern curses presuppose a situation where the potential offender is faced with a choice to obey or disobey an injunction. In most instances, if the hearer respects the terms of the inscription, the status quo prevails for the individual. In other cases, particularly so where one party is invited to enter into a formal relationship such as in the context of an international treaty or a personal oath of allegiance, if the first party accepts the conditions of the agreement, it receives the benefits that the new relationship entails. Should that party refuse or later violate the terms of the agreement, it becomes the object of the curses outlined in the treaty document or in the oath ritual. Such cases outline a situation where a people or an individual is positioned at a crossroads and compelled to make a choice. The outcome of such a decision, positive or negative, results in a completely new and irreversible situation for the inferior party. The treaty or the oath of allegiance may represent one of the best parallels to Adam and Eve's situation, especially when we consider that humanity is said to be created "in the image of God," a metaphor that alludes to its role as royal representative, and which is further echoed in 2:15–17, where the mandate to look after the garden is specifically linked to an invitation to be loyal to God.

If at first reading, we may have the impression that Adam and Eve were naturally in compliance as long as they did not eat of the tree of the knowledge of good and evil, it is, however, unlikely that this is what the text is describing. Based on the curse and blessing language used, the broader appeal to Hebrew wisdom, the description of humanity as God's representative on earth, and the ensuing necessity for Adam and Eve to confirm their loyalty to God, it is more likely that the text envisions a situation in which Adam and Eve were not considered to be in compliance but would need to formally declare their allegiance to God by participating in a critical test of obedience, a decision whose outcome would be irreversible and result in a new condition irrespective of the actual choice they would make. The account of the temptation in Gen 3:1–7 confirms this intuition.

> Now the serpent was more crafty than any other wild animal that the LORD God had made. He said to the woman, "Did God say, 'You shall not eat from any tree in the garden'?" The woman said to the serpent, "We may eat of the fruit of the trees in the garden; but God said, 'You shall not eat of the fruit of the tree that is in the middle of the garden, nor shall you touch it, or you shall die.'" But the serpent said to the woman, "You will not die; for God knows that when you eat of it your eyes will be opened, and you will be like God, knowing good and evil." So when the woman saw that the tree was good for food, and that

it was a delight to the eyes, and that the tree was to be desired to make one wise, she took of its fruit and ate; and she also gave some to her husband, who was with her, and he ate. Then the eyes of both were opened, and they knew that they were naked; and they sewed fig leaves together and made loincloths for themselves.

It should be noted that the narrative does not offer a precise chronological framework. There is no explicit information with respect to the time elapsed between the command uttered in 2:17 and Eve's encounter with the serpent. This would seem to indicate that the narrator did not consider such information essential to the understanding of the story. What we do know is that at a certain point in time, there arises an unprecedented situation that compels Adam and Eve to make a critical decision with respect to God and their allegiance to him.

Genesis ch. 3 opens with the introduction of a new actor. The serpent is described as "more crafty than any other animal that the Lord God had made" (3:1).[36] Within the framework of the narrative, the serpent is not strictly identified with Satan. Only later will Christian tradition establish a connection between the two protagonists.[37] In this context, the serpent is simply described as one of God's creatures. The narrative does not set up a dualistic universe in which the serpent represents a counterpart to the creator.

Is the serpent a literary device? A symbol of evil? As I have pointed out earlier, from a literary perspective, the creation account is an extraordinarily sophisticated text whose various elements may indeed have symbolic *and* historical significance. The one does not exclude the other. In this case, there is no compelling reason to limit the significance of the serpent to one or the other. If the use of the serpent image points to some archetypal significance, the narrative also portrays him as a real actor. The protagonist is a serpent and yet more than a serpent.[38] His primary role is to draw Eve's attention to the forbidden fruit and engage her in a debate on the exact nature of God's command and God's motives.

We also note that if it is a creature of God, it is not just any creature: It speaks! While some readers might not see anything unusual about such a wonder, theorizing that some animals may have had the ability to reason

---

36. André LaCocque's treatment of the serpent deserves attention. See LaCocque and Ricoeur, *Thinking Biblically*, 15–17. For a detailed treatment of the function of the serpent and the history of interpretation, see Westermann, *Genesis 1–11*, 237–40.

37. Cf. John 8:44; Rom 16:20; Rev 12:9; 20:2. For more details, see also Foerster, "*Diabolos*" and "*Satanas*," *TDNT*, 2:75–79; 7:152–56. Russell, *Satan*.

38. See Page, *Powers of Evil*, 12–23, and Blocher, *In the Beginning*, 151–54.

and to talk before the fall, the fact remains that the first recipients of this story, the Hebrews, did not live in a world where animals were customarily endowed with the ability to think and speak! If the introduction of such a vile creature would initially grab their attention, a talking serpent would keep them engaged with the story as surely as a bear trap snaps on its victim's leg. And that's the point. The entrance of this extraordinary animal on the scene signals that an event of momentous importance is about to happen.

The adjective used to describe the serpent is significant in two ways. While the meaning of the word "crafty" (*aroum*) is ambiguous and may refer to either the knowledge of the wise (Prov 12:16; 13:16) and to its reprehensible counterpart: guile and shrewdness (Job 5:12; 15:5). In this context, the word further emphasizes the importance of this new actor. The serpent is not only noteworthy because of its remarkable ability to converse, but also and chiefly because of what he is about to say. This is a *clever* serpent. The use of *aroum* demands we pay very close attention to the words of the serpent.[39] In the same way that the "knowledge of good and evil" hints at Hebrew wisdom,[40] the use of the word *aroum* further links this story to the same tradition. This is very significant, for wisdom is not simply about gaining knowledge. Hebrew wisdom is about choosing the way of life, i.e., God himself, and rejecting the way of death, i.e., idols or anything else that claims one's loyalty.[41] The serpent's entrance signals that something of immense significance is about to unfold. The conversation that follows perfectly mirrors the compressed character of the creation story. It is theoretically conceivable that the actual conversation between the serpent and Eve occurred over a period of hours or days, but the details of that encounter are of no interest to the author whose main concern is to provide what the reader minimally needs to understand the rest of the story.[42]

The serpent opens the conversation by means of a question directly related to the mandate spelled out in 2:15–17. From a literary perspective, the question is significant in that it reminds the reader that the mandate introduced in ch. 2 must be read in the light of ch. 3. "Did God say, 'You shall not eat from any tree in the garden'?"[43] At first sight, the question doesn't

39. See Wenham, *Genesis 1–15*, 72.
40. See Westermann, *Genesis*, 241.
41. See Gilbert, "Venus FlyTrap," 176–77.
42. C. S. Lewis offers a fascinating account of what such an encounter might have looked like in a fictional reenactment of the temptation of Eve in *Perelandra*.
43. The Hebrew is not entirely clear as to whether we have a question. The conjunction *af* could simply denote a strong emphasis: "Even though God said . . . " (see Speiser, *Genesis*, 23). Westermann notes that the expression is often used to introduce

seem particularly "crafty." As far as questions go, this strikes me as a puffball. It is neither clever nor subtle. In fact, Eve easily defuses it. But the serpent is a "clever" creature indeed. The purpose of this salvo is not to trick her, but to draw her into a conversation and get her guard down. The serpent doesn't appear as a formidable opponent. So much the better to lull Eve into a false sense of security. But as the dialogue unfolds, we recognize the accuracy of the serpent's description. He behaves much like a chess player whose first move is meant to trap the opponent. This innocuous question enables him to take control of the conversation and put the woman on the defensive.

The serpent's question represents a conspicuous misstatement of God's injunction. God's actual words are almost the exact opposite. In 2:16, God states that Adam is free to eat from any tree in the garden. The only proviso is that the first humans refrain from eating from "the tree of the knowledge of good and evil." In her response, Eve correctly notes that the injunction only applies to the tree "that is in the middle of the garden" (3:2). She incorrectly adds, however, that they are not only to refrain from eating it but from touching it as well. Eve also indicates that she is aware of the penalty that would result from violating the divine command. So far so good.

In vv. 4 and 5, the serpent comes back to the offensive: "You will not die; for God knows that when you eat of it your eyes will be opened, and you will be like God, knowing good and evil." There is nothing subtle about this second assault. He does not bother pursuing the matter of which trees may or may not be fair game. His sights are on Eve's last assertion. It has been said that the bigger the lie, the more likely people are to believe it. I don't know that it's always true, but in this case, it seems to have proven right.

The serpent's move incorporates two lines of attack. On the one hand, he explicitly challenges Eve's belief about the punishment that will be meted out to her and Adam in case of disobedience. His denial is emphatic, using the same grammatical form as in 2:17: Adam and Eve will surely not die.[44] He does not pretend to misquote God's words. He simply states that it is all a lie. On its own, this strategy may not have been sufficient to sway Eve. In v. 5, the serpent introduces the second leg of his strategy. He proceeds to redefine the totality of reality. The belief that they will die is not only false. It is false because God is lying. The oldest lie in the world has just been birthed. Now here is a plausible lie. The command not to eat of the forbidden fruit is all about God, not them. According to the serpent, God has ulterior motives for not wanting them to eat of the forbidden fruit. God is afraid. The creator does not want them to eat of the fruit because he knows that when

---

a statement (*Genesis*, 239).

44. The Qal infinitive absolute and the Qal imperfect.

they do, they will, in one critical respect, be like him. The real reason behind God's prohibition is to keep Adam and Eve from attaining a higher level of existence: "your eyes will be opened, and you will be like God, knowing good and evil." If what makes the serpent's lie so convincing is linked to the vigorous tone of his pronouncement, it is ultimately driven home by impugning the very person of God, his character, trustworthiness, and his integrity. It is a lie because God lied. He deceived them to keep something valuable from them.

The net impact of the serpent's words is twofold. First, Adam and Eve are thrust into a situation where they now have to make an explicit decision with respect to God's command. The "tree of the knowledge of good and evil" can no longer be ignored. If, before this encounter, Adam and Eve had the luxury of living in the garden without paying real attention to the forbidden fruit, this is no longer the case. At this point, Eve must make a judgment call as to who is telling the truth: God or the serpent. That decision entails an appraisal of God's very character. Will she trust the word of God or will she trust the word of the serpent? After his last statement, like a seasoned negotiator, the serpent falls silent. He has made his case. It is now all up to the woman. Adam and Eve have reached an infinite point of critical choice after which nothing will ever be the same one way or another. There is no use pondering any further the nature of the serpent. The point is that through his agency, Adam and Eve are now confronted with the issue that will determine their destiny and that of the entire human race.

Second, the serpent's statement reveals the true significance of God's injunction with respect to the tree of the knowledge of good and evil. In effect, it calls into question God's integrity and forces Adam and Eve to position themselves with regard to God. The real issue is not whether they will eat the fruit, but whether they will trust God and choose to be loyal to him at this critical juncture.

This text reveals the true significance of the injunction found in ch. 2. If we project back from the temptation narrative, it would appear that Gen 2:15–17 does not assume a situation in which Adam and Eve are automatically in compliance with God's command. Chapter 3 suggests that the earlier injunction hinted at a specific occasion when Adam and Eve would be compelled to make a formal decision with respect to God's command. It is at that point that Adam and Eve would realize the nature of free will, and that the curse and blessing formula would be fully implemented. The serpent is the instrument needed to "funnel," so to speak, Adam and Eve into the moment of critical choice. Without the serpent and the opportunity he creates, it is conceivable that the first two could have indefinitely remained in their original condition. Let us not forget that as long as the first two humans are not compelled to make a choice with respect to eating the fruit, they have not had a meaningful or formal opportunity to declare their allegiance toward God.

Before I move on to the next point, let me offer one clarification. To suggest that the serpent plays a central role in bringing Adam and Eve to a point of decision doesn't imply that God was directly or indirectly responsible for the choice they would make. The text doesn't link the serpent's actual presence in the garden or his discourse to God. While he is described as one of God's creatures, his actions are entirely his own. This point is reinforced when God singles him out for judgment along with Adam and Eve. If through his initiative, Adam and Eve would arrive at the point of critical choice, the serpent was not acting on God's orders. Adam and Eve were not *coerced*, either psychologically or physically, into disobeying God. The serpent offered nothing but a groundless attack on God's character. God's command was unambiguous and the consequences explicitly laid out.

That God may not be morally responsible for the serpent's actions does not preclude, however, the possibility of viewing the serpent as God's agent. While there is nothing in the text to suggest that God directed the serpent to deceive Eve, the serpent did nevertheless unwittingly become God's agent in facilitating the creation of an infinite point of critical decision for the first two. But here is a crucial distinction that must be maintained. The serpent *meant* to manipulate Adam and Eve into the sphere of death. God intended the test to be an opportunity to access the sphere of life. In that sense, he is indeed "that ancient serpent, who is the Devil and Satan" (Rev 20:2), who "was a murderer from the beginning and does not stand in the truth, because there is no truth in him. When he lies, he speaks according to his own nature, for he is a liar and the father of lies" (John 8:44).

The serpent's last statement is brilliant in that it is almost completely legitimate! The purpose of the "test" was indeed to complete the process of forming a creature that would be endowed with free will. In that respect, the serpent tells the truth. Once the test is over, Adam and Eve will, in one sense, be like God. The last component of the "free will program" will have been "downloaded." But there is undeniable deception. The serpent intimates that God has forbidden Adam and Eve from eating the fruit, because he does not want them to have their "eyes opened" and be like God, "knowing good and evil." There is also deception in that the serpent intimates that the knowledge that is just within reach is only accessible through eating the fruit, i.e., through disobedience. The reality is that, at this most critical juncture of human history, it is more accurate to state that this new knowledge is in fact accessible in two ways, either by eating the fruit or by *refraining* from eating the fruit. Either way, their "eyes will be opened." The difference between the one and the other lies in the consequences.

The terms of the blessing and the curse are abundantly clear to Eve. Even though she extrapolates a little, as shown by her reference to the interdiction to "touch" the fruit, the basic terms of the transaction are entirely transparent to her; she does not hesitate to interrupt the serpent to correct the assertion that God had in fact declared all the trees in the garden off limits.[45] She was perfectly aware of what God had said. The issue now is whether she and Adam will declare their willingness to trust God by refraining to eat from the fruit.

Verse 6 is once again one of those very compressed summaries of a process I suspect went for much longer than described here. "So when the woman saw that the tree was good for food, and that it was a delight to the eyes, and that the tree was to be desired to make one wise, she took of its fruit and ate; and she also gave some to her husband, who was with her, and he ate."

This passage indicates that the woman decided on the path to follow, not by betting on God's integrity, but by carefully considering the qualities of the fruit. She made two mistakes. She accorded more credibility to the word of the serpent though she had no evidence to do so, and she determined her decision on the basis of an aesthetic assessment: "good for food . . . a delight to the eyes . . . " The futility of this approach is obvious. There was nothing in and of itself about the fruit that could enlighten Eve. There was no objective criterion she could use to test the serpent's claims with respect to the fruit's attributes. The fruit did not appear to be unfit to eat. Why should it? What would be the point of forbidding a fruit that was obviously unfit for human consumption? Parental injunctions to young children always pertain to cookies not stones. The fruit's appearance did not betray any lethal quality as such, and there was of course the promise that the fruit would impart a special kind of understanding, which she now believed would be denied her if she chose to walk away. If she was not going to rely on the objective terms of God's offer, there remained no effective way of determining where truth lay. She needed and indeed possessed a transcendent word on the matter. But she chose to ignore it in favor of a subjective assessment of the fruit itself. She, like many today, abandoned objectivity in favor of subjectivity and autonomy in their appraisal of the nature of reality.

Her method ultimately proved to be futile and disastrous, for the problem was not in the fruit itself. She attempted to reason out a mechanism of cause and effect between the nature of the fruit itself and the divine curse,

---

45. See Speiser, *Genesis*, 23.

but there was none. The cause-and-effect mechanism resided in the decision itself: obedience (an affirmation of her loyalty to God) would lead to life, but disobedience (disloyalty) would lead to death.

At this moment of critical choice, Adam and Eve would discover and experience the real meaning of freedom with respect to God. Their "eyes" would "be opened" regardless of the decision they would make. It is in the process of choosing that "Free Will 2.0" would be downloaded and that a new species would be born. God gave Adam and Eve a clear and unambiguous choice: choose life or choose death. No tricks. No hidden agendas. No concealed motives. By distrusting God, by searching for hidden layers of meaning, by questioning the explicit intent of the test, Adam and Eve ended up opting for death. In order to determine the true nature of the ground of reality, they gave predominance to their senses over the objective word of their creator. While there is a perfectly legitimate and wonderful place for empirical inquiry, when it comes to defining ultimate reality, we will forever be dependent on divine revelation. Any other approach will prove to be a futile exercise in chasing one's tail.

To further explain what I think the text is trying to communicate with respect to the injunction found in 2:17, let me provide a personal experience that illustrates, even if imperfectly, important aspects of what is going on in this text. When our oldest son was four years old, he became fascinated with the kitchen stove. There was something about the appliance that he found irresistible. He would often be found trying to climb it in an attempt to reach the control knobs. Needless to say, we were not at all pleased with his newfound interest. And so, short of getting rid of the stove, we took every precaution we could to protect the boy. We sternly forbade him from playing with the stove. On a few occasions, we actually showed him what happens when one turns the knobs. He gave us the impression he understood the dangers inherent to playing with the appliance. We all made it as clear as we possibly could. He knew exactly what he was supposed to do. He could obey or disobey and then live with the consequences.

One day, early after supper when my wife and I were in the basement watching television, we heard a scream of agony coming from the kitchen. We flew up the stairs and found our son with one hand on one of the control knobs and the other on the one element that had been activated. While we were able to get to him before he was seriously hurt, what happened to him was nevertheless very significant. Our boy had been faced with a clear injunction and consequences in case of disobedience. Despite his well-meaning reassurances, for reasons unknown to us, one day he came to a critical juncture as to whether he was going to obey or disobey. Had he, at that moment, chosen to trust us and backed away from the appliance, he would have learned the meaning of freedom (as much as a four-year-old can I guess), and he would have been fine. He would have enjoyed both the blessing of an intact hand and have gained a valuable insight into the nature of his relationship to us. But he chose to disobey. In his act of disobedience, he also learned something about freedom and trust, as well as something about his parents' motives. Unfortunately, although the lesson was learned, his choice entailed unpleasant consequences that were integral to his action. He suffered a significant injury, didn't have full use of his hand for about three weeks, and experienced some degree of shame due to his defiant attitude.

Had my son chosen to obey my "command" at the moment of critical choice, he would have learned the meaning of freedom and trust, but would have been spared the "curse."

To summarize then, what these texts describe is not just some undetermined period of time during which Adam and Eve are in compliance with God's command, followed by the inevitable capitulation to temptation. The portrait we have is of Adam and Eve being funneled into an infinite moment of critical choice that would determine their future and that of the species forever; a one-way door in either direction.

4
Life and Death: The World as We Experience It

IRENAEUS, FOLLOWED MORE RECENTLY by John Hick, proposed that God created the world to serve as a "vale of soul-making" for the benefit of an immature species. Augustine believed that while Adam and Eve were created perfect in every way, God mysteriously chose to subject them to a test of loyalty that they tragically and inexplicably failed.

As we saw in the last chapter, in order to understand the creation of Adam and Eve, their primordial nature, and their act of disobedience, we need to define with greater precision God's intent for humanity. God's original objective was the creation of a creature that would be like him in one critical aspect: the creature would be endowed with free will with respect to himself. While the creation of a human being did not entail any significant difficulty for God, the formation of a creature that would effectively and meaningfully be free with respect to him represented a significant challenge, for it entailed the introduction of a decisional impulse that would need to originate from the creature itself. In fact, logic dictates, and the creation narrative itself confirms it, that such a creature could not only be the outcome of a divine act. The reason is simple and related to the nature of free will. If the creature were to be free with regard to God, some kind of initiative originating from the creature itself would be needed to complete the formation of that creature. The possibility of such an act was necessary in order to generate the distance needed for the creature to differentiate itself from its creator and in turn enter into a loving relationship with him.

The process required to create that space is outlined in Gen 2:15–17, and its implementation described in 3:1–7. The creation of a creature endowed with free will did not necessitate some lengthy, evolutionary-like development, but the participation in an event that would in effect represent a point of critical choice resulting in the formation of a free creature.

As I pointed out, the requirement for the completion of the last phase of the creation process of this creature was not, *per se*, the actual consumption of the fruit itself, but a decisional process that would enable Adam and Eve to fully implement their free will and test their loyalty to God. The full implementation of free will resided in the act of self-volition itself, not in its outcome. This perspective is significantly different from how this text is usually read. Readers often tend to associate the consumption of the fruit with the acquisition of forbidden knowledge or knowledge that is not appropriate for humans. The assumption is that the "Golden Apple" itself is the source of that knowledge. If, as I propose, this is more properly the tree of the experience of the curse and blessing, then I would contend that gaining access to some alleged forbidden knowledge is not what this is all about.

The purpose of the tree and its fruit was to provide an opportunity for Adam and Eve to trust God and declare their loyalty to him. As we learn from Genesis 3, Adam and Eve were funneled into a critical point of decision by the serpent and chose to violate his command. In doing so, they became truly free with respect to God. In some sense, God's intent to produce a species that would truly be like him in "knowing good and evil" was now fully implemented. If, however, God was successful in bringing into being a creature that would be free with respect to himself, why then is the world the way it is? Was the emergence of misery, pain, and chaos an intrinsic and necessary component of the rise of human free will? Is evil an inextricable component of what it means to be human?

A NEW SPECIES IS BORN

After Adam and Eve's decision to disobey God, they experienced a fundamental transformation that affected them and, in due time, the rest of humanity. This transformation was prefigured in the curse and blessing formula that appears in Gen 2:17. It was announced by the serpent in 3:5, where he predicts that if they eat of the fruit, their eyes "will be opened" and that they "will be like God." The transformation is confirmed in 3:22 by God himself: "Then the LORD God said, 'See, the man has become like one of us, knowing good and evil; and now, he might reach out his hand and take also from the tree of life, and eat, and live forever.'"

God's summative assessment offers several insights into Adam and Eve's choice. First, Adam and Eve have in fact experienced a fundamental transformation; they are described as being like God, literally "like one of us." There is no suggestion here that they have become gods. They are said to be *like* God in "knowing good and evil." They now have an intimate experience of the blessing and the curse. God's observation implies a difference between what they are now and their previous condition, confirming what the serpent had told Eve during their encounter (Gen 3:4–5). This is no longer exactly the same species that existed before the primordial act of disobedience. What we have now is a new kind of creature.

As I alluded to earlier, God's judgment on Adam and Eve has typically been associated with the acquisition of the "knowledge of good and evil," as if such knowledge was reprehensible in and of itself. The precise nature of this "knowledge" has been variously described as a desire for omniscience ("good and evil" representing the boundaries of all knowledge in the same way "heaven and earth" describes the boundaries of everything that exists), knowledge that is appropriate only to the divine, moral discernment, a loss of innocence, or the acquisition of sexual knowledge.[1] While some of the suggestions may offer some insight into the nature of this knowledge, they likely reflect a misunderstanding of the text.

As I have noted earlier, "knowing good and evil" is not necessarily an adequate translation of the Hebrew *ladaat tov vara* in this context. The knowledge of good and evil more likely alludes to the experience of the blessing and the curse. The forbidden tree is referred to as the "tree of the knowledge of good and evil" not because the fruit has any intrinsic property as such, but because it is the object that will be the focus of a test of confidence, trust, and loyalty with respect to God. The tree is simply the means by which Adam and Eve will demonstrate their allegiance.[2]

In 3:22, God observes that Adam and Eve have undergone a transformation: "See, the man has become like one of us, knowing good and evil." It is an acknowledgment that the test of obedience that was hinted at in 2:17 is now complete. As a result, a new "program" has been installed. Adam and Eve now have a full understanding of their status as free creatures with

---

1. For a review of the various options, see Wenham, *Genesis 1–15*, 63–64, and Westermann, *Genesis 1–11*, 242–48.

2. Derek Kidner offers a similar interpretation with respect to the significance of the tree: "The fruit, not in its own right, but as appointed to a function and carrying a word from God, confronts man with God's will, particular and explicit, and gives man a decisive Yes or No to say with his whole being" (*Genesis*, 63).

respect to God. Being in possession of this knowledge is not problematic as such or intrinsically reprehensible; they are, after all, described as being like God. Since the "knowledge of good and evil," however we decide to define it, is portrayed as a divine attribute, it follows that having such "knowledge" cannot be deemed, by definition, to be immoral or unethical. I don't think it is the "knowledge of good and evil," *per se*, that defines Adam and Eve's sin, or that it represents a negative outcome. Since said "knowledge" is not evil in and of itself, it is likely that Adam and Eve would have gained the same insight even if they had chosen to obey God.[3] The knowledge they gained through the test of obedience is the existential insight into what it means to be free with respect to God. For lack of a better expression, it is at that moment that they became truly human. In and of itself, this was good. The problem resides in that the insight was gained through an act of disobedience.

The second part of v. 22: "and now, he might reach out his hand and take also from the tree of life, and eat, and live forever," confirms this intuition by hinting at the ontological catastrophe that has now struck Adam and Eve. The swift expulsion from the garden and the positioning of a sentry with a "flaming sword" to prevent anyone from entering it in vv. 23 and 24 sharply point to an existential development. Kidner writes, "Every detail of this verse, with its *flame* and *sword* and the turning *every way*, actively excludes the sinner. His way back is more than hard, it is resisted: he cannot save himself."[4] This should not come as a surprise for the reader, as the text has already provided a detailed description of God's judgment in vv. 7–21. God forbids Adam and Eve from having access to the tree of life, which would enable them to live forever in their fallen state. This is an important observation, for it implies that in their previous, "neutral," condition, Adam and Eve were *not* immortal; left to their own devices, they would eventually have experienced physical death. Indefinitely avoiding the moment of temptation was simply not an option. *They were not meant to live forever without the "Free Will patch."* The prohibition to eat from the tree of life also implies that the kind of human that emerged from the test could not be allowed to live forever. As C. S. Lewis so aptly states: "According to that doctrine [the doctrine of the fall], man is now a horror to God and to himself

---

3. As I mention in the preceding chapter, this insight is not entirely new. As pointed out by Wilder in his commentary on Genesis, Calvin states that had Adam and Eve been faithful to God at that moment, they would have been elevated to a "better life" (Wilder, "Illumination and Investiture," 52).

4. Kidner, *Genesis*, 72.

and a creature ill-adapted to the universe not because God made him so but because he has made himself so by the abuse of his free will."[5]

The primordial act of disobedience represented more than an error of judgment resulting in a superficial rift between the humans and their creator. The severity of God's decree in 3:22 and the structural pervasiveness of the sentence in vv. 7–21 suggest that the test of loyalty envisioned in the text and the attendant choice Adam and Eve would need to make were somehow connected to ultimate reality and would reach into its very core. It is the kind of decision that I would characterize as structural as opposed to superficial. It hints at an inescapable, primary, and organic connection between the vertical and horizontal spheres of human existence. This is why the test outlined in 2:15–17 is of such magnitude and the consequences so profound and far-reaching.

Let me try to illustrate further. We all make decisions that have greater or lesser import for our lives. Some decisions are inconsequential. Whether I decide to have a Coke or a Pepsi, a hamburger or a steak for supper makes little difference. There are decisions, however, that are much more serious. The more fundamental a decision is, the more consequential it will be. What university I choose to attend will irrevocably change my life. The profession I choose. The company for which I end up working. All these decisions will have an equally profound impact. If what I eat for breakfast represents a trivial matter having but limited bearing on my life, getting married is a decision that literally changes everything. The process of conversion to Jesus Christ is yet another type of structural decision. It is the most fundamental of all the choices a person can make. It's the kind of decision that not only transforms one's outlook but one's very being. It initiates a process of transformation that starts in this life and will extend into eternity.

Adam and Eve's expulsion from the garden to ensure they would not eat from the "tree of life" also clearly implies free access to the tree and its fruit had they opted to trust God. The catastrophic character of the transformation that compelled God to expel Adam and Eve suggests that obedience would have transformed Adam and Eve into the kind of creature that would live forever. Like Gen 3:1–7, 3:22 offers an important hint regarding the interpretation of the curse and blessing formula attested in 2:16–17. This verse confirms that in ch. 2, the text envisions a definite event constituting the final step in the creation of a creature endowed with free will. Genesis 3 is both good news and bad news. A new species is born, but not in the way God had intended. It is a mutated species.

---

5. Lewis, *Problem of Pain*, 63.

In order to gain a greater insight into the kind of creature and world that emerged after the primordial act of disobedience, we will consider the description of the curse found in 3:7–21 and use the results to reflect what Adam and Eve would have experienced if they had instead obeyed God.

THE CURSE

Genesis 3:4 and 3:22 signal that Adam and Eve's participation in an infinite point of critical choice would have radical consequences for them. While 2:17 is not as explicit with respect to the character of the precise event in which Adam and Eve would be compelled to participate, the text unequivocally spells out the ultimate consequence of disobedience. While there is no doubt as to the inevitability of the outcome,[6] Gen 2:17 leaves the specific terms of the threat and its implementation entirely open. As I noted in the previous chapter, this kind of generic language is not unusual when it comes to the formulation of curse formulas in ancient Near Eastern literature and in the Old Testament. It would be incorrect to assume that death merely refers to physical death. Since 2:15–17 is part of a larger unit, it is imperative that we bring the context of the entire narrative to bear on the interpretation of these verses.

The full significance of the curse is made explicit in Gen 3:8–19. When Adam and Eve chose to disobey God, something both wonderful and dreadful occurred. On the one hand, they gained a definitive understanding of what free will means with respect to God. The encounter with the serpent created a space for Adam and Eve to differentiate themselves from the creator. In that critical moment of decision, they exercised their freedom of choice and self-determination and gained a pivotal insight into the nature of ultimate reality itself, which I believe likely expresses the true significance of the "knowledge of good and evil." In one respect, the test was successful. Adam and Eve and, through them the entire human race, became creatures endowed with a genuine ability to enter into a loving relationship with God. Unfortunately, the full implementation of their free will, the primordial test of loyalty that would seal their fate and that of their descendants, occurred in the context of disobedience. As forewarned in Gen 2:17, this primordial act of disobedience would *lock* humanity into a level of existence that would be characterized by death: "You will surely die." Paul echoes this outcome in Rom 5:12: "Therefore, just as sin came into the world through one man, and death came through sin, and so death spread to all because all have sinned."

---

6 As indicated by the use of the combination of the Qal infinitive absolute and the Qal imperfect (lit. "die you shall die").

This first act of disobedience entailed tragic consequences for the human race. According to Gen 3:8–19, it resulted in three forms of alienation: from God (vv. 8–10), from each other (vv. 11–16), and from nature (vv. 17–19).

Alienation from God (Gen 3:8–10)

While the text offers little information about Adam and Eve prior to their transgression, we do know that they were living in the presence of God and in fellowship with him (Gen 2:25). They had no fear of God and though they were naked, they had no concerns for their safety.[7] Since the primal act of disobedience was first and foremost a challenge to God's integrity and an act of rebellion, the fallout from their action first affected their relationship with God.

> They heard the sound of the LORD God walking in the garden at the time of the evening breeze, and the man and his wife hid themselves from the presence of the LORD God among the trees of the garden. But the LORD God called to the man, and said to him, "Where are you?" He said, "I heard the sound of you in the garden, and I was afraid, because I was naked; and I hid myself." (Gen 3:8–10)

Adam's immediate response is characterized by fear. The first clue that something of pivotal importance has happened to Adam and Eve is their apprehensive reaction to God's appearance in the garden. It's not the fact of God's presence as such that is problematic. The text describes God as casually strolling in his garden just like any earthly king might enjoy his royal "park" in the cool of the evening,[8] something that would presumably happen on a regular basis.[9] But this time, God's visit triggers a different reaction. Adam and Eve proceed to hide from God. The explanation offered by Adam hints at the extent of the transformation he and Eve have experienced: "I was afraid, because I was naked; and I hid myself" (v. 10).

---

7. Wenham notes that the Hebrew verb normally translated by "ashamed" (*bosh*) "does not necessarily carry the overtones of personal guilt the English 'shame' includes" (*Genesis 1–15*, 71). In Hebrew culture, the sense of "shame" could be entirely triggered by factors external to the individual experiencing it (Judg 3:25; 2 Kgs 2:17).

8. Victor P. Hamilton notes that the type of Hithpael used here to characterize the kind of action "suggests iterative and habitual aspects" (*Genesis 1–17*, 192).

For an insightful exploration of the anthropomorphic language used to describe God in the book of Genesis, see Smith, *How Human Is God?*, 7–12.

9. Wenham, *Genesis 1–15*, 76.

To some readers, the attribution of Adam's fear to his being naked may seem somewhat incongruous. If nakedness is the issue, why not refer to the feelings of shame that surely would have resulted from his sin? The author is very intentional in invoking Adam's fear (Hebrew *yara'*) rather than his shame (*bosh*), which is used in 2:25 to describe Adam and Eve's absence of "shame." There is no compelling reason to link Adam's sense of fear to the shame that might derive from appearing naked before Yahweh.¹⁰ That priests were to avoid bodily exposure in the context of the cult is undeniable (Exod 20:26; 28:41–43), but as Gen 2:25 intimates, this is not the issue here.

In the ancient Near Eastern world, nakedness often entailed negative connotations. To be naked was to be in an extremely vulnerable position. Those who were, for instance, abandoned in the wilderness without a garment would face a life and death situation, for while daytime temperatures could be very hot, at night, they could fall quite dramatically.¹¹

The problem at hand does not reside in whether Adam and Eve can appear unclothed before Yahweh. Adam's intense apprehension reflects rather a keen sense of vulnerability. Adam and Eve now perceive the creator as their mortal enemy. And with good reason! Hadn't God announced that they would die if they ate of the fruit of the tree of the knowledge of good and evil? Adam did not hide from God simply because he was "ashamed," but because he feared God's punishment for his transgression. Walter Brueggemann aptly describes the scene:

> What had been a story of trust and obedience (chapter 2) now becomes an account of *crime and punishment* (3:1–7). In brief limits, the dynamics are not unlike those of Dostoevski. There is a strange slippage between the crime and the punishment. The torture of Raskolnikov is in seeing what is not there, in hearing voices and imagining threats. The power of guilt takes on its own life. It works its own destruction. Death comes, not by way of external imposition, but of its own weight. So the nakedness of 3:7 and the hiding of 3:8 already manifest the power of death, even before the Lord of the garden takes any action. Serpentine

---

10. So Rad, *Genesis*, 91.

11. Job 24:7 describes the poor as those who "lie naked, without clothing and have no covering in the cold." In Ezekiel and Isaiah, "nakedness" denotes a state of extreme vulnerability and need. It is sometimes associated with military defeat (Ezek 18:7, 16; Isa 58:7; cf. Deut 28:48). For more details on the meaning of "nakedness" (*'arom*), see Seevers, "עָרוֹם (*'ārôm; ārōm*)," 532–33. For a detailed analysis of the concept of nakedness in the ancient Near East, see Sweeney and Asher-Greve, "Nakedness, Nudity, and Gender," 125–76.

distortion has set before the earthlings a destiny not envisioned by the Lord of the garden.[12]

Adam's newfound fear of the creator does not simply betray a sense of guilt deriving from the transgression of a divine decree and the ensuing punishment. As serious as the "legal" case against Adam and Eve might be,[13] I suspect there is something else at play. What happens next is more than the required punishment for an act of transgression. The extensive and thoroughgoing character of the curse against the first humans parsed in 3:15–19 coupled with the expulsion from the garden in 3:22 strongly hints at a development of catastrophic proportions with respect to Adam's nature. There is something going on here that reaches far beyond a relational breakdown. The text appears to signal a disruption of such intensity and depth as to preclude being in the very presence of God. Adam's primal act of disobedience triggered an ontological mutation that now prevents the entire human race from directly experiencing the presence of God.[14] Two factors account for this situation.

The first has to do with who God is and what we have now become. When Isaiah cries out, "Woe is me! I am lost, for I am a man of unclean lips," he underlines a fundamental incompatibility between the holiness of God (Isa 6:3) and human sinfulness. I seriously doubt that any human being is in a position to fully appreciate the chasm that exists between God and sinful humanity. As Lewis observes, "Now error and sin both have this property,

---

12. Brueggemann, *Genesis*, 48–49.

13. The legal character of Adam and Eve's transgression highlighted in Gen 2:17 and confirmed by the Apostle Paul in Rom 5:12–14 is occasionally overshadowed in discussions pertaining to the nature of sin and the theory of atonement. In an effort to unhook the sacrifice of Christ from any formal judicial requirement resulting from Adam's primordial act of disobedience and subsequent human transgressions, some authors have suggested that in the Old Testament, sin is essentially relational and the response to sin is fundamentally restorative. As theologian Mark D. Baker states, "The Hebrew concept of justice has a relational foundation" (*Religious No More*, 100). He adds, "To act justly is to be faithful to the people one is committed to by agreement or covenant. The relationship, not an impersonal law, is central" (*Religious No More*, 100). While there is indeed a very strong relational component inherent to the concept of law in the Old Testament, that does not in any way eliminate the notion of a legal transgression requiring judicial punishment. To suggest an opposition between the two is a red herring. The Old Testament evokes retributive as well as restorative justice. The Roman Catholic biblical scholar Roland de Vaux notes, for instance, that in several cases, the violation of certain laws does entail a punishment ranging from the death penalty to fines and imprisonment (*Ancient Israel*, 1:158–60). While there was a relational component to Adam's act of disobedience, his transgression was also "legal" in that it constituted an explicit violation of a divine prohibition.

14. See for instance, Exod 33:20; Isa 6:5; Rev 1:17.

that the deeper they are the less their victim suspects their existence; they are masked evil."[15] Here is the unsettling paradox true saints have been all too conscious of over the centuries. As we get closer to God, we also experience a growing awareness of the intense corruption of human nature and the frightening chasm that separates us from God. But the further we move away from God, the fuzzier our perception of sin and the absolute holiness of God become.

Not only are humans objectively alienated from God because of what they have become, there is also a kind of subjective alienation that compels men and women to withdraw from him in fear and suspicion (Col 1:21). As a species, we now experience what C. S. Lewis has called the terror of the "Numenous."[16] Not only do men and women veer away from the living God, they are compelled, either consciously or unconsciously, to create new gods, gods in their image they believe they can manipulate and use to legitimize their innate ideologies of death and further their own agendas. This, incidentally, constitutes the essence of idolatry (see Rom 1:18–32).

The fear of the divine is the most common and deeply seated of all human traits. As far back as we can assess, human beings have had an innate and fundamental fear of the gods. From ancient Mesopotamia to the most remote regions of the Venezuelan jungles,[17] human beings have devoted enormous resources to appeasing them. Animal or cereal sacrifices have always been but the tip of the iceberg. Whatever shape they may take, the gods always and ultimately demand the flesh and blood of their worshippers and offer nothing more substantive in return than vanishing mirages.

Even the ancient Hebrews, who were closest to the living God and to whom God revealed himself through Moses and the prophets, consistently moved back to the spiritual default position that emerged after the fall. Like a metal object pulled by an irresistible magnet, the Hebrews inevitably forsook God and found solace in the arms of Baal. Adam's experience and that of the ancient Israelites are endemic of the entire human race. From times immemorial, human beings have and continue to embrace the dreadful and blood-sucking idols that fill their imagination.

Idolatry is most commonly understood as the outward worship of the physical representation of one or more deities. Such a definition is simply too rudimentary. Idol worship is infinitely more serious than just bowing down to a statue and making an offering to some imaginary god. It is first

---

15. Lewis, *Problem of Pain*, 90.
16. Lewis, *Problem of Pain*, 5–11.
17. The first-hand account of a Yanomamö shaman who converted to Christianity in Mark Ritchie's *Spirit of the Rainforest*, is extremely evocative of the true character of idolatry and its horrific impact on society.

and foremost a projection of the diseased human self on the cosmos. In ancient Mesopotamia and ancient Rome, this phenomenon resulted in the creation of gods who were just like humans in their propensity to express the vices that we associate with human nature: pride, jealousy, lust, envy, arrogance, hubris, hatred, etc.

The Old Testament is unequivocal in its harsh condemnation of idol worship, not, as some cynics might contend, because of some narcissistic impulse in Yahweh's psyche. The injunction against idolatry does not emerge out of a weak and threatened divine ego. At the very core of idolatry, there is a set of ideas and values, a worldview that essentially negates life and promotes dehumanization and oppression. Moses and the prophets were determined to fight idolatry because idol worship represents and reflects at its core the allegiance of the mind and the heart to nihilism. Above and beyond all else, Baalism was an ideology of death. Is it then any wonder that the Israelite prophets, from Isaiah to Malachi, fought idolatry with every fiber of their being?

Idolatry can never be reduced to harmless cultural expression. If men will not worship the living God, they will worship something else, and that something always zeroes in on ideologies of death. The twentieth century witnessed the horrific consequences of idol worship. Nazism resulted in the deaths of six million Jews and countless others. Estimates are that between twenty and fifty million people died under Stalin's rule. Pol Pot also had his day. In some misguided effort to pull his people back from the brink of modernity, the leader of the Khmer Rouge had over one million of his own countrymen mercilessly exterminated through forced labor, starvation, torture, and execution. North Korea's Kim Jong-un, son of the notorious leader Kim Jong-il, may have the nuclear bomb but his people continue to face the threat of mass starvation. Most European countries have disastrous birth rates. Abortion is an accepted, almost routine, method of birth control in the former Eastern Bloc countries, China, Canada, and the United States. Radical Islamists enthusiastically teach their young men to embrace and inflict death in the name of Allah. These gods may not be known as Baal, Ashtoreth, or Marduk, but one thing is for certain: Moloch is alive and well today. Those who still entertain some doubts about that only need to view the series of videos recently released by a pro-life organization called Center for Medical Progress, which reveal how the United States federally funded Planned Parenthood profits from selling fetal tissue and body parts.

The seeds of the death cult that idolatry represents were generously sown on that fateful day when Adam and Eve knowingly and willfully embraced death rather than the source of all life.

Human Alienation (Gen 3:11–16)

Not only has the primordial act of disobedience introduced a rupture between humanity and God, human beings became alienated from each other and from their very own selves.

> He said, "Who told you that you were naked? Have you eaten from the tree of which I commanded you not to eat?" The man said, "The woman whom you gave to be with me, she gave me fruit from the tree, and I ate." Then the LORD God said to the woman, "What is this that you have done?" The woman said, "The serpent tricked me, and I ate." The LORD God said to the serpent, "Because you have done this, cursed are you among all animals and among all wild creatures; upon your belly you shall go, and dust you shall eat all the days of your life. I will put enmity between you and the woman, and between your offspring and hers; he will strike your head, and you will strike his heel." To the woman he said, "I will greatly increase your pangs in childbearing; in pain you shall bring forth children, yet your desire shall be for your husband, and he shall rule over you." (Gen 3:11–19)

The most evident sign of this alienation is the fundamental disruption that now characterizes all human relationships. The allusion, in Gen 2:17, to the judgment that would follow Adam's disobedience is here described as a virulent moral illness. Personal accountability and responsibility are replaced by accusation and scapegoating. Adam blatantly blames Eve for his disobedience, and Eve frantically turns against her slithery conversation partner. Gone are mutual trust and acceptance. Guilt and distrust now poison everything.

The extent of the contamination will become fully evident as the narrative unfolds. In 3:16, we read: "To the woman he said, 'I will greatly increase your pangs in childbearing; in pain you shall bring forth children, yet your desire shall be for your husband, and he shall rule over you.'" The harmonious relationship between man and woman envisioned in 2:20b–25 is now disrupted in several ways. The woman will be profoundly conflicted with respect to her husband. While childbirth will result in intense pain, she will be powerless to avoid the relationship that is the root cause of her suffering, "your desire shall be for your husband . . . " The woman is condemned to living in a hierarchical relationship in which the man has the upper hand.

It would be an error to think that the text is condoning or promoting such a model as an ideal. The overall narrative, especially 1:27, in which the text affirms both sexes as made in the image of God, is remarkably non-patriarchal. The curse against the woman is portrayed as a distortion of something that was not originally meant to be, and as an explanation for the way things have been and still are in many parts of the world. Throughout human history, women have generally been relegated to a subservient position and assigned a utilitarian role. It is mainly in the Christian West that the age of marriage for women was postponed and that women were given access to education.[18] In much of the rest of the world, a woman's primary function was to bear children. And as much as some are loath to admit it, this is the situation that prevails even today for millions of women throughout the world. Genesis 3:16b underlines the painful dissonance we feel between what is and what ought to be.

The curse against Eve is not just about one specific woman or womankind as a category. As a creation story, the narrative oscillates between the particular and the universal. The structural disruption created by the primordial act of disobedience doesn't only affect the first two humans; it's about humanity. It speaks to the disharmony that now prevails between our appetites, our desires, the imperatives that drive us, our ideals and our hopes. The allusion to the restlessness that would now characterize Adam and Eve's relationship is also intended to describe all human relationships. If conflict can be expected in the most intimate sphere of human existence, it will surely spread everywhere. The curse on Eve signals the emergence of a "virus" that will infect all human interactions, revealing itself through pettiness, pride, hatred, racism, oppression, slavery, war, exploitation, etc.

The judgment against Eve extends far beyond human relationships; the effect of the curse reaches into the very core of what we are. The reference to the increase of pain in childbirth is symbolic of the profound disruption humans experience within their very own nature. On a physical level, the body is no longer in subjection to the spirit. Hungers and passions wage war against the mind, the former often overriding the latter. Uncontrolled desires become addictive cravings that destroy people and communities. The exquisitely well engineered network of pain sensors that runs throughout the body to warn us when we approach or exceed its tolerances will sometimes eerily go out of control, hurling men and women into raging seas of agony and pain that only the most powerful narcotics can suppress. Over time, this rupture between mind and body will reveal itself as an irreversible process of self-destruction that leaves the mind reeling in disbelief.

---

18. See Chaunu, *Le chemin des mages*, 123–25. Chaunu addresses the question of the status of women in the Christian West in more detail in *Le temps des réformes*.

In an imaginary reconstruction of humanity's early origins, C. S. Lewis offers this vivid description of the fall and its disastrous impact on human nature:

> The process [of deterioration caused by the fall] was not, I conceive, comparable to mere deterioration as it may now occur in a human individual; it was a loss of status as a *species*. What man lost by the Fall was his original specific nature. . . . This condition was transmitted by heredity to all later generations for it was not simply what biologists call an acquired variation; it was the emergence of a new kind of man—a new species, never made by God, had sinned itself into existence. The change which man had undergone was not parallel to the development of a new habit; it was a radical alteration of his constitution, a disturbance of the relation between his component parts, and an internal perversion of one of them.[19]

Not only do we face a fundamental rupture between body and spirit, it is our very minds that are infected by sin, causing spiritual dysfunction, mental illness, emotional distress, and biological degradation. The body is at war with itself. Death is the universal end-result of this condition. This is why old age and death create such a terrible sense of dissonance. We fight the aging process and its attendant degradation with the frantic energy of a bird caught in the jaws of a cat until illness breaks our spirits. Only then, do we anxiously await death if only to be relieved of the pain and despair that grips us. The reality of death is in absolute conflict with our inner conviction that we should live forever.

Speculating on the mechanism that led to humanity's predicament, Lewis writes:

> Up to that moment the human spirit had been in full control of the human organism. It doubtless expected that it would retain this control when it had ceased to obey God. But its authority over the organism was a delegated authority which it lost when it ceased to be God's delegate. Having cut itself off, as far as it could, from the source of its being, it had cut itself off from the source of power. . . . I doubt whether it would have been intrinsically possible for God to continue to rule the organism *through* the human spirit when the human spirit was in revolt against Him. At any rate He did not. He began to rule the organism in a more external way, not by the laws of spirit, but by those of nature. Thus the organs, no longer governed by man's will, fell under

---

19. Lewis, *Problem of Pain*, 78.

the control of ordinary biochemical laws and suffered whatever the inter-workings of those laws might bring about in the way of pain, senility and death. And desires began to come up in the mind of man, not as his reason chose, but just as the biochemical and environmental facts happened to cause them.[20]

After the fall, the body ceased to be a submissive servant and became a cruel master. There is a force in our very nature, within our very cellular structure, at a level beyond what science can even begin to fathom, that is bent on our ultimate destruction. In his Epistle to the Romans, Paul provides an extraordinary description of the state of war that prevails in human nature:

> But I am of the flesh, sold into slavery under sin. I do not understand my own actions. For I do not do what I want, but I do the very thing I hate. Now if I do what I do not want, I agree that the law is good. But in fact it is no longer I that do it, but sin that dwells within me. For I know that nothing good dwells within me, that is, in my flesh. I can will what is right, but I cannot do it. For I do not do the good I want, but the evil I do not want is what I do. Now if I do what I do not want, it is no longer I that do it, but sin that dwells within me. So I find it to be a law that when I want to do what is good, evil lies close at hand. For I delight in the law of God in my inmost self, but I see in my members another law at war with the law of my mind, making me captive to the law of sin that dwells in my members. Wretched man that I am! (7:14-24)

It should be noted that some scholars contend that Paul is not describing his own personal struggle with the continued presence of the sin nature; he is said, rather, to be resorting to the rhetorical and collective "I" to refer either to all human beings, Adam, or Israel.[21] While none of the positions entirely resolves all the difficulties this text entails, it seems to me that the most plausible interpretation remains the one where Paul appears to be describing the struggles associated with the continued presence of the sin nature in his own life and, by extension, in the life of all Christians.[22] While there are no doubt hyperbolic elements in his exposition, his portrayal of

---

20. Lewis, *Problem of Pain*, 77-78.

21. For an extensive discussion of the rhetorical "I," see Jewett, *Romans*, 441-45; Aletti, "Rm. 7.7-25 encore une fois," 358-76; Stott, *Romans*, 205-15; Toews, *Romans*, 194-97.

22. For a review of the arguments supporting this position, see Osborne, *Romans*, 180-91; Mounce, *Romans*, 166-72.

the spiritual war that characterizes the life of the Christian is consistent with other such observations, most notably Gal 5:16–18, where he underlines the fundamental conflict that exists between the sinful nature and the Spirit as well as the persistent reality of temptation and sin in the Christian experience:

> Live by the Spirit, I say, and do not gratify the desires of the flesh. For what the flesh desires is opposed to the Spirit, and what the Spirit desires is opposed to the flesh; for these are opposed to each other, to prevent you from doing what you want. But if you are led by the Spirit, you are not subject to the law.

While Paul may have been concerned about defending the goodness of the law (7:7–13), he is equally concerned about reassuring his readers with regard to their continued struggle with sin, particularly so in the light of his forceful reminder in Romans 6 about believers having "died to sin" in v. 2 and being "no longer slaves to sin" in v. 6. He ensures that his earlier observation about the believer's new status in Christ not be confused with the absolute eradication of the sin nature that will occur on the day of resurrection.

New life in Christ brings with it a new and heightened awareness of the demands of the law and a new appreciation for the depth of our own corruption. That is just part and parcel of living in a spiritual kingdom that is and yet is still to come. We can respond in one of two ways to this paradoxical situation. We can become thoroughly despondent about our inability to perfectly fulfill the demands of the law and be paralyzed by guilt. Or we can choose to live joyfully despite the keen awareness of our inadequacy by recognizing the absolute efficacy of Christ's sacrifice. The reality of a sin nature that still has its claws firmly anchored in the deepest recesses of our soul need not bring us to the place of despair such a realization may entail, as evoked by Paul in v. 24: "Wretched man that I am! Who will rescue me from this body of death?" The sacrifice of Christ does not only represent an objective payment for all human offenses, but provides the foundation to overcome the sense of guilt that will sometimes emerge because of sin, thus enabling us to live with confidence and joyful thankfulness: "Thanks be to God through Jesus Christ our Lord! So then, with my mind I am a slave to the law of God, but with my flesh I am a slave to the law of sin. There is therefore now no condemnation for those who are in Christ Jesus" (Rom 7:25—8:1).

This inner and deadly conflict that is every person's lot finds its ultimate dénouement in physical death. In this respect, the apostle was no evolutionist who believed that death is a most desirable process designed by Mother Nature to take out those who have made their contribution to the genetic pool, in order to make room for the young. In his great chapter on the resurrection of the body in 1 Corinthians 15, Paul leaves no doubt about the total and absolute incongruousness of death. He also leaves no doubt about what needs to be done to rid humanity of this scourge. The old body must be destroyed. No superficial restoration will do. While we may not understand the scientific rationale for what he alludes to, the reality is that whatever it is that has contaminated humanity at the fall will die only if the old nature dies and is replaced by a new one. He writes:

> Listen, I will tell you a mystery! We will not all die, but we will all be changed, in a moment, in the twinkling of an eye, at the last trumpet. For the trumpet will sound, and the dead will be raised imperishable, and we will be changed. For this perishable body must put on imperishability, and this mortal body must put on immortality. When this perishable body puts on imperishability, and this mortal body puts on immortality, then the saying that is written will be fulfilled: "Death has been swallowed up in victory." "Where, O death, is your victory? Where, O death, is your sting?" (1 Cor 15:51–55)

The symbolic and archetypal character of the creation narrative should not be lost on the reader. The text does not just focus on a particular man or woman, but on *woman*kind and *man*kind; it targets the entire human race. The curse against the snake also hints at the archetypal character of this text.

Scholars are somewhat at a loss to explain the full significance of the serpent and the divine curse against it. The historical situation possibly underlying the symbolic language may be beyond our reach. Questions regarding the exact nature of this animal—physical, moral, and spiritual—and the precise implications of God's judgment may indeed be beyond the modern reader's ability to reconstruct. While I acknowledge our limits, several observations can nevertheless safely be made.

The "enmity" (Hebrew *'ibah*) that will exist between the serpent and the woman is intended to describe a condition that will prevail throughout history. This statement is not only intended for Eve and the serpent or womankind and the snake as a species. This text describes a reality that encompasses all of humanity: "and between your offspring and hers" (v. 15). The author is not only alluding to a sharp sense of discomfort women may feel at the sight of a snake, but to the reality of a cosmic conflict that will plague humanity.

But what kind of struggle is the author referring to? The answer must be sought in the symbolic significance of the serpent. While the serpent of Genesis 3 is not, technically speaking, equated to the Satan of the New

Testament, this serpent is nevertheless described as being "crafty." The word itself does not necessarily convey a negative connotation. But in our text, "craftiness" morphs into deceit. The serpent lies. His is the first lie. A lie pronounced to lure our first parents into disobedience. The lure? An offer to attain an enlightened state and a higher plane of existence. It's the ultimate temptation; the desire to gain control over the universe independently from God. Ironically, this is, I suspect, exactly what God was offering Adam and Eve, and by extension, to all of humanity, but the serpent promised that Adam and Eve could attain this goal without God. The lie was that God intended to keep them from accessing this higher plane of existence by forbidding them access to the fruit of the tree of the knowledge of good and evil.

This curse hints at the reality of the ever-present tug of war between resisting or giving in to the lure of the first lie. This existential struggle was originally meant to be a one-time event. Adam and Eve's disobedience made it a permanent fixture of human existence, one that just like the other elements of the curse, we are not free to lift.

In his insightful commentary on Genesis, Gerhard von Rad writes:

> One must, under all circumstances, proceed from the fact that the passage reflects quite realistically man's struggle with the real snake; but one must not stop there, for the things with which this passage deals are basic, and in illustrating them, the narrator uses not only the commonplace language of every day, but a language that also figuratively depicts the most intellectual matters. Thus by serpent he understands not only the zoological species (which in a Palestinian's life plays a quite different role from in ours), but at the same time, in a kind of spiritual clear-headedness, he sees in it an evil being that has assumed form, that is inexplicably present within our created world, and that has singled out man, lies in wait for him, and everywhere fights a battle with him for life and death. . . . A real serpent is meant; but at the same time, in it and its enigmatic relation to man, man's relation to the evil with which he has become involved becomes vivid.[23]

The comprehensive character of the curse is revealed in that it targets the most basic aspects of human life. Von Rad explains:

> As for the man, his punishment consists in the hardship and skimpiness of his livelihood, which he now must seek for himself. The woman's punishment struck at the deepest root of her being as wife and mother, the man's strikes at the innermost

---

23. Rad, *Genesis*, 92–93.

nerve of his life: his work, his activity, and provision for sustenance. Here again the curse is to be read as in the case of the serpent. It does not, however, strike the man himself, but goes, so to speak, through him. It goes more deeply to the lowest foundation of all human existence; it strikes the most elementary realm of male effectiveness, the earth. And here too is a cleft, a mutual recalcitrance that now breaks into creation as a profound disorder: Man was taken from the earth and so was directed to it; she was the material basis of his existence; a solidarity of creation existed between man and the ground. But a break occurred in this affectionate relationship, an alienation that expresses itself in a silent, dogged struggle between man and soil. Now it is as though a spell lay on the earth which makes her deny man the easy produce of subsistence."[24]

Alienation from Nature (Gen 3:17–19)

The third sphere of alienation reaches far beyond the domain of relationship, divine or human; in a way that reason cannot apprehend, it extends to the cosmos itself. The last curse stretches yet further the intuition conveyed by the judgment against the woman. The curse against the ground is symbolic of humanity's constant struggle to survive in a hostile world. Take, for instance, the relationship between humans and animals. We instinctively feel that, with a few exceptions, notably the dog, humanity's relationship to animals is no longer what it was intended to be. In this sphere again, we must admit to a discontinuity between what is and what ought to be.

> And to the man he said, "Because you have listened to the voice of your wife, and have eaten of the tree about which I commanded you, 'You shall not eat of it,' cursed is the ground because of you; in toil you shall eat of it all the days of your life; thorns and thistles it shall bring forth for you; and you shall eat the plants of the field. By the sweat of your face you shall eat bread until you return to the ground, for out of it you were taken; you are dust, and to dust you shall return." (Gen 3:17–19)

The natural environment constitutes an exceedingly hostile place for human beings. While modern science and technology may help manage and alleviate many of the uncertainties inherent to this world, it is impossible to avoid the material and human casualties that result from some of the natural disasters that occasionally sweep over our towns and cities. Throughout

24. Rad, *Genesis*, 93–94.

human history, men and women have had little choice but to submit, even if reluctantly so, to the homicidal whims of Mother Nature. And if truth be told, the reality is that, in the end, Mother Nature always wins. If she gives us life, she also takes it away. The death rate stands at an impressive 100 percent. In this regard, we also feel that things are not as they ought to be.

Genesis 3:8–24 lays out the consequences of Adam and Eve's act of disobedience. The text points to the emergence of three types of alienation: (1) alienation from God; (2) alienation from others and human nature; and (3) alienation from the cosmos. The far-reaching character of the curse points to a fundamental disruption in the very fabric of reality. While it most intensely affected human nature itself, like a nuclear detonation, the shock waves resulted in chaos and devastation far beyond the first point of impact (Rom 8:18–25). The Old Testament scholar André LaCocque describes the disaster that strikes the created order: "When the fall occurs, it is cosmic; it permeates the whole of creation from one end to the other and leaves no one and nothing innocent. The whole universe is in turmoil, 'sick unto death,' in Kierkegaard's words."[25]

THE EXTENT OF THE DAMAGE

That it is not an easy task to ascertain the extent to which human nature and the rest of creation were affected by Adam and Eve's act of disobedience is an understatement. Augustine, Calvin, and Reformed theologians advocated the doctrine of total depravity to describe the magnitude of the damage sustained by human nature. According to this view, humanity's rebellion against God is absolute. Sin permeates every dimension of human life. Humans are unable to submit to God or do good. This is not to say that every single human will give full expression to the worst manifestations of evil. The doctrine of total depravity teaches that all human actions are unacceptable to God because of an inward corruption that infects every fiber of human nature. This distortion is so comprehensive that no one can even accept God's offer of salvation apart from God's gracious intervention.

On the other side of the spectrum, some propose that human nature was not affected as such by some so-called "original sin." Mennonite New Testament scholar John E. Toews adamantly denounces the doctrine of total depravity as having any basis at all in the biblical text: "Mark Biddle was correct, the doctrine of original sin as formulated by Augustine and taught as dogma in the Western church since the Council of Orange (529) 'cannot

---

25. LaCocque, *Trial of Innocence*, 152.

be found in Scripture.'"[26] For Toews, sin is defined as "falling short of expectations in relationship with God and fellow humans, it is rebelling against God and breaking relationships with other humans."[27] Seeking support for his position, Toews also notes that the doctrine of original sin is absent from Jewish and Eastern Orthodox traditions.[28] He adds that the Anabaptist tradition also avoided the language of original sin, both because the expression itself is absent from Scripture and because Ezek 18:4 explicitly attributes guilt only to the person who sins.[29]

While I do not wish to address such a vast question in this context, I will offer a few thoughts. On the one hand, I think there is much to affirm in the Augustinian position. That a specific label may not be found in Scripture is not, in and of itself, an indication of its legitimacy or lack thereof. For instance, the absence of the word "Trinity" in Scripture doesn't invalidate the doctrine. The better question is whether there is biblical evidence to support the *concept* that is associated with the label.

The language that describes the consequences of Adam and Eve's act of disobedience in Genesis 3 goes far beyond a disruption in their relationship to God and to each other. The text portrays the outcome of their decision in categories that are akin to a structural and catastrophic dislocation affecting all aspects of human existence and reaching into the very fabric of reality itself. In Rom 8:19–23, the Apostle Paul alludes to the extensiveness of the damage inflicted on the universe at the fall:

> For the creation waits with eager longing for the revealing of the children of God; for the creation was subjected to futility, not of its own will but by the will of the one who subjected it, in hope that the creation itself will be set free from its bondage to decay and will obtain the freedom of the glory of the children of God. We know that the whole creation has been groaning in labor pains until now; and not only the creation, but we ourselves, who have the first fruits of the Spirit, groan inwardly while we wait for adoption, the redemption of our bodies.

To suggest, as Toews does, that sin is external to us, located out there in the "transpersonal and structural powers,"[30] thus inadvertently echoing the eighteenth-century French philosopher Jean-Jacques Rousseau, does not do justice to the intended reach of the curse language uttered in Genesis

26. Toews, *Story of Original Sin*, 95.
27. Toews, *Story of Original Sin*, 95.
28. Toews, *Story of Original Sin*, 96–99.
29. Toews, *Story of Original Sin*, 99–102.
30. Toews, *Story of Original Sin*, 108.

3, Paul's description of the impact of sin in Romans 8, and the emergence of physical death as the most extreme expression of the consequences of sin on human nature as expressed in Rom 5:12–13 and 1 Cor 15:21–22. Toews's characterization of sin also fails to take into account the description of God's encounter with Cain in Genesis 4, where Cain's impulse to murder his brother Abel is explicitly attributed to Cain and not to any external influence. Our Lord himself unambiguously localized evil within the very core of the human heart: "But what comes out of the mouth proceeds from the heart, and this is what defiles. For out of the heart come evil intentions, murder, adultery, fornication, theft, false witness, slander. These are what defile a person"[31] (Matt 15:18–19).

Moreover, that sin is not just something we do but a force or a principle that is intrinsic to human nature is much more consistent with our daily experience of sin as a personal reality than Toews's naïve view of sin as merely "volitional and political."[32] To observe that something is wrong with me rings true in a way that Toews's sin as "transpersonal and structural" obfuscations never will. Where does he and others who share this view think evil comes from? To concede that something is terribly amiss with me is as basic an observation as: "I like chocolate ice cream." It just *is*. On this point, I must side with Augustine, Calvin, and the Reformed tradition.[33]

Where I part ways with Augustine and Calvin pertains to the precise extent of the damage done to human nature. I am not convinced the Bible supports the contention that the fall entirely obliterated our ability to make moral choices. Genesis 1:27–28 and 2:15–17 represent, for instance, two passages that affirm humanity's status as created in the image of God and designed to work in partnership with God. These two passages, intended to clarify humanity's status and role, are given to the emerging people of Israel long after the fall. In that respect, the story of Cain and Abel is also revealing. As Cain, seething with anger after God rejects his offering, considers how he will respond, God enjoins him to resist the impulse to murder his brother Abel: "The LORD said to Cain, 'Why are you angry, and why has your countenance fallen? If you do well, will you not be accepted? And if you do not do well, sin is lurking at the door; its desire is for you, but you must master it'" (Gen 4:6–7).

---

31. See also Mark 7:20–23.

32. Toews, *Story of Original Sin*, 108.

33. For an extraordinary exploration into the nature of sin and the extent to which it poisons human existence, see Plantinga, *Not the Way It's Supposed to Be*.

While the language used to describe Cain's desire to murder his brother could be construed as an allusion to an external impulse,[34] it is highly unlikely. The image of sin "crouching at the door" is a figure of speech used to personify sin by attributing human action to a thing or in this case likely a predator animal.[35] The murderous desire that gnaws at Cain is a confirmation of the dark flaw that now afflicts human nature; the "death" sentence is not limited to Adam and Eve, but extends to their offspring, and hence to the entire human race.

If, on the one hand, Cain's desire to murder his sibling authenticates the presence of a fundamental sinful impulse in human nature, God's exhortation to Cain, on the other hand, confirms that while human nature may have been severely damaged as a result of the primordial act of disobedience, the ability of men and women to exercise their free will was not obliterated, at least not in the way Calvinism describes it. God's question to Cain assumes an ability to resist his impulse to kill his brother.

Free will remains an irreducible element of what it means to be human. Despite the structural damage inflicted on human nature, an ability to resist sin remains. This fact alone constitutes a monumental testimony to the resiliency of human nature. In contrast, it appears that the angels that rebelled against God were not so fortunate; they became what they chose to embrace: immaterial shadows condemned to eternal damnation.[36] Only a human being can rebel against God and maintain some degree of personal substance, integrity, and the capacity for redemption.

In a remarkable echo of Gen 1:26–28, Psalm 8 affirms humanity's royal status and intrinsic value:

> When I look at your heavens, the work of your fingers, the moon and the stars that you have established; what are human beings that you are mindful of them, mortals that you care for them? Yet you have made them a little lower than God, and crowned them with glory and honor. (Ps 8:3–5)

The Hebrew poets never exhibit childish naïveté about human nature. The Psalter is replete with grim and vivid descriptions of human wickedness.

---

34. Brueggemann states, for instance, that sin is not here described as a "breaking of rules. Rather sin is an aggressive force ready to ambush Cain" (Brueggemann, *Genesis*, 57).

35. Cf. Bullinger, *Figures of Speech*, 868. Brueggemann describes the image as sin "waiting like a hungry lion ready to leap" (*Genesis*, 57). While there are, as commentators note, several serious grammatical and semantic difficulties in this text, the overall picture that emerges is that of God inviting Cain to overcome his impulse to kill his brother. For a summary of the issues, see Wenham, *Genesis 1–15*, 104–6.

36. See Matt 25:41; 2 Pet 2:4; Jude 1:6; Rev 12:9.

When the Apostle Paul makes the case for the universality of sin in Rom 3:10–18, he quotes from Pss 14:1–3; 53:1–3; 5:9; 140:3; and 10:7. Even if one could argue that in their original context these passages specifically refer to rebellious men, Paul nevertheless discerns another layer of meaning that points to an underlying condition. The psalms entertain no illusions about humanity's brokenness and natural propensity to give in to its sinful impulses. Be that as it may, in Psalm 8, the psalmist unconditionally, forcefully, and unashamedly affirms humanity's glory. If there is something that is hopelessly broken in the very core of who we are, there is also something of incontrovertible worth that remains.

The essence of what constitutes the image of God in humanity was not entirely ruined. This intuition, as ill-defined as it may be, is confirmed by what we can daily observe about human behavior. If some individuals reach down into the darkest depths of depravity, others rise to the highest peaks of charity. In fact, most of us experience both the darkness and the dignity inherent to our nature as well as the ever-present tension between the two.

Let's summarize. On the one hand, Adam and Eve participated in an event designed to provide the last piece required for the full implementation of their free will. Participation in a critical moment of decision with respect to whether they would trust God provided a new and fundamental insight into the nature of their relationship to God. As the Genesis text states: "the eyes of both were opened" (3:7). They became like God "knowing good and evil" (3:22). Tragically, the insight needed to complete humanity's creation was acquired in the context of disobedience. As announced in the curse and blessing formula in 2:17, their act of rebellion irremediably led them into the sphere of death.

Disobedience was not, however, inevitable. The use of a curse and blessing formula presumes that Adam and Eve had a real choice. At this moment of critical choice, they could have chosen to obey and, in doing so, experienced the blessing.

THE BLESSING

Had Adam and Eve chosen to trust God, they would have received the insight that was to derive from obeying God. And this insight would have been gained in the context of obedience. In accordance with the normal use of the blessing and the curse in the ancient Near East, we can assume that if Adam and Eve had chosen to obey rather than disobey, the outcome of this decision would have been the opposite of the outworking of the curse in Gen 3:8–24.

In other words, as surely as disobedience locked humanity into the sphere of the curse, as predicted in 2:17, an act of obedience would have locked humanity into the sphere of the blessing. Inasmuch as disobedience irreversibly funneled humanity into the path of death, it is reasonable to assume that an act of obedience at this juncture would have locked humanity into a level of human existence characterized by life, shalom, harmony, prosperity, etc. At that point, Adam and Eve would have been given full and unfettered access to the tree of life and would have lived as free creatures in partnership with God for all eternity. The implication is inescapable. Had Adam and Eve chosen the path of life, humanity would never again have had the possibility of entering the sphere of death. Both options represented real options and "one-way doorways." Never again would humanity face death: the act of discovering freedom would have led into a whole new level of human existence, one that would be characterized by life.

Scholars who use the creation narrative as a starting point to reflect on the problem of evil consistently miss this point. They adopt, consciously or unconsciously, a fatalistic view of the test outlined in 2:15–17. As far as they are concerned, the fall was a foregone conclusion; even if Adam and Eve somehow managed to avoid eating the forbidden fruit, sooner or later, someone eventually would, thus precipitating the fall of humanity. Or, as John Hick does, they read the temptation, the disobedience, and the curse in the light of the present human condition, as symbolic of the adversity humanity must face in order to attain its full potential. The Creation account, however, makes it clear that the introduction of evil in human history was neither an ontological necessity nor was it something intended by God for a greater purpose. God never meant for men and women to experience suffering and death.

The most serious difficulty with my proposal resides in our inability to imagine what life in the sphere of the blessing would have been like and to consider it as a real option, as real as the possibility of disobedience was. Our major problem resides in the fact that we are standing on this side of history and can therefore only have but a dim view of what the alternative might have been. Had Adam and Eve obeyed, I suspect we would be speculating on the hypothetical consequences of a primordial act of disobedience and on what life might have been like under the curse. I am quite convinced such a project would be the target of a never-ending stream of skepticism. A Hitler, a Stalin, or a Pol Pot would be unimaginable. Men abusing women? Gratuitous violence? Mass murder? Abortions? Terrorism in the name of God? Unthinkable. Such philosophical speculations would be dismissed as quickly as yesterday's breakfast. And yet, it appears that this is exactly what the text states. Adam and Eve had a real choice. The curse and blessing formula indicates they could have chosen to obey, usher the human race into the sphere of life, and be transformed by the tree of life into creatures who would never know rebellion, sin, evil, violence, suffering, and death.

What would the world be like if Adam and Eve had trusted God? On a most basic level, humans would be in a perfect relationship with God. While they would deeply reverence him, they would not feel terror in his presence nor the threat of judgment and punishment. Men and women would never have experienced the terror of God. They would live in harmony with each other. Violence, deceit, wars, gossip, lust, pride, distrust, hatred, suspicion, and everything else that makes life so odious would never arise out of our nature to infect our relationships or taint our character. While these creatures would be perfectly cognizant of the theoretical existence of evil, they would never indulge in it.

But even as I write these lines, I find it difficult to imagine such a world. Not because it is intrinsically impossible, but because it assumes a different kind of humanity. Sin is like rust on a car. In colder climates, it eventually and always finds a hold. And once it does, there isn't much we can do about it. But as pervasive as it might become, we can easily imagine a car without rust: such vehicles exist. Cars do not come out of the factory with rusty doors. Nobody maintains that rust is necessary for the enjoyment of the vehicle.

Imagining sinless human beings is not as easy, for we never see such remarkable creatures. But is their existence intrinsically impossible? The New Testament testifies to one such person, Jesus Christ, who was without sin and fully human. There is also the promise of a new world inhabited by those who will have put their trust in Christ, and who will be forever without sin! We would be hard pressed to find even one Christian who would disagree with this. Why can't we envision the possibility of Adam and Eve giving birth to a sinless species? Any refusal to entertain even the mere possibility would imply that evil was in fact inherent to God's project for humanity.

Some might object that such a world would not offer the kind of opportunities for personal growth and character development as our present environment does. Perhaps! But if that is the case, wouldn't that objection be equally valid with respect to the perfect world God promises? If we accept the assumption that a world devoid of human sin could not offer meaningful opportunities for the development of virtues, then it follows that evil was an imperative and necessary component of God's project. To admit that God could not complete his project for humanity without the introduction of evil in human history would in fact be an admission of the necessity of an Edenic fall.

Based on the evidence we have examined, there is nothing in the text that would suggest that human disobedience was necessary or inevitable. To assert that a test of obedience requiring a decision that would solely emerge from the creature itself is not the same as postulating the necessity of a negative outcome. The former leaves open both obedience and disobedience as possible options.

This position is entirely consistent with what we otherwise know about God. The creation account itself describes everything God creates as "good" (1:4, 10, 12, 18, 21, 25) and "very good" (1:31). The New Testament portrays God as intrinsically good. The Apostle John best expresses this truth in his first epistle: "This is the message we have heard from him and proclaim to you, that God is light and in him there is no darkness at all" (1 John 1:5). Evil is parasitical. There is no such thing as absolute evil, for evil is always contingent on the good. Absolute goodness, however, stands on its own. Pure and unadulterated goodness existed in the person of God from all eternity and will continue to exist for all eternity when the plan of redemption is complete.

Why couldn't a world without sin offer real, significant, and meaningful challenges? I can't think of any reason that would prevent individual members of a species "locked" in the sphere of life from deploying those virtues that we associate with good character in a world uninfected by sin. By way of analogy, while citizens of a country under attack, such as England was during World War II, can perform heroic acts of valor, war is not a necessary precondition for the emergence of the kind of character qualities that presuppose such actions.

The difference between a world devoid of sin and the situation that now prevails would be twofold. First, every human being would start life free of the "mortgage" that sin now represents and would therefore be in an infinitely better position to navigate the challenges that such a world would still have offered. Consider the difference between an able-bodied athlete running a marathon and a man with broken legs attempting the same. The marathon is a challenge to both, but the one man is perfectly equipped to face it, whereas the other is severely impeded by his condition. Because of Adam's first act of disobedience, we are all like the man on crutches. Human existence is still possible and at times even exhilarating, but because we are no longer what God intended us to be, life is much more burdensome and grueling than it should be. Much of the spiritual, moral, and intellectual energy we deploy in this world is tragically focused on managing the evil that relentlessly emerges from our own nature.

We not only fight the spiritual illnesses that relentlessly arise from the human soul or the inevitable physical deterioration of the mind and body.

We also have to contend with ideologies of death that live on long after those who brought them into existence have passed on and continue to kill as efficiently as the deadliest viruses.

In a world without sin no one would suffer from a physical or mental disability. It would be a world without war and violence, without abuse or enslavement. A world where disease and death would be unknown. Imagine if you will, a world devoid of superstition and anti-human ideologies, and where everyone would live to his or her full potential. Every child would have kind, just, and responsible parents and would grow up to become a man or a woman of noble character fully embodying the image of God's imprint on his or her soul. Can we even begin to imagine what such men and women could accomplish under those conditions? The infinite possibilities and the limitless horizon that would forever unroll before us lie beyond human imagination. Instead of devoting most of our efforts to promoting or fighting evil, we would tirelessly deploy the powers of the three-pound brain to expand our understanding of the universe and exercise our virtues in the service of God and one another.

In our present condition, though we live with the illusion of natural progress, particularly so in the West, the reality is altogether different. Traditional cultures tend to be static, experiencing little change and technological advance. Great empires have risen and fallen with the regularity of a grandfather clock. Western civilization, which many would consider to be the greatest in terms of its accomplishments in every field imaginable, is, despite its veneer of permanency, showing serious signs of fatigue and may soon collapse under its own weight, one of most ominous signs being the disturbing demographic patterns we have witnessed in Western countries over the last forty years with most of them experiencing birth rates that are significantly below replacement rates. To echo the great quantitative historian Pierre Chaunu, how can an aging population that doesn't even have the will to reproduce itself maintain its scientific expertise, let alone innovate in any significant manner? Just to make myself clear, it will require a critical mass of young people to sustain the ever growing scientific and engineering specialization on which we now rely. It won't be long before we begin to feel the absence of those who should but never will be. The collapse may take a little while yet, but it may also come, as these things often happen, with the lightning speed of a runaway train. We will see.[37]

---

37. The below-replacement birth rates most Western countries have experienced in the last decades is a good example of a phenomenon that, at first, was perceived as a painless solution to the alleged threat overpopulation represented back in the 1970s. But as most governments are now painfully discovering, far from being a solution for anything, it is turning out to be a slow-motioned catastrophe. Pierre Chaunu described

In any case, my point is that in a world without sin, men and women would be free to be what they were designed to be, to love and to work in partnership with God on projects that right now, because of the blindness inherent to our condition and the spiritual disease that afflicts our soul, we are not free to imagine let alone pursue.

Before I conclude this chapter, I need to address at least one more objection. It is an issue that will surely not have gone unnoticed by the reader. To some extent this matter will be viewed as somewhat academic by some but will be considered seriously by many. If we admit the possibility that by a critical act of obedience, Adam and Eve and all of humanity would have been locked into the sphere of life, what might have been the implications for God's plan of redemption for humanity and for the Son of God? Does this mean that Christ's sacrifice would have been unnecessary?

The great Karl Barth himself addressed the issue. Two things to note about his position. First, Barth maintained the notion of a fallen humanity, not originally created as such, but as a condition that resulted from the misuse of human free will.[38] Second, Barth also believed that the fall was inevitable. While God did not will it as such, he permitted it.[39] In Barth's opinion, the fall was necessary in order to elevate humanity to the position to which it was destined through Christ.[40] It was necessary and inevitable in order to make the cross possible and in doing so, bring glory to God. Karl Barth specialist R. Scott Rodin explains:

> Clearly here Barth is ascribing a necessary place to the Fall. Evidence for this grows as Barth follows this discussion with a look to the future of reconciled humanity and finds its *eschaton* in the coming of God Himself in whom are found redemption and eternal intimate participation in and with God. What would have been the eschatological hope of pre-fallen humanity? It would not have been this glorious hope, for "this perspective

---

these low birth rates as "la peste blanche," the white plague, the Western world's suicide (see, for instance, *Un futur sans avenir*). For a more recent exploration of this issue and its implications for Western societies, see Last, *What to Expect*.

38. It should be noted, however, that Barth did not think of evil or the sin nature as originating from the fall as such. According to R. Scott Rodin, Adam's historical act of disobedience was simply the first manifestation of a preexisting reality. He writes, "Barth clearly saw the Fall not as one act in history but as a state of man in which the historical act of Adam was the first manifestation of that state." See Rodin, *Evil and Theodicy*, 113n16.

39. In this respect, Barth clearly maintained orthodox theology's distinction between the *voluntas efficiens* and the *voluntas permitten*. See Rodin, *Evil and Theodicy*, 105.

40. Rodin, *Evil and Theodicy*, 140.

does not belong of necessity to the essence and conception of creation as such." In fact, had there been no Fall, even the promise of everlasting life would be in question, . . . Barth anticipates the critical questions that arise from this line of reasoning, for he has certainly stated that the restoration made under the threat of death and eternal punishment far exceeds that which would have been possible if sin and its consequences had never been a factor in the relationship of Creator and creation. This implies that the eternal will of God was to save His creature from its sin through His acts of reconciliation, and that the Fall was predestined as a part of creation so that "such great salvation" could take place.[41]

Barth's position echoes the perspective of many with respect to the necessity of the fall and sin to fully reveal the glory of God in terms of his justice and grace. As Paul writes in Rom 5:20–21, sin has no doubt revealed God's grace in a way that would not have been otherwise possible: "But law came in, with the result that the trespass multiplied, but where sin increased, grace abounded all the more, so that, just as sin exercised dominion in death, so grace might also exercise dominion through justification leading to eternal life through Jesus Christ our Lord."

While Paul no doubt recognizes that sin provided God with an opportunity to show his grace in a way that might not have been possible otherwise, it does not necessarily follow that the introduction of sin was necessary for the completion of God's project. One is not a necessary corollary of the other.

I have argued in this chapter that neither the fall nor the introduction of sin in human history is portrayed as inevitable. But the major difficulty in accepting this position, and that's what I suspect is behind Barth's insistence on the inevitability of the fall, probably resides in what is perceived as a necessary link between incarnation and atonement. In other words, it is generally believed that the incarnation of God in Christ was the indispensable corollary of the need to redeem humanity. But is such an articulation between incarnation and atonement an ontological imperative? I'm not so sure that's the case.[42]

First, that Christ had intended to sacrifice his life from all eternity does not necessarily imply an unbreakable linkage between the incarnation and the atonement. It may only mean that God had planned from all eternity past the remedy for humanity's sin, because he also knew from all

---

41. Rodin, *Evil and Theodicy*, 86.
42. Philip Yancey pursues a similar idea in "Ongoing Incarnation."

eternity that Adam and Eve would disobey. If in our context, the incarnation and the atonement are inexorably connected, it may well be because in this timeline, the incarnation is in fact historically associated with the necessity to atone for sin.

Second, the other difficulty that arises in relation to the perception of a necessary link between incarnation and atonement is no doubt a function of the very limited horizon that the creation narrative provides with respect to a future locked into the sphere of the blessing. While the extent of God's glory and mercy would not have been expressed in quite the same way, who is to say what God had ultimately in mind for humanity and for the revelation of his own person? For instance, the potential to live forever and without sin is certainly hinted at in Gen 3:22. Can we not imagine the incarnation of Christ in the context of Adamic obedience? As critical as it was, I don't think the only purpose of the incarnation was to save humanity from sin; it was also a vehicle to reveal and apprehend God in a new and more profound way.

As the Gospel of John intimates, in addition to its atonement value, the incarnation was also God's means to bridge the near-infinite chasm that must exist between matter and absolute Spirit, "And the Word became flesh and lived among us, and we have seen his glory, the glory as of a father's only son, full of grace and truth" (1:14). God's desire to become one of us and to live among us was not primarily an outcome of humanity's sinful condition. If Adam and Eve had obeyed God, I suspect that God may have nevertheless planned to come in the flesh, not to die, but to bridge the chasm between him and humanity. In that context, the eventual coming of the Son of God would have been anxiously awaited, joyfully welcomed by all, and might have signaled a new phase in God's plan for humankind. I realize this line of thinking is somewhat speculative, but there is nothing in Scripture that precludes such a possibility. In the same way good is not contingent on evil, there is no reason to postulate the necessity of the atonement in order to imagine the possibility of God becoming man in order to reveal himself to his creature.

I understand that some may find this discussion entirely irrelevant and pointless. What is the point anyway? Whatever the possibilities may have been, the reality is that Christ came as a man in order to save us from our sins. This is true. But the question remains important, for ultimately it is our very understanding of the status and nature of evil that is at stake.

5
A New Equation to Resolve

MOST PEOPLE WOULD ADMITTEDLY recognize that there is something that is not quite right with humanity. Beside our propensity to engage in types of behavior that violate our most basic sense of what is just and good, death remains a universal, bewildering, and intractable reality of the human condition. The most critical question we face with respect to the continued and persistent presence of evil pertains to whether the sorry condition in which we find ourselves is the outcome of a strictly historical and evolutionary process or whether there is an inherent metaphysical factor at work. This is a crucial question, for the answer will determine whether we will look for a strictly historical cure or a metaphysical one.

JEAN-JACQUES ROUSSEAU

This issue was raised over two centuries ago by an eighteenth-century French philosopher, writer, and composer by the name of Jean-Jacques Rousseau (1712–1778). While most people may no longer be aware of Rousseau's significance, he nevertheless remains one of the most influential thinkers with respect to modern political and educational thought. The importance of Rousseau for our discussion lies essentially in his view of human nature.

Rousseau was born in Geneva and lived in that city until the age of fifteen, when he ran away after his father left the city due to legal problems. Soon after, Rousseau was introduced to Françoise-Louise de Warens, who was instrumental in his conversion to Roman Catholicism. He reverted back to Calvinism in 1754 to regain his Genevan citizenship. Rousseau's conversion to Catholicism is important to note, for it may signal a burgeoning discomfort with the doctrine of total depravity, one of the central tenets of Calvinism.

According to Harvard professor Leo Damrosch, "an eighteenth-century Genevan liturgy still required believers to declare 'that we are miserable sinners, born in corruption, inclined to evil, incapable by ourselves of doing good.'"[1] That later Rousseau came to reject this view is made clear in his complete repudiation of the doctrine of original sin in his treatise on education, *Émile*, published in 1762: "Let us lay it down as an incontrovertible rule that the first impulses of nature are always right; there is no original sin in the human heart, the how and why of the entrance of every vice can be traced."[2]

American moral philosopher Susan Neiman, author of *Evil in Modern Thought*, one of the most compelling reflections on the Jewish holocaust as the extreme incarnation of moral evil published in recent years, offers an insightful analysis of Rousseau's position and its implications for our understanding of the origin of evil and its solution.

The importance of Rousseau cannot be overestimated. Neiman states that Rousseau's reflection in its original context is "so new and profound that it radically changed our construction of the problem of evil."[3] Emmanuel Kant described him as a second Newton. Rousseau's significance resides in that he was the first one to treat the reality of evil as a philosophical problem rather than a metaphysical one. He was also the first to offer a solution contingent on historical rather than religious mechanisms.[4]

Before Rousseau, there were essentially two perspectives on evil. There was first the *optimist* position, which, echoing Leipniz, views this world as the best of all possible worlds. This position defined all manifestations of evil as merely apparent. Evil is viewed as a necessary condition for the completion of a greater plan. In the same way a painful medical treatment may be necessary to cure a patient of a serious illness, every instance of evil will lead to the good of the larger whole. This results in the belief that there is no genuine evil.

On the other end of the spectrum, there were those who claimed that evil is a mystery. "Those who acknowledged that evils are genuine found

1. Damrosch, *Jean-Jacques Rousseau*, 121.
2. Rousseau, *Emile*, 124.
3. Neiman, *Evil in Modern Thought*, 41.
4. Neiman, *Evil in Modern Thought*, 41.

that they literally defy explanation. Not only do all the resources of reasoning fail to explain them; the persistence of evil makes us doubt all the resources of reasoning itself . . . it is hopeless to analyze evil, and probably wrong to try. The best we can do is describe it."[5] Before Rousseau, either there was no problem of evil or there was no answer to it.

Even though Rousseau lands in a place that is diametrically opposed to Augustine and the Reformed position with regard to sin and the sinful nature, he nevertheless builds on Augustine in one respect. For Augustine, there is a straightforward connection between moral and natural evil: infinite punishment for infinite guilt. God gave humans free will, but its abuse was so thorough that only a miracle could save them, i.e., the death of Christ.[6] But if Rousseau adopts Augustine's formula with respect to a cause-and-effect connection between moral and natural evil, he entirely moves away from metaphysics. If Rousseau affirms human free will and the possibility of abusing it, he nevertheless moves away from the fall defined as a metaphysical phenomenon. He locates the fall strictly within a historical framework. In doing so, he replaces "theology with history and grace with educational psychology."[7]

In Augustinian thought, humanity is damned. After the fall, Adam and Eve and the rest of humanity are not free to lift the curse on their own. As Neiman points out, this position left Augustine open to the seventeenth-century French philosopher Pierre Bayle's charge that "generous donors don't offer gifts that will destroy their recipients."[8] While Rousseau maintains a strict relationship of cause and effect between moral and natural evil (we always deserve what happens to us), humanity is not inherently perverse. "The entire catalog of crimes and misfortunes can be seen as not fully intentional but mistaken. Thus knowledge, not penance is needed."[9] By reframing the "fall" as a historical phenomenon, Rousseau boldly challenged the notion of human nature as irrevocably damaged as a result of a primeval catastrophic event. In Rousseau's perspective, human sin doesn't simply explode on the scene at a given moment of human history. Because it is something that developed over time, its solution will also need to be implemented over time. As Neiman further clarifies, Rousseau's appeal to history was very useful, for it created a space between necessity and accident.

---

5. Neiman, *Evil in Modern Thought*, 42.
6. Neiman, *Evil in Modern Thought*, 43.
7. Neiman, *Evil in Modern Thought*, 43.
8. Neiman, *Evil in Modern Thought*, 43.
9. Neiman, *Evil in Modern Thought*, 43.

If the introduction of evil was necessary, we can be saved only by miracle. If it was an accident, then the world, where it matters, makes no sense. History, by contrast, is dynamic. If evil was introduced into the world, then it might also be eradicated—as long as its development is not fundamentally mysterious. After Rousseau, we need not deny the reality of evil. We can, rather, incorporate it into a world whose intelligibility is expanding. Exploring evil as historical phenomenon becomes part of our efforts to make the world more comprehensible in theory, and more acceptable in practice.[10]

Rousseau's task consisted in positing the cause-and-effect relationship between moral and natural evils and shedding light on the nature of the mechanism that connects the two. His project was all about confirming and demonstrating that there is meaning and justice in the world. A failure to complete this task would in effect confirm the nihilistic character of human existence. The assumption that humanity's nature was not inherently perverted was premised on the theological conviction that a good God could not create something inherently bad: "God makes all things good; man meddles with them and they become evil."[11] In his original state, man was free from perversity or vice. As long as "savage man," as Rousseau refers to him, lived in relative isolation living off what he could produce himself, he lived happily. It is only when such men found themselves in need of assistance from others and began to gather in small groups, and later larger ones, that the natural men began to experience desires that put them in competition with one another. Rousseau writes:

> So long as men remained content with their rustic huts, so long as they were satisfied with clothes made of the skins of animals and sewn together with thorns and fish-bones, adorned themselves only with feathers and shells, and continued to paint their bodies different colours, to improve and beautify their bows and arrows and to make with sharp-edged stones fishing boats or clumsy musical instruments; in a word, so long as they undertook only what a single person could accomplish, and confined themselves to such arts as did not require the joint labour of several hands, they lived free, healthy, honest and happy lives, so long as their nature allowed, and as they continued to enjoy the pleasures of mutual and independent intercourse. But from the moment one man began to stand in need of the help of another; from the moment it appeared advantageous to any one man to

---

10. Neiman, *Evil in Modern Thought*, 43.
11. Rousseau, *Emile*, 10.

have enough provisions for two, equality disappeared, property was introduced, work became indispensable, and vast forests became smiling fields, which man had to water with the sweat of his brow, and where slavery and misery were soon seen to germinate and grow up with the crops.[12]

The implications of Rousseau's "myth" were staggering. If the introduction of evil was indeed the result of a lengthy and gradual historical process, then its cure could also be located in history. The key to eradicating evil from human experience now resided in an educational process rather than a spiritual one. Rousseau further proposed that human nature was not fixed. In contrast to Augustinian theology, which maintained that human nature had undertaken a radical and irreversible change at the fall, Rousseau maintained that human nature, just like history, could be reshaped.

In this lies the importance of examining Rousseau. While the French philosopher has for the most part been forgotten, his ideas have not. Much of the theoretical framework that undergirds Western educational theory finds its source in Rousseau's understanding of human development, particularly so as articulated in *Émile*. I am not suggesting that this is a problem in and of itself. Children do undergo profound changes, physical, emotional, and mental, and these transformations have an extraordinary impact on how they learn.

The real problem is more specifically linked to the contemporary understanding of evil and its cure. Today, most educators embrace Rousseau's position with respect to the essential goodness of human nature and view education as the key to overcoming the foibles that poison human existence. While they may believe, like Rousseau, that human beings can commit evil acts, they do not attribute this capacity to a catastrophic mutation resulting from a spiritual mishap that occurred at the very beginning of human history. They do not therefore locate its ultimate cure in a divine intervention. Why should they? If the presence of evil in the world can be linked to a natural cause, then it will follow that the cure will also be seen as emerging from a historical process. The only question that remains lies in identifying the mechanisms that will bring about the "redemption" of humanity. It is to this task that *Émile* is dedicated.

This benign view of human nature and the notion of "salvation" by education have become deeply entrenched assumptions that are no longer challenged. Their truth is simply assumed and form part of a canon every bit of which is as authoritative as any religious axiom. This view of human

---

12. Rousseau, *Social Contract*, 216.

nature has become so predominant and pervasive that hardly any sector of human inquiry has been spared.[13]

Rousseau's impact on theological discourse has been considerable. While it may be unfair to lay it all at Rousseau's feet, the view that human beings are naturally good became a mainstay of twentieth-century liberalism. Those who embraced the notion that sin was essentially the outcome of social factors could not in good faith hold to the need for spiritual salvation and a divine redeemer.

Even if such a view of human nature keeps clashing with reality, its currency continues to grow. A significant number of theologians from a variety of denominational backgrounds have virtually discarded the orthodox view of original sin, and sin as innate to human nature.[14] In a manner consistent with such a position, the traditional view of Christ's death as satisfaction for humanity's sin has also waned. Christ's sacrifice is frequently reduced to the level of a political incident and its significance to an affirmation of nonresistance as a strategy for dealing with violence.[15] In a manner that eerily echoes Rousseau, these theologians substitute a historical process for a theological mystery, and moral education for grace. No wonder the traditional notion of evangelism understood as an invitation to repent and turn to Christ for salvation tends to fade away in circles that adopt this paradigm.[16]

Is humanity's present condition the result of a catastrophic metaphysical event or simply the outcome of an unfortunate series of historical missteps? Here is the question that every generation needs to examine anew. The first option will necessarily assume that only a divine intervention can set things right. Those who embrace the second will look for a strictly scientific answer for the problems that plague humanity.

A FUNDAMENTAL RUPTURE IN THE FABRIC OF REALITY

The author of the Genesis creation narrative goes to great lengths to portray Adam and Eve's act of disobedience as resulting in a fundamental rupture that reaches into the deepest recesses of human nature. The Canadian sociologist Fernand Dumont masterfully describes the extent of the disruption

---

13. For an assessment of Rousseau's far-reaching influence on educational philosophy, see Darling, *Child-Centred Education*, 17.

14. See, for example, Biddle, *Missing the Mark*; Toews, *Story of Original Sin*.

15. See, for example, Weaver, *Non-Violent Atonement*, and Seibert, *Disturbing Divine Behavior*.

16. Dintaman, "Spiritual Poverty," 205–8.

that affects humanity. He writes, "Something is wrong with human nature. It is as if humanity had remained stuck in a primordial choice: a choice none of us is free to revoke. A mortgage we cannot repay."[17] But the creation account does not describe the precise mechanisms that led to this tragic situation. The author confronts the reader with the aftermath of the event, not the underlying process that connected the act itself to the outcome that is now our burden to bear.

The Bible frequently alludes to the notion of a catastrophic event affecting human nature. In addition to the texts we have examined (Gen 2:17; 3:7, 8–24), in Genesis ch. 4, we have the well-known story of a man who slays his brother. This first murder is both a dramatic example of the structural disorder that immediately infected human relationships and a terrifying harbinger of things to come. In chs. 6–8, we are given a vivid description of the self-destructive evolution of human history. The situation is described as so severe as requiring a radical reset: humanity's destruction by means of a universal flood. Genesis 6:5 is particularly evocative: "The LORD saw that the wickedness of humankind was great in the earth, and that every inclination of the thoughts of their hearts was only evil continually" (see also 6:11–13).

What could motivate God to destroy the human race at this early stage of its history? The text provides an important hint. We are dealing with the first post-fall generation, a species of men and women who are probably still closer to Adam and Eve than us in terms of their intellectual and physical capabilities. While it is a species that knows few limitations, it is nonetheless profoundly flawed. This is no longer the creature God had intended to bring into being. This is a species that is grossly misshapen and distorted. These creatures use the vast resources at their disposal to spew evil on an industrial scale.

Just to give us some perspective, think of the massive destruction and havoc Adolph Hitler or Joseph Stalin could have wreaked upon the earth if these men could have lived six or seven hundred years. Imagine the knowledge, expertise, political power they could amass. One such man could trigger a war that would dwarf all that we have seen in the twentieth century. Two such men could create hell on earth. Failures would be temporary setbacks, platforms from which they would learn and push further in their next attempt to impose their will on the world. Imagine what a thousand such men could do, the plagues they could unleash upon the world. This is

---

17. Quelque chose ne va pas tout au fond de l'homme. Comme si l'humanité était restée coincée dans un choix premier : un choix que chacun de nous n'est pas libre d'effacer. Une hypothèque que nous ne pouvons lever." See Dumont, "Après le système Chrétien," 191.

the terrible situation that Gen 6:5, 11–13 seeks to describe. This is a species that lives far too long for its own good.

If God was to allow such a creature to live, he would need to engage in a some genetic engineering. He put an end to the super race and created a being that would be more limited, at least in terms of its longevity. This is what Gen 6:3 signals: "Then the LORD said, 'My spirit shall not abide in mortals forever, for they are flesh; their days shall be one hundred twenty years.'" Following the destruction of the antediluvian generation, human life spans gradually decrease to reach what we are now accustomed to.[18]

The allusion to men living upwards of five to six hundred years is often invoked as a reason to challenge the historicity of these texts. Be that as it may, we should keep two things in mind. First, these references to such extraordinary life spans are not just instances of the type of textual problems associated with the transmission of numbers in the Hebrew Bible.[19] The narrator is very conscious of the contrast in life span before and after the flood. These numbers are used intentionally. Neither do they parallel the fantastic numbers attributed to the earlier, predynastic monarchs listed in the Sumerian King List. There is a sobriety in the biblical text that is absent from the Sumerian list in which some of the kings' reigns range from approximately eighteen to forty thousand years.[20] Second, while the biblical numbers may still seem outlandish to us, the reality is that scientists still do not understand the mechanisms underlying the aging process.[21] Some of them even suggest that we may be on the verge of piercing some of the mysteries surrounding this most unpleasant fact of life, and that we will soon be in a position to extend the human life span far beyond what it is today. Not only are we potentially positioned to break the 120-year barrier, some visionaries go so far as to claim that scientists may one day unlock the safe that holds the secrets to immortality.[22]

Despite the wild optimism of some, the reality is that we inexorably age and die. It's interesting that those more sober scientists who claim that we will be soon be able to extend human life can only, and that in their wildest

---

18. See Wenham, *Genesis 1–15*, 142.

19. For a detailed discussion of the difficulties inherent to the transmission of large numbers in the Old Testament, see Wenham, "Large Numbers," 2–36.

20. See Jacobsen, *Sumerian King List*, and Young, "Incredible Regnal Spans," 23–35.

21. For a succinct description of the aging process, its possible causes, and the state of research, see Tosato et al., "Aging Process," 401–12.

22. For instance, such organizations as the LongeCity (http://www.longecity.org/forum/page/index2.html/_/feature/about-r28) and senescence.info (http://www.senescence.info/cure.html) promote the belief that human life spans can be extended far beyond what is considered normal today.

dreams, hope to reach 120! Let's face it, our very obsession with living longer, healthy living, and safety is a proof that old age and death are not germane to who we are. If it were, it would not even register as a concern at all.

The idea that aging is an aberration is nothing new. It is echoed in some of the oldest texts to appear in human history. For instance, in the ancient Babylonian myth *Atrahasis*, we are told that in the process of fashioning humanity, the gods mixed clay with divine material to ensure that the human creatures would not live forever.[23] In the *Epic of Gilgamesh*, the main protagonist, driven by despair and seeking to avoid the fate of his companion, Enkidu, goes on a journey to find the elixir of life only to have it snatched from him by a serpent.[24]

Biblical allusions to the presence of an aberration in human nature are not limited to the book of Genesis. Other Old and New Testament passages allude to a critical flaw in fallen humanity. Considering the extent to which the doctrine of the fall and original sin have come under fire, a brief review of some of these texts is warranted.[25]

In Isa 6:5, the prophet, realizing his inability to stand in the presence of the divine king, cries out: "Woe is me! I am lost, for I am a man of unclean lips, and I live among a people of unclean lips; yet my eyes have seen the King, the LORD of hosts!" In Jer 31:33, the prophet refers to a time when God will put his law "within them" and write it "on their hearts." This text implies two things. One, that something is fundamentally and structurally wrong with the people of Israel, and two, that a radically new approach is necessary to deal with their problem.

Jesus's own assessment of human nature, which sees the heart as the ultimate source of what is wrong with the world, bears mentioning again: "But what comes out of the mouth proceeds from the heart, and this is what defiles. For out of the heart come evil intentions, murder, adultery, fornication, theft, false witness, slander" (Matt 15:18–19).[26]

In John 3:19, the apostle describes an inherent human attribute, a default position that denotes a fundamental tendency to gravitate toward evil: "And this is the judgment, that the light has come into the world, and people loved darkness rather than light because their deeds were evil." In Rom 1:18–32, Paul highlights the most flagrant signs of the diseased human heart. In 3:10–26, the apostle reasserts the same idea using vivid images

---

23. For more details, see Bottéro, *Mesopotamia*, 99.

24. *ANET*, 96.

25. For an insightful study of the notion of original sin in the Bible, see Blocher, *Original Sin*.

26. The Gospel of Mark reports a similar declaration by Jesus in 7:18–23.

from the Old Testament and establishing the universal principle in 3:23: "Since all have sinned and fall short of the glory of God . . . "

It is, however, in Rom 5:12 that Paul refers most explicitly to the principle of a critical flaw in human nature: "Therefore, just as sin came into the world through one man, and death came through sin, and so death spread to all because all have sinned . . . " In this passage, Paul makes it clear that whatever ails humanity is not just an issue of individual morality but is tied to something that was "transmitted" from Adam to the entire race. But here a note of clarification is needed. The last part of the translation is somewhat misleading. In its present form, there is an apparent tension between the first part of the verse where Paul states that "death came through sin," i.e., through one act of disobedience. In the latter part of the verse, Paul seems to be indicating that death came because all sinned: "and so death spread to all because all have sinned."

The actual expression that Paul uses is not well rendered by the NRSV's "because all have sinned," which leaves the impression that death spread to all because all have sinned. This is not what this text says. The logic of this verse goes like this. First, Paul states that sin came into the world through one man. Second, death came as a result of sin. Third, death spread to all human beings. But how do we know that sin actually affected the entire human race? Simple. We know because all men and women experience death. What Paul is saying is that it is because of the transmission of sin from Adam to all human beings, and the subsequent universality of death that we can declare that "all have sinned." Paul here is not referring to specific sinful actions as such; he can declare all men sinners, because they all share in the principle of death through their filiation with Adam. The point of the argument is that since all men die, we know therefore that all men are infected by sin, for sin is the cause of the introduction of the death principle in human experience. This translation clarifies Paul's intent: "Therefore, just as sin came into the world through one man, and death came through sin, and so death spread to all. It is on that basis [that we can declare] that all have sinned."[27]

In Rom 7:14-24, where Paul alludes to the internal conflicts that the Christian experiences, the apostle reiterates his conviction that something is fundamentally wrong with human nature: "Now if I do what I do not

27. The heart of the debate centers on the meaning of the expression *eph ō*. While a majority of scholars today have settled on translating it as a causal "for this reason, because" (see Dunn, *Romans 1–8*, 273–74), the preposition *eph* (from *epi*) with the dative is best translated here by "on that basis." Not only does the latter translation more accurately reflect the preposition *epi*, but it also provides a more logical transition between the preceding statement and this one. Note the King James Version: "Wherefore, as by one man sin entered into the world, and death by sin; and so death passed upon all men, for that all have sinned."

want, it is no longer I that do it, but sin that dwells within me" (Rom 7:20). Ephesians 2:1 parses out the central implication of the condition that afflicts us, "You were dead through the trespasses and sins . . . " In Col 1:21, the apostle refers to the hostility that human beings have toward God: "And you who were once estranged and hostile in mind, doing evil deeds . . . "

To summarize, these passages appear to refer to an innermost disruption in human nature that taints every aspect of human experience and ultimately prevents human beings from gaining free and unfettered access to God's presence.

HUMAN EVIL

Moral evil and much of human suffering are the direct consequences of the condition into which humanity was hurled following the primordial act of disobedience. Several factors account for the persistent deployment of evil.

The rupture to which Genesis 3 witnesses has resulted in what one could describe as a structural tendency toward evil. Generation after generation, human beings generate ideologies of death that in time become conduits for the expression of the evil that is inherent to the human heart. In ch. 4, I referred to this process as an expression of idolatry: the rejection of the true God in favor of nonentities that eventually, consciously or unconsciously, come to embody destructive human impulses. Despite the circuitous road that may lead there, idolatry always turns out to be a tautology, the self worshipping the self.

Idolatry also expresses itself as a fundamental attitude of suspicion toward God or whatever is perceived as the embodiment of ultimate reality. Human beings deal with this suspicion by domesticating the deity, converting it into something they understand and that they can control to advance their own interests. Tragically, one of the most destructive manifestations of this phenomenon is when the divine is entirely subsumed to the state. German Nazism, Italian fascism, Japanese imperialism, and now radical Islam in its al-Qaeda or ISIS incarnations represent such examples. In fact, every form of totalitarianism is an expression of the ultimate belief in the supremacy and divine character of the state.

In the Western world, there has been a concerted effort to evacuate the Judeo-Christian notion of God, and to replace it with an ideological construct that privileges the ever-growing presence of the state and its reach into the sphere of the individual. Western Europe has boldly followed this impulse for well over a half century. Even the United States, a country founded on principles of limited government and individual freedom, appears to be headed in the same direction.

Wherever the notion of a personal and moral God, as found in the Judeo-Christian tradition, is dislodged from a culture, chaos is never far behind. The German philosopher Friedrich Nietzsche famously announced, near the end of the nineteenth century, that God was dead. This had, of course, nothing to do with whether God was literally dead. Nietzsche's observation was more akin to a state of the union address. It was a dramatic way to note that as far as the educated class was concerned, belief in the Judeo-Christian God had essentially vanished. Nietzsche had provided the eulogy. But for the philosopher, this wasn't necessarily a bad thing, for the death of God would provide an opportunity for the rise of a new kind of human whose horizons would no longer be limited by the constraints of divine law. Those who can't quite appreciate the significance of this declaration and its consequences need look no further than Hitler. Nietzsche knew exactly where the death of God would lead. He predicted, and rightly so may I add, that the twentieth century would be characterized by a kind of brutality and violence never seen before.[28] And the twenty-first century would be worse![29]

In addition to the primordial brokenness from which evil flows, individual freedom of choice plays a central role in the recurrence of evil. For free will to be meaningful, men and women must have the ability to make decisions that are ultimately determined by the individual rather than an external agent. God has created an environment where human beings are free to carry out actions that are self-generated and in which they can genuinely interact with each other. The range of what humans can do is remarkable. In this world, a man can choose to get drunk, drive a car at breakneck speed, and be killed in an accident. The world in which we live allows for an extraordinary range of action, be it for good or for ill. We may bemoan it when tragedies occur, but were it not the case, free will would be but an illusion.

Some Christians will no doubt resist the notion of an environment where human beings have the ability to act freely, as such an idea will be seen as a challenge to God's sovereignty. The latter inference is not necessary. At the heart of the issue is a matter of definition. The biblical text does not ever set human free will and God's sovereignty in opposition to each another. God is described as sovereign as creator and sustainer. But God's sovereignty does not necessarily denote absolute control. In other

---

28. See Copleston, *History of Philosophy*, 405–6; Heller, *Importance of Nietzsche*, 5–6. The Canadian journalist Mark Steyn eloquently examines the implications of Nietzsche's observation in *After America*, 323–24.

29. Implied from Nietzsche's preface to *The Will to Power*, 3.

words, divine sovereignty does not imply a universe in which God is the only significant agent. God could, of course, have chosen to exercise his sovereignty in this fashion. But such is evidently not the case. We do not live in the kind of universe where God determines every action. Even animals appear to benefit from a limited but significant level of self-determination in terms of responding to their environment. This principle is implied in God's command to the animals to reproduce themselves in Gen 1:20–25, where God is described as creating an undetermined number of creatures that are then released with the mandate to multiply. As for humans, not only do we have the impression of being self-determined, but Scripture also supports this notion. This is most clearly expressed in the temptation account where Adam and Eve are depicted as playing out the full extent of the freedom God has given them.

This is not to say there is no tension between God's sovereignty and human free will. In their fallen state, men and women do indeed tend to move away from God and his laws and to feed the well of chaos that is now part of the human heart. In some cases, they may use their free will to inflict pain on others or engage in self-destructive lifestyles. If the history of God's dealings with ancient Israel teaches us anything, it is that God does act in history to mitigate evil. Because of God's absolute goodness, there will be a profound tension between human free will and God's sovereignty. But that tension, for it is real, is not due to God's inability to impose his will. It is due to the space he has provided for humans to exercise free will even in their fallen state. While God does at times intervene to limit evil, there is an extremely fine line he chooses not to cross.

The ultimate line God will not cross is the exercise of human free will with respect to his own person. God is in the process of forming a people composed of men and women who will love him. By definition, love implies freedom. While God could easily manipulate our brain chemistry to forcibly induce "love," it would not be real; it would simply reflect a programmed response. This God won't do. While some people might be skeptical when it comes to the degree of free will human beings generally have, I submit that its exercise is absolute when God is the object. And that is the root cause that necessitates the existence of what Christian tradition refers to as hell. When it comes to the point zero of conversion, human beings are given the greatest power in the universe: the ability to embrace or reject God.

The primordial rupture in human nature does not imply the annihilation of humanity's ability to choose God and to resist evil. While the doctrine of total depravity teaches that every dimension of human existence has been contaminated by sin, the biblical text suggests that even in the sphere of the curse, human beings retain the ability to exercise their free will. This principle is well illustrated in the Cain and Abel story, where God reminds Cain that he has the freedom to say no to his murderous impulse (Gen 4:7). It is also an intrinsic assumption of the Sinai covenant, which gives the people of Israel the choice to obey or disobey its stipulations (cf. Deut 30:11–20). The use of the curse motif in the prophetic literature unambiguously underlines the recipient's freedom to act on God's indictments (cf. Amos 4:4–13). In the New Testament, the proclamation of the gospel and the genuine character of the invitation to receive or reject Jesus Christ are predicated on the recipient's ability to make a legitimate choice. Again, while I do not wish to minimize the effects of sin on humanity, God has nevertheless chosen to keep working in partnership with men and women despite the structural damage inflicted on human nature by Adam's disobedience. The point is not to blunt the impact of the primordial act of disobedience, but to highlight the remarkable resiliency of human nature, particularly as it pertains to our ability to relate to God.

I have stated earlier that the option to obey or disobey God's primordial command was intended to lock humanity into the sphere of the blessing or the curse. Now of course two questions arise. The first one has to do with Adam and Eve themselves and the outcome of the test God engineered for them. Considering the pain that resulted from the first primordial choice, we may be justified in asking why God could not simply do away with Adam and Eve and start again with a new pair. Surely the painless elimination of the First Two would have been but a small price to pay to avoid the hurricane of suffering and death humanity has experienced since then.

As speculative as this question might be, I think the answer must ultimately reside in the very nature of God himself. The Apostle John states that God is love (1 John 4:8), which implies that love is intrinsic to God's very being. God's love is infinite love. Since love entails commitment, it follows that God must be infinitely committed to what he initiates. When God launched the project to form a people composed of individuals that would love him, he instantly grasped that the First Pair would disobey him and hurl humanity into the sphere of death. God knew that the species he intended to create could come out of the test tainted by death. And he knew from all eternity that these two would in fact fail the test. Logic might have dictated that God snuff them out and try again with another couple. Who would ever know? But God was infinitely committed to the project and to the man and woman through whom he would initiate it. The answer to this question has to do with the nature of infinite love and infinite commitment, two concepts that are nearly impossible for humans to fully comprehend. The closest we sometimes come to it is when parents give birth to a severely handicapped child. While "common sense" might dictate terminating the "defective" fetus, there are those who vehemently reject such an option. When they decided to have a child, they were committed to having and raising the child that would emerge regardless of the challenges a difficult outcome might entail. Once God was committed to the human project, he would not, he could not go back. His nature dictated that he would pursue it to the end even if the cost proved to be infinite.

The other question we need to ask relates to the nature of the curse that was imposed on humanity. Did Adam and Eve's disobedience condemn humanity to be forever locked in the sphere of death? If we were to follow the intuition offered by major world religions or even science, we would have to conclude that humanity is indeed condemned to live in this condition for as long as the universe stands. But intuition and reason are insufficient guides. If God had indeed foreseen the possibility of the fall, as I believe he did, he had also foreseen the catastrophic conditions that would proceed from it and had devised a solution to resolve the new problem humanity was facing.

If the creation of a being endowed with free will required the resolution of an equation of infinite complexity, the redemption of the broken creature would prove to be infinitely more difficult, for it would necessitate the involvement of God himself in the person of God the Son. The mind-bending solution to the new problem created by human disobedience would require the incarnation of the Son of God, his death, and his resurrection.

THE SACRIFICE OF CHRIST

The necessity of the incarnation and the sacrificial death of Christ represents Christianity's most shocking and impenetrable mystery. While the New Testament uses a variety of images to characterize the sacrifice of Christ, the precise rationale behind the absolute necessity of Christ's death is shrouded in a mystery that lies beyond the limits of reason.

The New Testament offers a variety of reasons to account for Christ's death. From a political and sociological perspective, Jesus died because he was rejected by those to whom he came (John 1:5, 11). From a salvation perspective, Jesus died to give us the right to become children of God (John 1:12–13), to give men and women eternal life (John 3:16), to save the world (John 3:17), to enable life to expand (John 12:23–25), to bring redemption (Rom 3:24), to justify humanity (Rom 3:23 and 5:12–21), to remove the curse from humanity (Gal 3:13), and to cleanse our conscience from acts that lead to death (Heb 9:14).

The author of Hebrews states that Jesus died on our behalf as a sacrifice for sins (Heb 10:12). Even here the author is careful to point out that Christ's sacrifice is not identical to the Old Testament sacrifices. There is a fundamental and unbridgeable difference in the nature of the one and the other. The sacrifices offered under the old covenant did not really take sin away. They were only a symbol, a shadow, a foreshadowing of a greater reality:

> Since the law has only a shadow of the good things to come and not the true form of these realities, it can never, by the same sacrifices that are continually offered year after year, make perfect those who approach. Otherwise, would they not have ceased being offered, since the worshipers, cleansed once for all, would no longer have any consciousness of sin? But in these sacrifices there is a reminder of sin year after year. For it is impossible for the blood of bulls and goats to take away sins. (Heb 10:1–4)

In the following verses, the author explicitly states what he only hints at in vv. 1–4, namely, that God did not require offerings and sacrifices, and Jesus's death did not fit into the simple category of a blood sacrifice for sins.

> Consequently, when Christ came into the world, he said, "Sacrifices and offerings you have not desired, but a body you have prepared for me; in burnt offerings and sin offerings you have taken no pleasure." (Heb 10:5–6)

When it comes to Christ's death, the central element was not the consummation of a blood sacrifice. As Heb 10:7 and 9 state, the issue was linked to a deeper reality, the imperative to do God's will: "See, I have come to do your will" (Heb 10:9).

As I pointed out at earlier, a debate has emerged regarding the nature of the atonement. Some theologians have, for instance, objected to the legitimacy of the substitutionary atonement theory partly on the basis that it portrays God as a bloodthirsty and vengeful God who required the death of his own son to be appeased.

This caricature of Christ's sacrifice is wrong on at least two fronts. First, as the author of Hebrews makes clear, the sacrifice of Christ was fundamentally different from the sacrifices required under the Mosaic covenant. Second, God the father is not portrayed as a vengeful God who requires blood to be satisfied, and Jesus is never presented as a victim of "child abuse."[30] A trinitarian perspective makes such an inference implausible, absurd, and simply impossible. Jesus cannot be the defenseless victim of child abuse, as he himself is fully God. As the Apostle John succinctly states in ch. 10, Jesus gave his life of his own volition: "For this reason the Father loves me, because I lay down my life in order to take it up again. No one takes it from

---

30. See, for instance, Weaver, *Non-Violent Atonement*.

me, but I lay it down of my own accord. I have power to lay it down, and I have power to take it up again. I have received this command from my Father" (John 10:17–18; see also John 6:51). Hebrews 10:9 portrays Jesus as willingly making himself available to do God's will: "See, I have come to do your will" (see also 10:7).

The reality is that none of the images found in the New Testament can fully do justice to the underlying rationale behind Christ's death. They only provide glimpses and approximations. I also do not believe any single theory can completely account for the reasons that required Christ to die for the sins of the world. Some theories are no doubt closer to reality than others,[31] but ultimately reason and language must fail us.

The reason for this confession of humility is linked to the nature of reality. The deeper we probe into the fabric of reality, the more complex it proves to be. The following illustration is not completely adequate, but it will give an idea of what I am trying to say. A paper cut will usually require no more than a bandage. The body's self-healing mechanisms are such that a small injury will only require a simple treatment. Skin cancer, on the other hand, reveals a much deeper problem requiring a sophisticated, demanding, and rigorous protocol. This holds true in every aspect of human experience. A car engine that is running poorly because of bad spark plug wires will require much less attention than an engine with damaged valves. Most children recover quite easily from the occasional belittling from other kids, but victims of sexual abuse will be more deeply affected and will require much more time and extensive counseling to function normally later in life. The reality is that whenever we begin to scratch below the surface, so to speak, we discover that nothing is quite as simple as it first seems.

ULTIMATE REALITY

The necessity of Christ's death to save humanity is no doubt linked to the nature of ultimate reality itself, namely, that which is grounded in the very person of God and is most intrinsic to his essence. The closer something is to the core of reality, the more "rigid" and intractable it becomes. For

---

31. In my opinion, substitutionary atonement theories provide a more accurate insight into ultimate reality than the increasingly popular political or peace theories that state that Jesus died to denounce "empire" or to defeat violence by "absorbing" it into himself. While these explanations may offer additional insights into the significance of Christ's sacrifice, in and of themselves, they remain inadequate in terms of addressing the justice issue presupposed by human disobedience. For a helpful summary of the main issues, see Boersma, "Disappearance of Punishment." See also McKnight, *Jesus and his Death*; Marshall, *Aspects of the Atonement*.

instance, can God simply forgive and forget offenses we commit against him and against each other? The way God responds to sin in the Old Testament and the New would strongly suggest that it's not that simple.

Why is something considered sinful? On one level, we can understand sin as a violation of a divine law. This is a definition that is easy to grasp, as it parallels what happens when we break the law. But when it comes to God, I suspect that something is deemed sinful, not simply on account of a law that was broken, but because the action or the attitude that is so qualified "slices into," "etches," or "sears" the ground of reality. This "damage" cannot simply be wished away. In the same way a scratch on a car cannot just be wiped off, but must be repaired, offenses committed in the realm of ultimate reality must also be "repaired." God cannot just "wish" sin away. For God to forgive sin, an action reaching into the ground of reality itself is required.

In contrast, actions that do not transgress God's moral requirements or are otherwise inconsequential, such as ordering a cup of coffee at the restaurant, do not affect ultimate reality and do not therefore require repair. In a house, there are structural elements such as the foundation and load-bearing walls, which cannot be carelessly altered without serious consequences. There are, however, nonstructural elements which can be modified at will without causing any problem whatsoever.

This may explain why Moses could debate with God when God first called him (Exod 3:1—4:14) and, in some sense, get away with it. While his resistance to partnering with God in delivering the Hebrews from Egypt could be viewed as being offensive to God, it did not constitute a moral violation. Adam and Eve's act of disobedience, however, represented a type of action that reached into the essence of ultimate reality and incurred commensurate consequences.

When God decided to create a species that would be like him in the most significant manner in which any creature can be like God, i.e., by being endowed with free will, I suspect the project involved and necessitated reaching into the deepest layer of reality. Adam and Eve's violation of God's command represented a type of action that stretched into the very fabric of reality and affected, as such, the very structure of reality. By analogy, Adam and Eve's action was to the universe what radiation is to the human body. In the same way radiation reaches into the body's cellular structure and requires a corresponding treatment to mitigate its effects, Adam and Eve's act of disobedience reached into the very "DNA" of reality. Because the damage reached into the very fabric of reality, the cure would also need to extend to the very core of reality itself.

Only one course of action could undo the damage done and bring about humanity's redemption: the incarnation of the Son of God, his death, and resurrection.[32] The sacrificial death of Jesus Christ was an imperative required by ultimate reality's very exigencies. Jesus himself alluded to the absolute nature of those demands when, in the garden of Gethsemane, he asked whether there was some other option available to him: "And going a little farther, he threw himself on the ground and prayed, 'My Father, if it is possible, let this cup pass from me; yet not what I want but what you want'" (Matt 26:39).[33] As the narrative makes clear, there was indeed no other option. Christ's sacrifice was not the expression of a capricious and vengeful God. It was, on the contrary, an imperative required by ultimate reality. There are two things that we need to keep in mind when we deal with reality. The deeper we reach into its fabric, the more extensive and far-reaching an action will be, and the more demanding and rigid the conditions of that reality will be.

In the same way humanity could only be introduced to free will by a precise process, fallen humanity could only be redeemed by one and only one mechanism, Christ's sacrifice. The cross cannot be reduced to a critique of empire or to an extended lesson on the merits of nonviolence, for they fail to take into account the infinite gravity of the ontological rupture that occurred in the fabric of reality when Adam and Eve disobeyed and the imperative to intervene at the same level to fix the structural brokenness that was introduced by sin.

I realize that the notion of an ultimate reality that imposes its terms may be difficult to grasp and to accept. And yet, our own experience tells us that it must be that way. In the physical realm, we constantly face the unbending realities of the most basic laws of physics. If I fall from the eleventh floor of an apartment building, I will be killed. If I carelessly cross the street and get hit by a bus, I will be seriously harmed.

The mistake we often make, as postmodern secularists, is to believe that the spiritual sphere matters little and is less demanding than physical reality. To accept this assumption is to make a grave error. Take forgiveness, for instance. We have all been faced with situations that required forgiveness on our part. As Pastor Tim Keller insightfully explains in his book *The Reason for God*, human forgiveness is never extended carelessly or fleetingly. Whenever we need to extend forgiveness, there is always a "cost" associated with it. The more serious the offense, the greater the cost, emotional or otherwise.[34]

---

32. See Matt 16:21; Mark 8:31; Luke 9:22; 17:25; 24:7, 26, 44, 46.
33. See also Mark 14:36; Luke 22:42; John 18:11.
34. See Keller, *Reason for God*, 194–200.

When Adam and Eve disobeyed God, they not only toppled the first of a catastrophic chain of dominos, they offended God himself. They sinned against God. The offense was infinite and all-encompassing in scope. It is in the very nature of ultimate reality to demand compensation for sin. Justice demands it for God demands it, and God is, at his very core, just. If God could simply waive aside a fundamental transgression of his righteous will, God would cease to be God. There was nothing the First Two could do to make amends (Rom 5:6). Since the offense was infinite and structural, payment would also need to be infinite and structural. Only God could set things right. While the precise rationale may be beyond human reason, the New Testament points to the necessity of a divine intervention to redeem humanity and identifies Christ's death on the cross as its absolute corollary. The death of Christ was the great solution needed to resolve the new problem created by the fall (Rom 8:23; Titus 2:13–14).

I earlier compared God's intent to create a creature that would be free with respect to himself as a near-infinitely complex equation. The key to solving the equation consisted in setting up a test that would provide one critical opportunity for the creature to make a choice that would originate from the creature itself. If Adam and Eve had chosen to trust God, they would have become the kind of creature God had envisioned. But they disobeyed. While the primordial test fulfilled its purpose in terms of producing a species that would be endowed with free will, the act of disobedience brought into existence a fallen creature.

This new situation in effect created a new equation for God to address. As the New Testament reveals, Christ's sacrifice represented the key to resolving the new equation. But that is not all. While Christ's sacrifice creates the conditions necessary for humanity's redemption, just like Adam and Eve had to personally participate in God's protocol for the full development of a free creature, to benefit from Christ's sacrificial death on the cross, each human being is required to make a personal decision. That is the one piece of the puzzle that must remain out of God's hands if humans are to freely enter into a loving relationship with God.

6

Parsing Out a Biblical Theology of Evil

THIS CHAPTER WILL EXPLORE the implications of our study of the creation account for some of the difficult questions that are often asked in the face of the persisting presence of evil in the world: What is evil and how can we recognize it? Why did God create a world that had the potential for the kind of suffering we experience? Is this the best God could do? If justice is a critical component of God's character, why do some good people suffer through no fault of theirs? Is there a relationship between morality and happiness? Are there moral rules we can follow that will guarantee a good life? Since pain is often viewed as necessary for the development of character, does that mean that evil is in fact necessary for the development of virtues?

I will also reflect on the difficulty inherent to turning to the only true source of healing in the universe. Evil, pain, and suffering are a constant reminder of our vulnerability as human beings. Men and women do their best to stay off its path and would in fact give anything to avoid death, which must certainly qualify as the worst manifestation of evil. While the Bible claims to offer the only viable solution to the presence of evil, the biblical option often appears to be unacceptable. I will explore why that is.

ON THE NATURE OF EVIL

Defining evil seems like an easy task until, that is, we attempt to do so. Even though we may intuitively recognize it when we see it, there is surprisingly little consensus with respect to what exactly constitutes evil. If recent history proves anything at all, it's that naming evil is a lot more complex than it appears at first sight. In great part, that may explain why C. S. Lewis chose to write about the problem of *pain* rather than the problem of *evil*. Unlike the more abstract concept of evil, it is much more difficult to theorize endlessly about whether something is painful or not.

The challenge inherent to defining evil comes from two directions. On some occasions, evil is loosely used to describe unexceptional actions that result in harmful outcomes or to characterize challenging situations. In other words, something is described as evil, not because it is evil in and of itself, but on account of objectionable elements associated with it. Some, for example, argue that the world would not necessarily be a better place if all evils were eliminated. University of Colorado professor of philosophy Michael Tooley explains:

> Thus, some would argue, for example, that the frustration that one experiences in trying to solve a difficult problem is outweighed by the satisfaction of arriving at a solution, and therefore that the world is a better place because it contains such evils. Alternatively, it has been argued that the world is a better place if people develop desirable traits of character—such as patience, and courage—by struggling against obstacles, including suffering. But if either of these things is the case, then the prevention of all evil might well make the world a worse place.[1]

At first glance, the scenario Tolley describes makes sense, but one question immediately emerges. Should the mere prospect of facing a difficult problem or a situation requiring the deployment of moral virtues be defined as evil in and of itself? Not necessarily. There is no compelling reason for considering the challenge of climbing a mountain or solving a mathematical problem as evil *per se*. How can we possibly equate solving an engineering challenge with something as morally reprehensible as murder? In fact, to characterize such examples as evil may result in creating a theoretical framework that makes the task of providing even a partial solution to the problem of evil virtually impossible. While it may seem tempting to define such cases as evil, as the failure to find ready solutions to such challenges may result in pain and death, we must remember that our all-too-common

---

1. Tooley, "Does God Exist?," 101.

propensity to unsuccessfully navigate the constellation of life-threatening problems that human existence entails is not, according to Scripture, inherent to human existence *per se*. It is but a consequence of the rupture that occurred at the dawn of human history.

There are situations, however, that most naturally strike us as morally evil but may not be universally defined as such. For instance, common sense dictates that the slaughter of six million Jews under the Nazi regime must certainly rank as a manifestation of radical evil. But common sense doesn't always win the day. The destruction of the Jews was perceived as a fundamental good by much of the Nazi apparatus before and during World War II. In some sectors of the Arab world today, the Holocaust, if not altogether denied, is not necessarily viewed as reprehensible. In fact, with the growth of radical Islam in the Middle East and other parts of the world, we note a proportional rise in the kind of ideology that led to the persecution of the Jews during the Nazi era. The Allied forces may have eliminated the Nazis but not anti-Semitism.[2]

It should be obvious to all that abortion as a crude method of birth control should rank at or near the top of whatever evil scale we may have at our disposal. At the very least, third trimester fetus dissections should unanimously be viewed as a form of radical evil that only heartless and barbaric people would condone. And yet, judging by the amount of attention this issue receives compared to such fashionable causes as the fate of baby seals or the many environmental causes that scream for our attention, one might conclude that the termination of hundreds of thousands of healthy babies is, at best, a great good on par with feeding the poor, at worst, like the presence of toilets and sewer systems, an awkward and slightly embarrassing fact of life.

The French Reformed theologian Henri Blocher, in his insightful book *Evil and the Cross*, attempts to offer a comprehensive and universal definition of evil as that which ought not to be. He writes:

> What do people mean, when in a real-life situation they use the word "evil"? They are talking about its *unjustifiable reality*. In common parlance, evil is "something" that occurs in experience and *ought not to*. It has occurred, but it is not what you would expect. Spontaneously and whole-heartedly we say "No!" to it,

---

2. The rise of anti-Semitism among Arabs in the Middle East and in Europe is well documented. For example, see Bastani, "Iranians 'Least Anti-Semitic in the Mid-East.'" For an informative treatment of the rise of anti-Semitism in France and its implications for the French Jewish community, see Goldberg, "Is It Time."

like Jackie Kennedy when the assassin's bullet hit her husband by her side in the open car.³

While such a definition may be entirely appropriate and reflective of what evil is, in reality, as soon as we position ourselves within the broader horizon of world religions and philosophy or even within the narrower confines of Christian theology, agreeing on a definition of evil, whether in an abstract or concrete manner, remains as elusive as discovering the proverbial Holy Grail.

As we head further and further into the so-called postmodern era, which incidentally would be more accurately described as the post-reason and anti-Christian era,⁴ I am appalled at our increasing inability to recognize evil even when it is right in front of our eyes. We are losing our ability to distinguish between the vicious grin of the assassin and the benevolent smile of the grandmother. We have become hopelessly naïve sheep that deny the existence of the wolf and confuse the violent potential of the sheepdog with the murderous impulses of the wolf.⁵

The task of finding a definition that would receive unanimous assent is as futile as trying to warm our feet in a bucket of dry ice. We live in the kind of ideological world that makes it virtually impossible to arrive at the type of common definition that is necessary both to accurately identify evil and to act against it. For here lies the uncomfortable edge of the sword: We will act against evil, both in our lives and in the world, only if we can unambiguously identify it.

Despite the inherent difficulty of the task, I would like to propose a definition that, I believe, emerges out of the creation account. The primordial test described in Gen 2:15–17 represented a choice between life and death. God's intent was to give Adam and Eve the opportunity to choose life and to usher humanity into eternal life. But Adam and Eve chose the path of death and thus introduced the human race to the age of misery. As we have seen, the creation account presents itself as paradigmatic and historical. It addresses the human condition, but it also describes a historical situation; it is both archetypal and specific. As a *creation story*, it intends to provide a basic definition of what evil is. If we follow the trajectory suggested by this text, then we could propose that *evil is that which obstructs, obliterates, and*

---

3. Blocher, *Evil and the Cross*, 10–11.

4. For an insightful and incisive critique of postmodern thought, see Plantinga, "Christian Philosophy," 328–52.

5. This imagery is borrowed from a short article by Lt. Col. (Ret.) Dave Grossman, entitled "On Sheep, Wolves, and Sheepdogs."

negates life. Within the creation account's framework, to choose evil is to choose death over life.

This definition may seem simple enough. Unfortunately, choosing life over death is not always self-evident. The Nazis were convinced they were on the path to a glorious future, and to the extent that they succeeded in cleansing and protecting the purity of the Arian gene pool, they would guarantee a better future for themselves. The efficient, albeit horrific, implementation of their poisonous ideology was the unavoidable step toward the emergence of the super race. But as readers may no doubt realize, the Nazis always represent an easy target. Time has a way of sharpening our focus. If only such moral clarity could always be maintained. But as is often the case, the closer we are to a situation, the hazier our eyesight becomes. For instance, why is it that an otherwise healthy concern for the environment can morph into a quasi-anti-human movement? In some circles, the simple fact of having children, something that has generally been viewed as inherently good, is now depicted as an intractable evil, a shameless imposition upon the earth.[6]

Those who embrace evil are not always aware of doing so. In fact, the more we cultivate the fertile ground of evil that is inherent to the human heart, and the more we give expression to it, the more limited, it seems, is our ability to recognize it for what it is.[7] In turn, this further enhances our potential to engage in ever-greater expressions of evil.

In the case of our post-Christian society, the loss of confidence in reason is further undermining our ability to recognize evil. Like the proverbial frog being gradually boiled to death, the Western world is slowly dying in the rising heat of the toxic stew of its own ideological pot.

Despite the difficulties inherent to articulating a definition everyone could accept in this post-reason age, I still maintain that the definition we

---

6. The notion that humans are outstripping the earth's capacity to support them is so widely accepted today that it has almost become a self-evident truth. Back in 2007, one John Feeney, who is described as an environmental writer and activist, in an article originally posted on the BBC News website, entitled "Humanity Is the Greatest Challenge," openly expressed what many radical environmentalists only dare say behind closed doors. He writes, "We must end world population growth, then reduce population size. That means lowering population numbers in industrialized as well as developing nations. Scientists point to the population-environment link. But today's environmentalists avoid the subject more than any other ecological truth. Their motives range from the political to a misunderstanding of the issue. Neither justifies hiding the truth because total resource use is the product of population size and per capita consumption. We have no chance of solving our environmental predicament without reducing both factors in the equation. Fortunately, expert consensus tells us we can address population humanely by solving the social problems that fuel it."

7. M. Scott Peck, the well-known author of *The Road Less Traveled*, extensively develops this thesis in *People of the Lie*.

can derive from the creation account can provide an adequate starting point. But if we do not share some basic assumptions about what defines "life," and what might favor or obstruct it, is there any hope of arriving at a common understanding of the nature of evil? While the problem is daunting, I'd like to propose some principles that may offer a way forward.

A WAY FORWARD

First, hardwired in the deepest sectors of their moral encoding, human beings have a natural law that provides the broad parameters of right and wrong. As C. S. Lewis points out in *Mere Christianity*, this universal law, which in *The Abolition of Man* he calls the Tao, may not express itself in identical ways in all cultures, but it does generally entail a number of basic elements that are common to all cultures.[8] It is, for example, universally understood that it is preferable to save a child from drowning than to gleefully watch the tot thrash in the water until he suffocates. The number of wives a man may lawfully have differs from culture to culture, but everyone would agree that no man can have any woman he wants. Human conscience normally provides some sense of what is morally right or wrong. A man may choose to murder another, but unless he is a psychopath, he will have some notion of the reprehensible nature of the act he has committed.

Human conscience, however, is not foolproof. While it can effectively alert us to the presence of unethical behavior, it does not guarantee consistent moral comportment. Unlike Isaac Asimov's three laws of robotics,[9] and in what must represent an ironic confirmation of human free will, men and women can, given some ideological tinkering, engage in the kind of moral deconstruction that can eventually lead to the inversion of previously stable ethical standards. Such deconstruction is not handily done, but over time, a generation or two, sometimes less, it can be achieved. The moral reprogramming engineered by the Nazis, the emergence of a death cult in radical Islamic circles, most recently reincarnated in ISIS, and the near-routine use of abortion as a means of birth control all bear witness to humanity's ability to modify its moral encoding.

Second, any ideology that pretends to favor humankind or the community at the cost of individual men and women should always be viewed with suspicion. The great "isms" of our time have one thing in common.

---

8. See Lewis, *Mere Christianity*, 3–32, and *Abolition of Man*.

9. The concept of robotic "moral" laws that determine the behavior of robots was first introduced by Isaac Asimov in his short novel, "Runaround," published in 1942, and reused in several novels and short stories.

Communism, fascism, socialism, evolutionism, and utopianism, to name a few, are ideologies that purport to seek the betterment of humanity as a whole, but ironically, their strict implementation has consistently resulted in the impoverishment, if not the destruction of millions of "peasants" unsuitable for whatever utopia these ideologies promise.

Third, always bet on freedom, the intrinsic dignity of the individual, personal accountability, and self-reliance. Whenever an ideology threatens to obliterate these truths, we should beware, for wherever these principles are undermined, people die, and cultures degenerate into chaos or morph into some form of totalitarianism. But here again, there is no shortage of North American and European intellectuals who will scoff at identifying such concepts as freedom and self-reliance as fundamental. But how do we know whether such truths are indeed fundamental and worth defending and fighting for? There is nothing esoteric about it. It has everything to do with the worldview that underpins the biblical text.

Fourth, trust Scripture. While the natural law can be deconstructed, and our natural moral compass decommissioned, Scripture remains. From an ethical perspective, the Bible does not just provide a law code. It reaches far beyond the legal realm. The biblical text offers a revolutionary worldview, one that radically departs from anything humans have articulated throughout history.

Scripture offers a life-affirming worldview that accomplishes two things. It provides a benchmark to evaluate the various ideologies that surreptitiously emerge with each generation. In cultures where the most critical elements of the biblical worldview are adopted, the yield is consistent: life abounds. In cultures where these truths are ignored, opposed, or undermined, people consistently sow the seeds of death and oppression. Shocking abstractions? Not really. Even the most cursory comparison between South and North Korea will dramatically illustrate this principle. In the former, churches thrive, democracy rules, innovation and prosperity pervade the culture. In the latter, totalitarianism reigns. Citizens live in fear, constantly face the prospect of starvation, and are fed to the ever-expanding gulags. As the French historian Pierre Chaunu never tired of pointing out, consider the status of women in cultures that have been significantly influenced by the Bible and those that have not. In the former, and that pretty well includes the entire Western world, women benefit from the same rights as men. Just about everywhere else, women wish they were so lucky. Under Sharia law, the body of Islamic law that regulates life under Islamic rule, women have precious few civil rights. The contrast with the Western world is stark but mostly ignored by the Western intellectual elites.[10]

As can be seen from our discussion, no definition of evil will ever satisfy everyone. But all things being equal, I maintain that the notion of evil derived from the creation account as that which opposes life is probably as useful an understanding of evil as can be achieved in our context. While not everyone will agree on what constitutes life, I think there is sufficient overlap between the biblical understanding of life and that found in popular culture to serve as a legitimate starting point. But having a working definition of evil is not enough. If we are to avoid slipping into pantheism, where evil is no longer distinguished from the good, or Manicheism, which views evil as eternal and ontologically distinct from the good, then it is necessary to clarify the question of origin.

ON THE ORIGIN OF EVIL

Where does evil come from? The creation account locates the historical emergence of evil in Adam and Eve's primordial choice in the garden of Eden. As far as humanity is concerned, this is where it all starts. Evil emerged as a consequence of the first humans' decision to distrust their creator. This choice resulted in a catastrophic chain reaction that affected human nature and every aspect of human life. Cain's murderous inclinations and the explosion of violence that came to characterize the antediluvian civilization are linked to Adam and Eve's act of disobedience. All the misery and the suffering experienced by men and women throughout history ultimately derives from that first act of disobedience. According to Gen 3:16–19 and Rom 8:20–21, Adam's disobedience also introduced a fundamental disruption in the very nature of the universe itself.

But many Christians are not satisfied to leave the matter rest there. Are we not to find the ultimate origin of evil, the point zero of its emergence, in a prehistorical angelic insurgency? Christian tradition teaches that evil was born in the heart of Lucifer and spread throughout the ranks of those angels who rebelled against God. Tradition also teaches that it was Satan, disguised as a serpent, who was instrumental in humanity's downfall.

Isn't it reasonable to posit the hypothesis that evil must ultimately be located in the person of the Adversary himself? The matter of what demons

---

10. Professor Emeritus at Paris IV-Sorbonne, Pierre Chaunu, was one of the few French leading intellectuals of his time to highlight the differences between the status of women in the (Christian) West and the rest of the world, most notably the Middle East. See, for example, Chaunu and Renard, *La femme et Dieu*.

are, where they come from, and the nature of their relationship to the human world are important questions. The easy way out would simply be to define Satan as a personification of evil, a psychological projection originating from our need to find a scapegoat for the unbearable burden of guilt that plagues us. I wish it were that simple. But spiritual reality is not so easily domesticated. It is as stubborn as a bull-headed dog gagging on a chicken drumstick.

If the Old Testament provides little information about the devil and his servants, the New Testament, however, offers some key information about the pesky creatures that are said to pollute humanity's spiritual and moral atmosphere. The most pernicious issue with respect to demons resides in their origin and whether the cause of human evil can be traced back to them.

As far as we can tell from the few texts that address the demonic, there appears to have been a catastrophic event, a rebellion that induced the emergence of these entities. While we know little about the precise mechanism that led to this situation, Scripture does view these creatures as objectively real. They have the ability to interact with human beings and to "infect" them under the right conditions. The testimony of our Lord and the apostles leaves no doubt about these matters. While some New Testament passages and later Christian tradition have associated the serpent of Genesis 3 with the devil of old, thus confirming demonic involvement even at this earliest stage of human history, the root cause of evil in human history must nevertheless be laid, as the creation account unmistakably does, at the feet of Adam and Eve. The ultimate responsibility for the primordial act of disobedience they committed belongs to them and them alone.[11]

IS THIS THE BEST OF ALL POSSIBLE WORLDS?

King Alfonso X infamously claimed that if he had been at God's side at the time of creation, the world would have been a better place. In response to Pierre Bayle, who picked up on Alfonso's critique, Gottfried Wilhelm Leibniz strenuously attempted to demonstrate that since God is perfect, this universe could not be anything but the best of all possible worlds God could have made. David Hume, vehemently maintained, however, that this universe showed every sign of having been designed by, at best, an incompetent being and, at worst, an evil God.

While we may debate whether this is the best of all possible worlds, the creation account is categorical in one respect: this world is not as God had

---

11. For more details on the nature of the demonic and the character of their relationship to humans, see Gilbert, *Demons, Lies & Shadows*, and Page, *Powers of Evil*.

originally intended it to be. This is perhaps why most of us never quite feel like this is where we belong. While there is continuity between the world we know and the world God had envisioned, they are not the same. For one, the world as originally imagined and created by God was not tainted by sin. The divine assessment is massively and gloriously unequivocal. On six occasions in Genesis 1, God declares his creation "good" and once "very good."

Does this pronouncement imply finality? Was the universe completed in the same sense a wood sculpture might be? Yes and no. While the text signals the completion of an overall infrastructure, the creation of the universe was not an end in and of itself. The purpose of this gigantic undertaking was to provide a framework to support human existence. As such, it is also a dynamic system in which everything, from the tiniest subatomic particle to the largest galaxy, is in perpetual movement. For reasons I would rather not speculate on, the creation account appears to link humanity's destiny and that of the universe. The narrative hints at some fundamental change, either favorable or detrimental, that would occur when Adam and Eve would face the primordial test of allegiance. As Gen 2:17 intimates and 3:8–24 confirms, obedience to God's command would lock humanity and the entire universe into the sphere of life. If we can assume that the outcome of obedience would have resulted in a reversal of the scenario attached to disobedience, the implication is that both the human race and the universe would have been propelled into a new phase of existence that would have transformed the universe in ways we cannot imagine. But when the First Two disobeyed, they committed an act that reached into the very core of reality itself and triggered a deadly chain reaction that affected them first and then the rest of creation. Thereafter, the world became effectively locked into the sphere of the curse.

The creation narrative goes to great length to establish the distinction between God's original intent and the world that emerged after Adam and Eve's sin. The universe was indeed created good. But the world we know, contaminated as it is by sin, no longer strictly reflects the world as originally devised by God. It does, however, remain the best of all possible worlds for a species contaminated by sin. If God is infinitely good and powerful, then we must assume that this is the best of all possible worlds *in the context of the fall.*

The impression that this is not the best of all possible worlds imaginable is perfectly accurate. This world is under a curse. To presume that the world as we know it was intended to be the *best* of all possible worlds is delusional. In that respect, Alfonso X, Bayle, and Hume were right. Where they were wrong was in their belief that this was the world God had originally imagined.

Even if we assume that this may indeed be the best of all possible worlds for a fallen race, there are nevertheless several issues that need to be addressed if only because they represent formidable objections to this assertion. The first relates to why good people suffer and the other to what is often referred to as natural evil, the kind of pain that results from nonhuman causes such as hurricanes, earthquakes, diseases, droughts, etc. These topics are important, because they offend our sense of justice. That evil people may suffer is not an intractable problem. It is the notion that good people may suffer through no fault of theirs that represents a major stumbling block.

ON WHY GOOD PEOPLE SUFFER

It is to respond to this dilemma that Rabbi Kushner wrote *When Bad Things Happen to Good People*.[12] The book was written in response to the painful death of the author's son, Aaron, at the age of fourteen, eleven years after being diagnosed with progeria, a disease that causes children to age prematurely. It was Kushner's way of dealing with the questions his son's condition raised and the spiritual crisis that ensued. This book does one thing well, but the other quite poorly.

On the one hand, it debunks many of the simplistic answers that are often offered to explain why good people suffer. Like Gregory A. Boyd in *God at War* and *Satan and the Problem of Evil*,[13] Rabbi Kushner challenges the various versions and offshoots of what Boyd calls the "blueprint" position, the belief that God is the ultimate cause of suffering, and that all instances of evil have a God-ordained purpose.

It is important to note that in traditional Jewish theology, God is the only effective cause.[14] Unlike Christian theology, which can divert some of the responsibility for evil to Satan and demons, Jewish tradition offers no such safety valve. While God is not held as the source of moral evil, there is no attempt at elucidating the mechanism that permits the juxtaposition of the notion of God's absolute sovereignty and the presence of evil in the world. They are just laid side by side without logical articulation as a quasi-antinomy: God is the cause of everything, *and* God is not the cause of everything.

As Rabbi Kushner himself concedes, what he learned in seminary turned out to be inadequate. In an effort to resolve the painful dilemma his son's death forced him to face, Kushner virtually rushes headlong into

12. Kushner, *When Bad Things*.
13. Boyd, *God at War* and *Satan*.
14. See Goldberg, "Providence," 32–42.

oncoming traffic! He ends up articulating a position that turns out to be worse than the original problem he sought to resolve. Kushner manages to douse the theological fire that rages in his soul by serving his readers a powerless God. Kushner's God is good and benevolent but is worth no more than a whole boat of beans when it comes to dealing with evil. The rabbi unveils Santa Claus. A God who is undoubtedly good but stripped of any power. While the book may and has in fact offered solace to thousands of people, it ultimately fails to maintain a Christian orthodox view of God and to resolve the classical dilemma Christians face. I'm convinced that whatever comfort his thesis may offer will ultimately prove to be as effective as a picture of a fireplace on a blistery winter day.

Why do good people suffer? That's a fair question, and one that most of us have or will ponder at some point or another. On November 11, 2006, Winnipeg (Canada) inner-city pastor Harry Lehotsky died at the age of forty-nine, following a long battle with pancreatic cancer.

Pastor Harry and his family had moved into the "North End," often described as one of the poorest and most violent neighborhoods in Winnipeg. If Harry had many friends, his relentless lobbying on behalf of his neighborhood against a faceless bureaucracy sadly gained him a few enemies as well. Harry was the kind of man who could bust a drug dealer one moment and share the gospel with him the next.

By any standard, Harry was a good man, better than most. And then, out of the blue, he gets hit by the proverbial bus. He is diagnosed with terminal pancreatic cancer. The doctors give him a few months to live. In an article he wrote soon after his diagnosis, he asked the question many of us were wildly dancing with. Why him? Couldn't the Angel of Death pick one of the drug-dealing scumbags that litter the neighborhood?

But after further reflection, he began to ask, why not me? By all accounts, he should have died a long time ago of a drug overdose. God spared him and gave him a second chance, an opportunity to live a useful life and leave a worthy legacy. At the age of forty-nine, Harry had lived more than many who get to live to twice his age.

Harry could face his own mortality with courage and fortitude, because this good man had resolved to deal with reality, not wishful thinking. And that, by the way, is one of the surest signs of leadership, personal integrity, and spiritual health there is. Great leaders do not set up shop in la-la land. Harry had a sound theology of evil. When disaster struck, he resisted the urge to self-destruct. His faith in Christ and an adequate theological foundation carried him to safety.

And that is the point of articulating a biblical theology of evil. I entertain no illusions about the human condition or the so-called goodness of human nature. Living conditions can change in the blink of an eye. One night you quietly fall asleep in "Hobbiton" and brutally awake in "Mordor." A good theology of pain and suffering is not intended to anesthetize the mind. On the contrary, it is designed to help us maintain hope in God and our belief in his goodness. It also ensures we do not fall apart at the seams when tragedy strikes, as it inevitably does. If responding to cancer is the forty-two-kilometer marathon, walking the theology-of-evil treadmill is the training that is necessary to win that race.

To get a handle on why good people sometimes unjustly suffer, it will be helpful to consider Augustine's threefold categorization of evil: moral evil, amoral evil, and metaphysical evil.[15]

Moral evil is generally defined as the kind of evil that derives from the action of a moral agent. It is a form of gratuitous suffering that results from malevolent human action, and whose sole purpose is to satisfy the self-centered impulses of the agent inflicting the pain. The need to inflict pain and death on others often emerges out of utopianism—examples are Stalin's communism, Pol Pot's "green" revolution, and Hitler's dream of a Third Reich. Another is greed and lust. And last but not least, there is pleasure. Some people are cruel simply because they derive intense gratification from inflicting pain on others. These three impulses are often as hopelessly entwined as vipers in a snake pit during mating season. Moral evil is by far the greatest source of suffering in the world.

C. S. Lewis attributes most of human pain to human action:

> When souls become wicked they will certainly use this possibility to hurt one another; and this, perhaps, accounts for four-fifths of the sufferings of men. It is men, not God, who have produced racks, whips, prisons, slavery, guns, bayonets, and bombs; it is by human avarice or human stupidity, not by the churlishness of nature, that we have poverty and overwork.[16]

Sometimes decent men and women suffer because of someone else's malevolent action toward them. What makes this possible is the range of freedom God grants human beings. While God did not create a world that allows individuals to act on every single impulse they may have, he nevertheless allows a significant, even if limited, degree of moral self-determination.

---

15. Augustine explores the problem of evil in *Concerning the Nature of Good*. For an informative survey of Augustine's view of evil, see Willimon, *Sighing for Eden*, 38–49. For a more detailed treatment, see Hick, *Evil and the God of Love*, 43–95.

16. Lewis, *Problem of Pain*, 86.

To qualify as moral evil, the suffering must be *intentionally* caused by human action or inaction. Suffering that is the outcome of an unintentional act does not technically fall in this category.

Amoral evil denotes suffering that is not directly caused by a moral agent. This includes pain that is caused by natural disasters such as earthquakes, tsunamis, floods, tornadoes, etc. This is not to say that earthquakes and tsunamis are morally "evil" *per se*. The word "evil" highlights the devastating impact that such occurrences have on human life; it's not intended to characterize the moral status of the events themselves. They are described as "amoral" because there is in fact no moral agent involved.

As with the likes of Alfonso X, Pierre Bayle, David Hume, and countless others, it is tempting to accuse God of criminal negligence for creating a world where men and women are subjected to such natural disasters. Why did God create a world where human beings would need to contend against forces that often prove to be overwhelming and deadly? There are several factors to keep in mind as we consider this question.

First, according to Gen 3:17–19, the environment was irremediably affected by Adam and Eve's primordial sin. While it may be impossible to specify in what ways and to what extent, Scripture leaves no doubt about this tragic reality (see also Rom 8:20–22).

Second, the universe in which we live is not some matrix-like computer simulation; our world is *real*. In order to maintain the kind of environment that is required to support life, a number of natural forces must constantly be at work. Earthquakes, for example, are not primarily instruments of God's anger. While the Bible sometimes describes God as using them to express his judgment,[17] we also know that they naturally occur as a result of large-scale motions in the earth's lithosphere. Other potentially destructive phenomena such as hurricanes and tornadoes develop when certain atmospheric conditions are met. As distressing as such occurrences may turn out to be, they are simply expressions of the natural forces needed to maintain the earth's environment.

Third, God has created a world in which there is space for the free and random interaction of the elements of nature. There is no reason to believe that this "space" was the outcome of the fall. While the fall may have affected some key features of the environment and humanity's ability to navigate the challenges inherent to such a world, as signalled in Gen 3:16–19, nothing in the text suggests that a world without sin would have been devoid of risk or might have precluded the unimpeded expression of the elements of nature

---

17. See, for instance, Exod 19:18; Amos 1:1; 8:8; 9:1, 5; Isa 2:19–21; Mic 1:3–6; Rev 16:16–20.

and their free interaction. If a universe in which everything were perfectly predictable might be of some obvious benefit, particularly with respect to avoiding accidental deaths, I suspect such a world would not have had the capacity for the kind of freedom all living beings seem to enjoy and the infinite number of possibilities our universe entails in terms of how humans interact with each other. There have never been two identical days, cloud formations, or baseball games. The potential for limitless diversity is written in the very code of reality.

I would contend that there is no absolute discontinuity between a world with sin and one without; the distinction resides essentially in the severity of the conditions that now prevail in a fallen world and the ontological flaw introduced in human nature as a result of disobedience. Much of the suffering we experience results from the free interaction of the elements that constitute our world. People often die from accidents simply because they find themselves in the wrong place at the wrong time. As difficult as it may be to accept, there may be no other reason for a bicycle mishap or of a child struck with leukemia as bad luck.

This principle does not in any way offer a challenge to God' sovereignty. If God had wished to create a universe where every single atom, every molecule, every organism was under his direct control, he could have easily done so. This is not what he wanted. As a being endowed with free will, he put a premium on creating a world engineered in such a way as to permit the exercise of free will. The creation of such a universe would require a strategic modulation of God's sustaining power both with respect to maintaining its basic integrity (Col 1:17) and allowing for a meaningful degree of self-determination on the part of his creatures. It should be noted that there is no contradiction between postulating a degree of free interaction between the various elements of the universe and the concept of God's sovereignty. Boyd offers a helpful explanation. He writes:

> The point is that the law of God's providence is a moral law, not a deterministic law. To say that "God regulates all things" is not to say that "God controls all things." Rather, God's governance is one that is consistent with "the preservation of freedom of will in all rational creatures." Hence, God's sovereign will "regulates all things" not by controlling events but by imposing a moral law on them, such as the law that sin has consequences.[18]

Sin is another factor that contributes to the presence of natural evil in the world. Human beings are not what God originally intended them to be; their very nature being now affected by sin. God created a world that

18. Boyd, *Satan*, 44.

required that humans act responsibly. This was to be the case with or without sin. I suspect that even in a world unaffected by sin, the earth would still exhibit large scale and potentially destructive natural phenomena such as earthquakes, hurricanes, and tornadoes.

It is important we not confuse the idyllic conditions prevailing in the garden of Eden with what may have been the case in the world at large. The careful delineation of the royal garden's geographical boundaries in Gen 2:8–14 points to a distinction between the two. While the text provides little information about the precise nature of the environment outside the garden, the divine command to "subdue" (*kabash*) the earth in Gen 1:28 is more forceful than the invitation to "till" (*abad*) the garden and "keep it" (*shamar*) in 2:15. In this context, the Hebrew verb *kabash* denotes an action intended to bring into subjection a wild, untamed, and challenging environment.[19] In contrast, when used in an agricultural context, the verbs "to till" and "to keep" allude to work that is typically and routinely required to maintain and manage a field, a vineyard, or in this case, a royal garden.[20] The garden of Eden may well have been intended to serve as a sheltered environment, an incubator, designed to provide a safe place for humanity to live and develop the skills that would eventually enable men and women to colonize the rest of the planet. The effects of an untamed world on an unfallen and adequately prepared humanity would have been greatly mitigated. Humans unaffected by sin would have presumably managed the harsher conditions prevailing outside the garden of Eden with such competency and expertise as to preclude any loss of human life.

As I have stated on several occasions, Adam and Eve's eviction from the garden of Eden implies that they would have been allowed to eat of the tree of life if they had obeyed God and would have henceforth lived forever. But here is the rub. Sin entered the world and so debased human nature that the adverse consequences of natural phenomena on human life will at times be much worse than they normally would, not only because some people are in the wrong place at the wrong time, but also because they find themselves on the wrong end of human incompetence, stupidity, and carelessness.

---

19. *Kabash* is most used to refer in reference to the subjugation of a nation or a person. See, for example, Num 32:22, 29; Josh 18:1; 2 Sam 8:11; 1 Chr 22:18; 2 Chr 28:10; Neh 5:5; Esth 7:8; Jer 34:11, 16; Zech 9:15.

20. For *abad*, see Gen 2:15; 3:23; 4:2, 12; Exod 1:14; 2 Sam 9:10; Isa 30:24; Jer 27:11; Zech 13:5; Prov 12:11; 28:19. The verb *shamar* doesn't so much denote the work itself as the responsibility a person might be entrusted for something or someone else (see Gen 4:9; 30:31; 1 Sam 17:20; 2 Sam 15:16; 2 Kgs 22:14; Ps 121:3–4; Neh 12:25).

In addition to moral and natural evil, unjust suffering can also derive from what is sometimes referred to as metaphysical evil.[21] Metaphysical evil is that which derives from the intrinsic nature of the world as it is now.

Our universe is, for instance, subjected to the inexorable laws of thermodynamics. The first law tells us that the universe is running down. This process is inevitable and irreversible. One day, far into the future, the entire universe will be cold, inert, and lifeless. But such an eventuality is so remote that compared to paying the rent or making the next car payment, the first law of thermodynamics constitutes but an infinitesimally small concern for most people. The second law is, however, more problematic in terms of its immediate effects on human life. It states that everything seeks a state of disorder. Each day dramatically brings us face to face with this inexorable principle. From our city infrastructures to our own bodies, everything requires constant maintenance. Unlike Superman, we are vulnerable to a broad array of elements. Extreme heat or cold, water (as in I-fall-in-the-ocean water), impact forces (as in I-am-about-to-get-hit-by-the-bus), and hurricane winds have the potential to do us in. We can unexpectedly be struck by a stealthy virus or slowly ravaged by old age. Such is human existence. And no one is exempted.

We all eventually die, not because there is necessarily something morally reprehensible in any one person's life, but because this is the way the world is now designed. The grim reaper shows no favoritism; saints and sinners alike fall to his sickle. It is important to understand that much of the suffering we experience has nothing to do with individual morality as such. We may, either by neglect or bad habit, exacerbate the aging process or our personal genetic predisposition for one disease or another, but in the big scheme of things, decay is a process that is intrinsic to our universe and to our nature. It's nothing personal. It's just part of living in a fallen world. While we can easily identify specific reasons that might account for some types of suffering, in many cases, there may not be any precise moral cause-and-effect mechanism to explain why a child is diagnosed with cancer or why a responsible high school or college student suddenly develops signs of schizophrenia. And to make matters worse, there may be no rational or clearly discernible purpose for much of human suffering. If only we could always identify both the precise cause and the purpose of the pain we experience, that would be immensely helpful, but such is not the case. The sad fact is that whether it's driving to work or assessing the genetic threat of heart disease, we are all constantly playing the odds. It's part and parcel of

---

21. For a detailed discussion of the various ways in which metaphysical evil has been defined, see Antognazza, "Metaphysical Evil Revisited," 112–34.

living in a real world in which God allows the elements of nature to freely interact with each other.

Why do bad things happen to good people? The most basic answer has to do with the nature of the world in which we live. Good people sometimes suffer at the hands of evil people. On occasion, innocent people happen to be in the wrong place at the wrong time. Sometimes they suffer simply because of the very nature of human existence. Good people can also experience pain because of their own actions and attitudes. Lest there be any confusion on the matter, it is crucial to keep in mind that while we may use adjectives like as "good" or "bad" to characterize a person's character, these value judgments are relative. This is where Rabbi Kushner's thesis is woefully inadequate. The title of his book, *When Bad Things Happen to Good People*, assumes the existence of some idealistically upright class of people we describe as "good," and who should therefore be spared from pain, at least gratuitous pain. It's not that simple.

While some people may be more righteous than others, everyone is infected by sin. As Jesus reminds his hearers in Matt 15:19, everyone carries the seeds of chaos in the deepest recesses of their soul. While the extent to which we give in to these impulses differs from person to person, the reality is that we are all contaminated. Sometimes "good" people suffer, because they choose to fall prey to the evil within. In *The Problem of Pain*, Lewis observes that while there may not always be a specific moral cause behind every instance of human suffering, God has allowed pain to be an immutable part of human experience to impress upon us the fact that we are *all*, without exception, spiritually sick and need a spiritual remedy. "God whispers to us in our pleasures, speaks in our conscience, but shouts in our pain: it is His megaphone to rouse a deaf world."[22]

Lewis has no illusion about human nature. Whether we are upright citizens who generously give to the poor or thieves who unashamedly steal from them, the need for personal redemption remains the single most critical fact of human existence. Sin is a force that is intrinsic to human nature. While it manifests itself in a multitude of ways, every man, woman, and child is infected by it. Its outworking may be more visible in some than in others, but its debilitating and corrupting presence is universal and inevitable.

Lewis further states that the most basic manifestation of the sin nature resides in a state of rebellion against God (cf. Col 1:21). In some people, this impulse overtly, visibly, and explicitly manifests itself. In others, it's subtler, nearly undetectable, but present nevertheless. Sin is integral to who we are. To simply associate it with bad behavior, annoying habits, or the occasional

---

22. Lewis, *Problem of Pain*, 91.

flare of anger represents a grave misrepresentation of spiritual reality and what Scripture teaches. Sin infects every single cell of our mind and body. This is why the Bible always describes the cure we need as nothing less than thorough transformation: "So if anyone is in Christ, there is a new creation: everything old has passed away; see, everything has become new!" (2 Cor 5:17). Lewis writes, "In the world as we now know it, the problem is how to recover this self-surrender. We are not merely imperfect creatures who must be improved: we are, as Newman said, rebels who must lay down our arms."[23]

If God uses a vast array of strategies to compel us to recognize our spiritual condition, the presence of pain constitutes the final argument in his effort to help us see our ruin for what it is and to seek his help. This is why "good" people are not and cannot be exempted from the requirement to repent from sin and turn to God. Nice and upright people also need the cure. Unfortunately, they may not have as keen a sense of their spiritual "cancer" as more obviously degenerate people do. Lewis further explains why God allows nice people to experience pain:

> We are perplexed to see misfortune falling upon decent, inoffensive, worthy people—on capable, hard-working mothers of families or diligent, thrifty little tradespeople, on those who have worked so hard, and so honestly, for their modest stock of happiness and now seem to be entering on the enjoyment of it with the fullest right. How can I say with sufficient tenderness what here needs to be said? It does not matter that I know I must become, in the eyes of every hostile reader, as it were, personally responsible for all the sufferings I try to explain. . . . But it matters enormously if I alienate anyone from the truth. Let me implore the reader to try to believe, if only for the moment, that God, who made these deserving people, may really be right when He thinks that their modest prosperity and the happiness of their children are not enough to make them blessed: that all this must fall from them in the end, and that if they have not learned to know Him they will be wretched. And therefore He troubles them, warning them in advance of an insufficiency that one day they will have to discover. The life to themselves and their families stands between them and the recognition of their need; He makes that life less sweet to them. I call this a Divine humility because it is a poor thing to strike our colours to God when the ship is going down under us; a poor thing to come to Him as a last resort, to offer up "our own" when it is no longer worth keeping. If God were proud He would hardly have us on

---

23. Lewis, *Problem of Pain*, 88.

such terms: but He is not proud, He stoops to conquer, He will have us even though we have shown that we prefer everything else to Him, and come to Him because there is "nothing better" now to be had. The same humility is shown by all those Divine appeals to our fears which trouble high-minded readers of Scripture. It is hardly complimentary to God that we should choose Him as an alternative to Hell: yet even this He accepts. The creature's illusion of self-sufficiency must, for the creature's sake, be shattered; and by trouble or fear of trouble on earth, by crude fear of the eternal flames, God shatters it "unmindful of His glory's diminution." Those who would like the God of Scripture to be more purely ethical, do not know what they ask. If God were a Kantian, who would not have us till we came to Him from the purest and best motives, who could be saved? And this illusion of self-sufficiency may be at its strongest in some very honest, kindly, and temperate people, and on such people, therefore, misfortune must fall.

The dangers of apparent self-sufficiency explain why Our Lord regards the vices of the feckless and dissipated so much more leniently than the vices that lead to worldly success. Prostitutes are in no danger of finding their present life so satisfactory that they cannot turn to God: the proud, the avaricious, the self-righteous, are in that danger.[24]

The threefold categorization of evil as moral, amoral, and metaphysical does not necessarily reflect airtight compartments. It is not as if the root cause of any specific instance of suffering is perfectly transparent to the human observer. This inability to make sense of the particular is probably what leads some people to give up on their attempts at articulating a comprehensive response. In other words, because they cannot make sense of little Billy's medical condition, they choose to find refuge in an agnostic bubble. In reality, those three broad categories often overlap with one another and all contribute, in varying degrees, to specific instances of suffering.

For instance, while there is some validity in attributing the brutal death of 230,000 people in Southeast Asia in 2004 to a giant tsunami wave and thus neatly categorize it as an instance of amoral evil, there is more to it.

Soon after the catastrophe, it became clear that many of those unfortunate souls may have had a premature appointment with the Angel of Death. Had there been an early warning system designed to detect tsunamis and warn the population at risk, thousands would have been spared. While there was an early detection system in the Pacific Ocean, there was nothing

---

24. Lewis, *Problem of Pain*, 94–96.

comparable set up in the Indian Ocean. Even though geophysicists at the Pacific Tsunami Warning Center were aware of the massive earthquake that had occurred, their attempts at warning the population of the imminent threat were in vain.[25]

Even if people had done something as simple as recognize the telltale signs of an imminent tsunami, such as rapidly receding waters, the death toll would have probably been lower. An emergency broadcast would have likely saved hundreds if not thousands of lives. I am not unaware of the difficulties inherent to preparing against such disasters. The point is that the high number of casualties suffered on that day was not inevitable. This dangerous phenomenon resulted in many more deaths than necessary through a combination of neglect, ignorance, and incompetence. If, in fact, there was a massive failure of communication, it shows again that the biggest challenge humans face may not so much be tied to environmental factors as to our own inherent weaknesses and shortcomings.

While we may not be able to avoid pain and death, most of us live with the assumption that if we live morally, we will experience a significant measure of happiness. Is such an equation justified?

ON THE RELATIONSHIP BETWEEN MORALITY AND HAPPINESS

One of the nagging questions that most of us ask at some point or another is whether there is a correlation between morality and happiness, and if so, can the mechanism that governs this relationship be identified and appropriated? Even though it may at first seem like a trivial matter, it remains one of the most profound, disconcerting, and frustrating questions we will ever encounter. Even as I ponder this problem, my immediate response fluctuates wildly between various alternatives. Much of the reason for that has to do with the unpredictability of human life, which makes it nearly impossible to derive the kind of clear and reliable principles needed to frame the relationship between morality and happiness, and the Bible itself, which, on this issue, doesn't always seem to be consistent.

With respect to the Old Testament, whereas some passages unambiguously herald a clear cause-and-effect relationship between virtue and happiness, others unceremoniously undermine any such connection. For its part, the New Testament frequently reminds readers that even conscientious Christians are as likely as not to suffer. And if we can believe James, not only should Christians expect trials and difficulties; they should "consider

---

25. TenBruggencate, "'Ewa Center Tried in Vain to Help."

it nothing but joy" (Jas 1:2). But before we throw our hands up in despair, it may be wise to consider whether these difficulties are as formidable as they appear.

In the Old Testament, several passages do indeed suggest a direct cause-and-effect relationship between virtue and happiness or, to use biblical language, obedience and blessing. The book of Deuteronomy frequently uses the language of blessing and curse. Deuteronomy 28:2 is a good example: "All these blessings shall come upon you and overtake you, if you obey the LORD your God." The principle that blessing and happiness will inevitably follow faithfulness and virtue (or its corresponding opposite) is frequently echoed throughout the rest of the Old Testament. Wisdom literature, particularly so in the book of Proverbs, often reiterates this principle (Prov 2:7-8, 21; 3:1-10; etc.). Many psalms declare that the righteous will prosper, and the wicked will be destroyed (Ps 1; 5:5-6, 12; 37:3-4, 20; etc.). The prophetic literature evokes the same theme from a twofold perspective. As in Deuteronomy, the prophets frequently promise God's blessing to the people if they will obey God's commands (Isa 1:19-20). But they also explore the negative side of this equation. These men of God go so far as to specify the people's covenant unfaithfulness as the factor behind the various disasters that plagued ancient Israel. From lethal droughts to defeats at the hands of ferocious and invincible invaders, the prophets have only one explanation and corrective: sin and repentance (Amos 4:4-13). For the prophets, if obedience to the covenant prescriptions will draw God's blessing, disobedience will attract his judgment as surely as a magnet attracts a nail.

According to these passages, the key to happiness is as simple as taking a walk in the park: be faithful to God, and all will be well. But is it really that simple? Those who even have but a sketchy knowledge of the Hebrew Bible know the Old Testament writers were plainly aware of the fact that this rule did not always apply. In the book of Ecclesiastes, for instance, the Preacher comments on the unfairness of life (Eccl 7:15). In contrast to the explicit promise of blessing for the righteous and loss for the wicked in Psalms 1 and 2, in Psalms 37 and 73, the psalmist keenly observes that sometimes, and against all expectations, the wicked prosper.

That the biblical writers note grave inconsistencies in the application of the law of retribution should not surprise us. Who has not noticed that too often the righteous suffer and the wicked prosper? Unless we are as blind and foolish as Job's three friends, life will have long ago taught us that the engine that drives the law of retribution regularly misfires.

The apparent inconsistency of the Old Testament's message is not, as some scholars have surmised, evidence of competing ideologies or traditions.[26] In fact, a strong case can be made with respect to the unity and consistency of the Old Testament message.[27] As it pertains to the law of retribution, many of the apparent contradictions can be resolved by a careful consideration of the context in which they appear.

The blessing and curse passages such as found in the book of Deuteronomy are set in the context of the Sinai covenant. The intent is straightforward. Yahweh, as the suzerain savior, will ensure that Israel will thrive as a nation as long as the people are faithful to the terms of the covenant. But should they violate them, God will abandon them and carry out his judgment. The purpose of the curses does not simply consist in announcing the destruction of the people but to compel Israel to reflect Yahweh's character.

There is scant evidence that the Israelite theologians differed in their assessment of the application of the curse and blessing formula. The prophets, for instance, go to great lengths to demonstrate the justice of God's severe judgments against Israel. The oracles of judgment almost invariably include a catalogue of Israel's offenses justifying God's actions against her (Hos 2:1–13; Isa 1:1–9; etc.). If there are inconsistencies, they do not lie in whether Israel deserves her fate, but in the unexpected and undeserved mercy God eventually shows toward his people. God regularly overrides the immediate imperatives of the covenant curses to ensure Israel's survival as his people.

Wisdom literature and the Psalms generally affirm the validity of the law of retribution. This law did not only apply to the nation; God's blessing extended to the faithful individual as well. Proverbs 3:5–10:

> Trust in the LORD with all your heart, and do not rely on your own insight. In all your ways acknowledge him, and he will make straight your paths. Do not be wise in your own eyes; fear the LORD, and turn away from evil. It will be a healing for your flesh and a refreshment for your body. Honor the LORD with your substance and with the first fruits of all your produce; then your barns will be filled with plenty, and your vats will be bursting with wine.

While such a passage and others like it would seem to suggest a near-mathematical correspondence between faithfulness and blessing, some nuances apply. First, the prosperity of the individual is nearly always contingent on the prosperity of the community. In theory, if Israel as a collective fell into disobedience and came under judgment, all Israelites, the faithful and the unfaithful, would bear the consequences of the nation's disobedience.

---

26. See, for example, Brueggemann, *Theology of the Old Testament*.
27. See Osborne, *Hermeneutical Spiral*, 347–73; Martens, *God's Design*.

This is a principle that has held true throughout human history. When Hitler became chancellor of Germany and proceeded with his plan to establish the Third Reich, multitudes of innocent people, both in and out of Germany, suffered a great deal because of the Nazis' dance with madness.

Second, the law of retribution, as variously parsed in the Old Testament, does not represent an absolute principle that comes into motion regardless of the historical situations the people find themselves in. It is more akin to a general principle that will generally prove to be valid but may not always be so depending on a variety of factors. For example, consider the maxim found in Prov 23:13–14: "Do not withhold discipline from your children; if you beat them with a rod, they will not die. If you beat them with the rod, you will save their lives from Sheol." The proverb clearly states that judicious discipline will save a child from destruction. As most of the original readers would have readily understood, the wisdom writer is not suggesting that no child will ever go wrong if properly disciplined. He is only giving expression to a well-known principle with respect to child rearing. Will it always turn out to be true? Of course not. There are children who grow up in good homes and who still turn to a life of crime. And there are children who are born and raised in abusive homes who turn out to become exemplary citizens.

People who faithfully follow God will usually experience a good life, and those who rebel against his commandments will generally experience grief. But there is no guarantee one way or another. Sometimes godly people get a raw deal, and the violent avoid their just reward.

It is the author of the book of Ecclesiastes, otherwise known as Qoheleth (the Preacher) who perhaps best captures the tension that exists between, on the one hand, the Old Testament allusions to the law of retribution, which suggests a close linkage between faithfulness and blessing, and, on the other hand, the inescapable reality of metaphysical evil, namely, the type of pain that results from the limitations inherent to human nature. His conclusion is surprising. In chs. 11 and 12, Qoheleth rejects the appeal to nihilism one might expect and instead invites the reader to enjoy all that life has to offer while remaining loyal to God.

A twofold rationale is offered. First, for Qoheleth, the only meaningful way to enjoy what life has to offer is to do so within a framework of faithfulness to God. It is only when we live with the conviction that there is a God, and that he is the source of all good things, that we can enjoy all that life has to offer without compulsively trying to hang on to the good things of life, as we age and gradually lose our ability to appreciate them. Human existence intentionally lived outside of the divine sphere, "under the sun," as Qoheleth would say, rapidly and inexorably becomes meaningless and pointless.

Second, the absolute limits of human life, old age and death, are not the direct consequences of specific moral failures. They are inherent to and an unavoidable part of life in a fallen world. If old age and death may point to the absurdity of human existence "under the sun," for Qoheleth that is not the case at all. Qoheleth's advice is to enjoy the good things life has to offer as gracious gifts from God, and to view the vagaries of life as intrinsic to a fallen world and reminders of our mortality and moral accountability toward God.[28]

The New Testament is equally lucid on the relationship between virtue and happiness. While some aspects of the law of retribution reappear,[29] New Testament writers entertain no illusions about the possibility that Christians may suffer and die. Christians can suffer because of their own foolishness (Acts 5:1–11; 1 Cor 5:1–5; Heb 12:5–10), persecution (Matt 5:10–12; 1 Pet 2:19–21), or simply because, like everyone else, they have bodies that are prone to disease, age, and death (1 Cor 15:22, 50, 56).

Before I move on, I need to say one more thing with respect to why bad things sometimes happen to good people, or why there is not always a direct cause-and-effect relationship between morality and happiness. This is a point Rabbi Kushner highlights well.

As I pointed out earlier, God has created a *real* world. What I mean to say is that this world is no virtual matrix-like universe, subject to be controlled for the benefit of some, and in which everything is illusion. This is no computer game we can reset when we "die." God created a real world in order to allow for the effective exercise of human free will, personal responsibility, accountability, and character development. As C. S. Lewis points out, this is the way it must be. He writes:

> So it is with the life of souls in a world: fixed laws, consequences unfolding by causal necessity, the whole natural order, are at once limits within which their common life is confined and also the sole condition under which any such life is possible. Try to exclude the possibility of suffering which the order of nature and the existence of free will involve, and you find that you have excluded life itself.[30]

We can have a world in which God exercises his sovereignty over some things, while still leaving the space necessary for humans to exercise their free will. It is impossible, however, to have a universe that allows for the

---

28. For more details on Ecclesiastes as a response to nihilism, see Gilbert, "Fighting Fire with Fire," 65–79.

29. See, for instance, 2 Cor 9:6–11; Gal 6:7–9; Heb 10:35–36.

30. Lewis, *Problem of Pain*, 25.

free interaction of individuals *and* one in which God controls all things. By definition, this is impossible, for these two statements constitute a formal contradiction in terms, and no amount of equivocation can change that.

A *real* world such as the one in which we live allows for two equally wonderful and awful truths. On the one hand, this world gives each one of us the ability to act freely. Or perhaps more accurately with respect to evil, and on a most fundamental level, we can use our free will to starve or feed the impulse to engage in evil. The potential for the one and the other may be affected by a variety of factors such as opportunity, resources, and intelligence, but ultimately it is determined by one's own self. On the other hand, the framework provided for human action requires an irreducible degree of randomness in the physical universe. If we deny the necessity or reality of chance, then we need to revert to the notion of God effectively controlling all things. In such a universe, there can be no "accidents." Every rock that falls off a cliff onto a highway is purposely caused by God. Every earthquake, tsunami, hurricane, and tornado is specifically ordained by God. In such a universe, every event carries moral freight, for each one is the outcome of a divine intent, regardless of how good or disastrous it turns out to be. Moreover, if God literally regulates everything, it becomes impossible to speak of human free will in any meaningful way at all; we must postulate God as the only effective cause.

A few years ago, Joni Eareckson Tada wrote a remarkable book in which she shares her faith struggles following a personal tragedy.[31] Joni had suffered a debilitating back injury in a 1967 diving accident in Chesapeake Bay. The accident left her paralyzed from the neck down. In her book, she describes how for many years she painstakingly sought an answer to why this terrible accident had happened to her.

The human brain has a fiery longing to make sense of the world. It unceasingly attempts to establish cause-and-effect relationships between events and will go to great lengths to do so. Unfortunately, while our three-pound thinking organ may be programmed to look for cause-and-effect relationships, it's not always so efficient at positing the correct cause behind every effect.

In that respect, this remarkable woman was no different from anyone else. For years, she tirelessly sought to make sense of the accident that left her entirely dependent on others. But here is the problem. She attempted to make sense of what ultimately could not be rationalized in any other way than as a simple accident caused by a moment of carelessness. Joni unwisely chose to plunge headfirst into shallow waters. The laws of physics being

---

31. *Joni.*

what they are, when human neck meets hard rock, neck breaks. This fact alone accounts for this horrible catastrophe. Nothing else. But sometimes, the simplest truths are the most difficult to accept.

I am in no way suggesting that I would have responded any differently. The need to give meaning to personal tragedies is virtually overwhelming and can remain so for years. Joni could not accept such a simple explanation for her accident. She feverishly kept looking for a better answer. And she devised one. The answer was simple and made sense of what appeared senseless and devoid of any possible significance. She found an answer that put this horrible accident into a broader perspective.

Joni eventually concluded that this accident was not the manifestation of blind fate. This event was in fact the demonstration of God's sovereignty. This was part of God's loving plan for her. In her own words, "Now I believe that God's purpose in my accident was to turn a stubborn kid into a woman who would reflect patience, endurance and a lively, optimistic hope of the heavenly glories above."[32]

What Joni is giving expression to reflects what Boyd calls the "blueprint worldview."[33] According to this view, everything that happens to human beings reflects the outworking of God's plan. Once we accept this view, our only challenge of course is to discover how horrific events fit into the greater picture. By any human standard, Joni is a most remarkable woman. Her life, her books, and her ongoing ministry, *Joni and Friends*, have touched and brought encouragement to millions of people around the globe. There is no doubt this accident played a determining role in the development of this remarkable organization. It's also plainly evident that Joni allowed God to use this personal misfortune to transform her into the kind of person that would eventually be used to touch the lives of countless broken men and women. It may well be, though I have no way to tell, that without this tragedy, Joni would have never become the person she is, and it's unlikely that *Joni and Friends* would have ever seen the light of day.

We need, however, to ask an important question: Was God the primary cause of the accident, or did God use it to produce something good?

This is where our relentless drive to establish cause-and-effect relationships can get us into trouble. Scripture clearly teaches that God can indeed transform evil into good.[34] The best-known statement to that effect is provided by Paul in Rom 8:28: "And we know that in all things God works for

---

32. Eareckson, "Victory through Suffering."

33. See Boyd, *Satan*, 11–14.

34. Philip Yancey offers an interesting perspective on this issue in "Chess Master," 112.

the good of those who love him, who have been called according to his purpose." The Bible also provides numerous illustrations of God using evil men to accomplish his will. The Egyptian Pharaoh, Joseph's murderous brothers, the Assyrians, even the traitor Judas, just to name a few, unwittingly became instruments of God's will. To state that God can produce good out of evil is one thing. To postulate God as the primary cause of evil turns the entire universe into a deterministic puppet stage where any semblance of freedom is no less illusionary than a thousand Sahara mirages.

We can thank God for Joni's remarkable and exceptional determination to overcome this personal tragedy. The accident revealed Joni's strength of character, God's love, and his power. We can thank God for opening windows of opportunity that enabled her to build a great organization. But to hold God responsible for the accident itself and to be thankful for it is not only bad theology but renders the very concept of love completely meaningless. Such a view makes God the author of the worst atrocities ever committed in human history. And if indeed God had no choice but to insert a strategically placed rock in the formation of the earth's crust and cause some perfectly timed distraction that would result in a catastrophic series of events, only to deal with a young woman's character flaws, then we should all be in wheelchairs.

Joni's accident was no more part of God's cosmic plan than the time a friend of mine inadvertently walked into a light post simply because he let himself be briefly distracted by two stunningly beautiful women on the other side of the street. Had God planned for these women to appear at the appropriate moment, so my friend would successfully smash into the post and learn some valuable lesson? I doubt it. Did my friend learn something from this unfortunate event? You bet he did!

And that leads us to another controversial and confusing subject. It is generally assumed that some degree of pain is necessary for the development of human virtues. This is an important question, for should it prove to be true, it would imply that the introduction of evil into human history was indeed necessary. But is that really so? What role does pain play in the development of virtue?

ON THE RELATIONSHIP BETWEEN PAIN AND VIRTUE

Many of those who have read C. S. Lewis's *Problem of Pain* often find themselves confused by the link Lewis creates between pain and virtue in the chapter entitled "Human Pain." I wish I could say that the confused only have themselves to blame. Though I am a great admirer of the Christian apologist, perhaps Lewis must bear some responsibility for some of the confusion emerging out of this discussion. I suspect Lewis himself had some misgivings about that chapter, as he thought it necessary to write an additional one on the same subject to expand further and possibly clarify some of the concepts introduced in chapter 6.

Readers are occasionally left with the impression that Lewis teaches that pain is good in and of itself. Pain is not only a tool God uses to produce better humans; it is viewed as a necessary element of the process that leads to the perfecting of human beings. While I can see how some may arrive at this conclusion, I would argue that this is not quite what Lewis meant. First, Lewis categorically denies that gratuitous pain is good in and of itself. He writes:

> But if suffering is good, ought it not to be pursued rather than avoided? I answer that suffering is not good in itself. What is good in any painful experience is, for the sufferer, his submission to the will of God, and, for the spectators, the compassion aroused and the acts of mercy to which it leads.[35]

This is entirely consistent with what the creation account teaches about the emergence of pain and evil in our world. The fundamental disruption created by the curse in Genesis 3 is unequivocally evil.

Second, while gratuitous pain may have no intrinsic value, it does nevertheless play an important role in signaling that something is amiss in the world. In the same way our nervous system will generate impulses that draw our attention to possible life-threatening situations,[36] on the spiritual plane, pain may also signal a condition that, if left unattended, may result in our ruin. Even if God may not be the effective cause of all human suffering, it is nonetheless because of his love for us that he refrains from completely removing every possible instance of pain from our existence. Were God to insulate humans from all pain, very few would turn to him, for it is because of the unfiltered experience of all that life offers, the unpleasant as well as the pleasant, and the sense that things are not as they *ought to be*, that most men and women turn to Christ in search of redemption. As the Canadian sociologist Reginald Bibby points out, "Here, as I noted in *Restless Gods*, we are recognizing with St. Augustine not only that our souls are restless, but also that we perhaps are being pursued by One who makes us restless."[37]

---

35. Lewis, *Problem of Pain*, 110.
36. Philip Yancey thoroughly explores this idea in *Where Is God?*
37. Bibby, *Restless Churches*, 2.

In other words, and that's how I understand Lewis, God does not allow us to suffer simply to satisfy the notion that pain is good for us *per se*, but as one way to make us restless, to make us realize that there is something fundamentally wrong with us and the world around us. If God, in some misguided kindness, designed mechanisms that would effectively insulate us from all pain, the odds that any of us would even seek his healing touch would fall dramatically. We would live like happy fools until the very bitter end. Just like parents may refrain from shielding their children from the consequences of their reckless behavior, God has determined it was better to let humanity experience, at least to some degree, the consequences of sin.

Third, Lewis's strong emphasis on this point, coupled perhaps with some lingering ambiguity in his own thinking, may leave the reader with the impression that some form of pain is indeed intrinsic to spiritual growth. This impression may derive from Lewis's own understanding of conversion.

We generally view conversion as a decision to embrace God. While conversion is synonymous with choosing God, the alternative may not be as simple as rejecting God. Why would anyone choose to reject God? God offers all that is good: life, joy, hope, meaning, significance. Why would anyone be so foolish as to consciously reject such great gifts? Many, however, do just that, and it is, I suspect, because human beings are not, as Jewish theology has traditionally maintained, in a morally, spiritually, and ontologically neutral position. There is something else going on.

Throughout his writings, Lewis suggests that conversion is not so much a choice between choosing and rejecting God, but a choice between God and the self. This is very different and infinitely more complex than having to choose between God and nothing. "From the moment a creature becomes aware of God as God and of itself as self, the terrible alternative of choosing God or self for the center is opened to it."[38] It is an existential choice between two powerful poles, one being God toward whom we entertain a natural hostility because of our sin nature (Col 1:21), and the other, the infected self, which offers a nearly irresistible attraction away from God.

When Adam and Eve gave credence to the serpent's word rather than the word of God, humanity was hurled into the sphere of sin. One of the consequences of this decision was its impact on our very nature. As the creation account teaches and human experience confirms, after the fall, a monstrous distortion was introduced into the human psyche. I am but too aware of the difficulties inherent to describing how human nature became corrupt. A comprehensive and precise description of the disorder is hopelessly beyond the reach of reason. However it came about, the reality is that

38. Lewis, *Problem of Pain*, 70.

the seeds of evil have found themselves in the fertile soil of the human heart. The human self was not destroyed but distorted in such a way as to create a new center of gravity, or perhaps more accurately a spiritual "black hole," that fiercely competes against God for our allegiance. While we cannot explain the mechanisms that led to its formation, the reality of the infected self is as blistering as the sun on a summer afternoon in Phoenix.

The distorted self is hopelessly bloated, self-preoccupied, self-important, and more afraid of the living God than death itself. It takes infinite pleasure in itself. Given a chance, it will gleefully feed on the limitless supply of empty calories this world dishes out. It thrives on pleasure, lust, lasciviousness, illusion and delusion, destruction, even self-destruction. The self best runs on hatred, particularly hatred for God, Christ, and his followers. We are as captivated by the self as Gollum was transfixed by his "precious." The distorted self is an abyss of terror. It is only through the grace of God that we are not wholly swallowed by it.

In this respect divine grace expresses itself in two ways. On the one hand, God made humanity out of extraordinary materials. As catastrophic as the fall may have been, it did not completely obliterate humanity. Human nature's remarkable resiliency is flagged in Genesis 2 and 3, and wonderfully affirmed in Psalm 8. On the other hand, the black hole of the self is not the only center of gravity in this world; God is forever working at attracting us to himself (John 12:32; 16:8).

There are indeed two centers of gravity in this universe: God and the self. We are not in a neutral position. The decision to love God and his son is done in the presence of a colossal force that drives and compels us to keep beholding the mesmerizing darkness of our soul. It is often observed that most conversions occur before adulthood. Small children most graciously embrace the living God; old men resist it the most. The older we are, the more imperative the lure of the black hole in us becomes. The choice is not really between accepting and rejecting Christ. It is ultimately between embracing God or forever embracing the self.

In his discussion, Lewis also refers to the kind of pain men and women experience when they come face to face with an opportunity to embrace God. The pain is of two kinds. There is the focused pain associated with recognizing the wrongness in us. When Isaiah comes face to face with the living God, an experience described in Isaiah 6, his response is devastating. "Woe is me!" cries the prophet. This expression denotes Isaiah's dismay at the realization of his true condition in the presence of a holy God. The prophet entertains no illusions about himself: "I am ruined," he adds.[39] "My

---

39. New International Version (1973).

destruction is sealed," as the New Living Translation dramatically puts it. Isaiah contemplates the glory of God but there is no praise coming from his lips. Instead, he recoils in horror, not at God, but at himself. Isaiah realizes that there is something frightfully wrong with him. The face of God reveals the serpent within (cf. John 1:4–5).

Isaiah's words point to human nature's dreadful condition. Regardless of the moral standards anyone may hold, every single human being is fatally marred by that brokenness the Bible calls sin. Conversion assumes a recognition of the fundamental "wrongness" that is in every one of us. There can be no real conversion without the painful appraisal of what we really are.

The other source of existential pain that accompanies conversion derives from the discomfort associated with relinquishing the control of our lives into God's hands. The self does not freely give up this authority. This is something that goes against its very nature. It will fight such reorientation of the whole person with everything it has. It will grasp at any straw. It never gives in without a fight.[40] Turning to the living God involves a most intimate and vulnerable process. It demands complete honesty about oneself and a sincere surrender to the person of God.

The willingness to recognize this fundamental "wrongness" in us is what makes it so difficult to turn to Christ. This is particularly so for the very religious or those have high moral standards. Their natural goodness is their greatest weakness, for it provides a shield of delusion in regard to their true nature and their desperate need for redemption. In the end, turning to God represents the most difficult decision men and women ever have to make, for it implies a conscious decision to make God, rather than the self, the center of reality. For some, the lure of the ruling self is so surreptitiously enticing that they will, for all eternity, wallow in its vampiric embrace. This, in a nutshell, is what the Christian doctrine of hell is all about.

---

40. C. S. Lewis's *The Great Divorce* is a fictional book that depicts a group of damned men and women who are afforded an opportunity to visit heaven and possibly be redeemed, if only they will be persuaded to abandon their false beliefs about themselves and the nature of reality. For most of these individuals, such a conversion proves impossible, for they prefer to hang on to their delusions and return to what turns out to be hell.

Conclusion

THE ORIGINAL PROBLEM

THE PRESENCE OF EVIL, suffering, and death, especially premature death, the death of little children and the demise of virtuous men and women cut down in their prime, is grievous to the soul. While I'm not inclined to get into the usual litany of real-life cases to make my point, as I write these lines, I can't help but remember the picture of a little girl I saw at the end of an article about the Islamic State's (ISIS) advance in Iraq in late October 2014. The piece was prefaced by a warning about graphic subject matter immediately following the article. I didn't want to see the accompanying pictures, but I scrolled too far down.... What I saw seared my mind and my soul. A little girl, no more than five or six years old, maybe younger. There she lay on the ground, dead, her head lying in the dirt about two feet from her body. Her life had brutally been cut short just because she was with Christians.

Several thoughts instantly exploded in my mind. I still have a hard time containing them. Where, first of all, was the political will or the sense of compassion required to eradicate those who kill the defenseless to satisfy the dictates of their ideology and their own thirst for blood? I was then immediately overwhelmed with pity for this poor little girl. Her life was over. She would never grow up, get married, and have children. If only we could blame an earthquake or a terminal illness. But that won't do. She died because a man decided she would. I have unfortunately been cursed with a vivid imagination. And from time to time, I see that picture and imagine how it all likely came down: The terror in the little girl's eyes as she sees the knife and feels it slicing her throat open, the screams of despair from her parents who would soon be next. I was also struck by a profound sense of powerlessness. I could do nothing for her and her people.

Now and then, I enjoy watching the odd superhero movie. *Captain America* and *Ironman* are my favorites. The most obvious problem with superheroes is that they don't exist. If, like Tony Stark, I only had an iron suit, I would surely be in a position to protect innocent people, but as things stand, I'm not of much use. The other problem lies in what seems to be an inversely proportional relationship between the number of superheroes that fill the Hollywood universe and the number of regular heroes on the streets.

When the West faced the rise of Nazism, Japanese imperialism, and Italian fascism, millions of heroes, regular men really, of the kind you could routinely meet just about anywhere, rose up to face that existential threat. It is difficult to imagine how we would respond to a similar threat today. Western culture has not produced such heroes in any significant number for some time. The ground is sterile; it only grows weeds. The so-called snowflakes, as Millennials are often labeled, quickly withdraw into their "happy places" whenever they encounter an idea that challenges their fragile ideological universe. God forbid we ever have to stare down the kind of peril the Greatest Generation faced. Singing John Lennon's "Imagine" while holding hands as a response to terrorist acts is just absurd and only empowers the West's self-declared enemies.

If many will still ask where God is when witnessing the kind of cruelty I evoked earlier, others will instead focus on why there are so few real-life heroes. Why are those who have the power to do something do nothing and express but the lamest platitudes when publicly responding to such brutality. Even if we should refrain from ascribing responsibility to God for such actions, which are plainly ours, we still need to reflect on why history landed where it did. Considering everything, was the creation of the universe, the earth, and humanity worth it? Didn't God anticipate the mess that would emerge? If he did, can't the responsibility of it all be laid his feet? Try as we might, avoiding the God question remains nearly impossible.

I began this book by asking the God question. If God is perfectly good, loving, and all-powerful, why does evil and suffering exist? As we saw in chapter 1, the range of answers for this most wrenching dilemma is not as broad as we might have expected. There do seem to be only two options: either God is morally defective, incompetent, evil, or downright nonexistent, or if God is good and all-powerful, as Christian tradition maintains, then evil is necessary to fulfill his plan for humanity. To simplify further, either evil is eternal, an intrinsic component of ultimate reality, or it simply doesn't exist, as what is generally defined as evil will in time prove to have been but the necessary precondition to a greater good.

THE THESIS IN A NUTSHELL: GENESIS 1-3

The creation story offers an alternative view. It unambiguously portrays God as both good and all-powerful. God's creation is also described as good, an assessment that covers the entire universe and humanity itself (Gen 1:31). But if the creation of the universe, the "heavens and the earth," could be accomplished by fiat, i.e., simply by God saying so, it was otherwise with humanity.

Humanity's full emergence was contingent on what I can best describe as a two-step process. On the one hand, God needed to form a creature that would be uniquely equipped to fulfill its assigned role. The creation of this special creature and the articulation of its mandate as God's partner are described in Gen 1:26-30 and 2:4-25. But this is only one-half of the equation. God intended for men and women to be much more than smart animals. They were to enter into a relationship with God that would be characterized by love. If humans had been intended to be just like any other creature, creation by divine fiat would have sufficed. But God's plan for humanity involved something more. In a sense, the creature would be of a totally different order. This difference is expressed by both the allusion to humanity being made in the image of God in 1:26-27 and by the reference to God breathing into Adam "the breath of life" in 2:7. These two actions uniquely pertain to the human species.

In order to be what God intended for humans to become and to have the ability to love God, the creature would have to be endowed with free will. This is where the rubber hits the proverbial road. God can create anything; he wills it and there it is. As long as it isn't nonsense, such as wishing God would create a square circle, God can do it. If creating a man was well within God's purview, designing a creature that would be endowed with free will and be free with regards to God, that was an entirely different proposition. The emergence of such a creature required a decision that would originate from the creature itself and independently from any divine coercion. The necessity of such a decision was inherent to the kind of relationship God wished to have with this particular creature. In this respect, the required action was similar to a marriage proposal or to initiating a friendship. In such cases, the relationship will flourish only if both parties willingly enter into it. When one party imposes itself on the other, it becomes tyranny.

A crucial question now arises: what process would a creature need to undergo in order to enable the emergence of a self-conscious sense of freedom with respect to God? While the creation account does not offer a philosophical rationale, it does describe the test that would produce the desired outcome (Gen 2:17), and Genesis 3 recounts how it was implemented, thus offering an insight into the precise significance of the test.

It is critical to keep in mind the open-ended nature of this test. There is nothing in the text to suggest that its outcome was predetermined by God. If God were to determine the outcome of such a test, it would essentially invalidate it entirely and make God the primary cause of sin, evil, and suffering. The test is fundamentally expressed as a curse and blessing formula, a literary form that leaves the outcome entirely undetermined. While God no doubt knew from all eternity how Adam and Eve would respond, the final dénouement was entirely up to them.

What this means is that God never originally intended for men and women to experience death. In other words, evil and suffering were not necessary for the full unfolding of God's project for humanity.

THE NATURE OF REALITY

In order to become the kind of creature God intended, Adam and Eve were required to make a decision that would constitute the last step of the process necessary to become free creatures. This final step would be implemented by means of a test of allegiance representing an infinite point of critical choice, which is described in Gen 3:1–6.

The outcome is well known. Adam and Eve chose to distrust God's word and they ate of the forbidden fruit. As announced by God in 2:17 and further described in 3:7–24, this single act of disobedience entailed consequences that reached into the very core of human nature and reality itself.

Why did such a seemingly trivial action have such repercussions? Eating some fruit, even *forbidden* fruit, must surely pale in significance when compared to murder or torture. But this was no trivial action. The author portrays it as an elemental choice that would determine the destiny of Adam and Eve and humanity. But why? It goes without saying that no one can hope to elucidate the precise nature of this critical event. As is often the case, there is indeed a chasm between affirming something and explaining it. All I can realistically hope to do here is reaffirm the cosmic significance of the test and its outcome.

There are at least two reasons that can be invoked to explain this unexpected outcome. They are intricately related to each other and may, in the end, represent just two ways of looking at the same truth.

On the one hand, the process that would lead to the full realization of God's intent for humanity was irremediably linked to the nature of reality and was intended to reach into its very fabric. I have made the argument earlier that the more fundamental a decision is, the more far reaching the consequences of that decision will turn out to be. The choice of a marriage partner, for instance, is infinitely more significant than deciding whether to have a hamburger or a tuna sandwich for lunch. The test set before Adam and Eve belonged to the first category, for the decision they were called to make would determine the type and quality of the relationship they would have with the Ground of all being.[1] There could be no decision more fundamental than the one they were invited to make. If the process into which the first humans were invited to participate reached into the core of reality, its outcome would necessarily have a corresponding and proportional impact on that same reality (perhaps Newton's third law of physics has its counterpart in the spiritual realm: For every action, there is an equal and opposite reaction).

On the other hand, the choice Adam and Eve were to make also entailed a moral and, in a certain sense, a legal dimension. The garden of Eden was God's property. God had given them access to everything except the tree of the knowledge of good and evil. The injunction established a legal foundation with respect to God's property rights as the garden's owner. To eat of the fruit would constitute a violation of God's sovereignty.

The gravity of Adam and Eve's act of disobedience was infinitely more grievous than some temporary fallout between two friends. The transgression represented a formidable challenge to God's will and integrity, a terrible abuse of his friendship. Because the offense was directed at God himself, it entailed infinite ramifications in terms of its moral and legal implications. God, being the foundation and the source of all justice and truth, could not pretend it had not happened. Because this action belonged to the realm of ultimate reality, it would, by necessity, alter it one way or another. The curse announced in Gen 2:17 constitutes the logical and inevitable outworking of an action that was inexorably connected to the structure of reality itself.

Adam and Eve were given the opportunity to make a real choice that would impact their destiny. If God is indeed the God of truth and the ground of all reality, as he must surely be, it logically follows that any choice God

---

1. I am echoing Paul Tillich's use of the same expression (see, for instance, *Systematic Theology*, 1:155–59).

offered would be real and entail consequences appropriate to each option. If, however, it turns out that the outcome of the test was from all eternity determined by God, as Karl Barth forcefully proposed, then what we have is a set up where Adam and Eve only had the illusion of a choice.

Everything in the majestic creation story points away from the inevitability of rebellion. Only the consequences of disobedience would turn out to be inevitable. This assessment is entirely consistent with the choice Cain is given with respect to his impulse to kill his brother Abel. In the same way Cain was not predetermined to kill his brother, Adam and Eve were given a real opportunity to obey the divine injunction. The living God is not into puppet shows.

LIFE GOES ON

Whereas Adam and Eve's act of disobedience entailed devastating consequences for humanity, God's judgment in no way signaled the end of history. While death would plant its flag, it would not reign over all of reality. While sin infected every facet of human existence, it did not, however, obliterate humanity.

The curse was not the end of the story. That the human race could withstand such a brutal blow is a testimony to God's grace. Despite the severity of the language used to characterize the judgment that would follow human transgression, God never intended to wipe humanity out. God's grace was exhibited in his continued willingness to relate to Adam and Eve. It was further expressed in the promise that the conflict initiated in the garden would one day end with the victory of the woman's offspring (Gen 3:15). God's mercy was exhibited in the provision of "garments of skin" to clothe them (Gen 3:21). While God had every right to let the first humans feel the full blow of their new vulnerability, he chose instead to provide some basic protection against the hostile environment they had conjured into existence. Finally, God showed his grace by ensuring they would not live forever as fallen beings. While some readers may not be entirely persuaded, I maintain that this is the best way to read Adam and Eve's expulsion from the garden of Eden (Gen 3:22–24). A mutated race bent on murder, violence, and war, as displayed in the Cain and Abel story (Gen 4:1–8) and later in the horrid portrayal of the antediluvian generation (Gen 6:5), could not be allowed to live forever in this condition.

God's desire for the human race to endure is also a testimony to his faithfulness. God had from all eternity intended to have a people composed of men and women who would love him. God could have easily aborted the entire project, deciding to end it all or start over again with a new couple, but the author of all reality, truth, and justice would not, or perhaps more accurately, could not, do so. He would press on regardless of the outcome.

The power of faithfulness driven by infinite love is incomprehensible and unimaginable. We sometimes get a small glimpse of this when parents who learn that their unborn child suffers from a serious congenital condition still choose to have and care for the baby. Why do they do it? Because they loved the child even before he or she was conceived. If human beings can exhibit this kind of self-sacrificing love, could God do any less for us?

That human history could go on despite what humanity had become is a witness to the resiliency of the human race. People sometimes ask why God would make human beings of such poor material that they would so easily go wrong. C. S. Lewis addresses this question in *Mere Christianity*. He writes:

> The better stuff a creature is made of—the cleverer and stronger and freer it is—then the better it will be if it goes right, but also the worse it will be if it goes wrong. A cow cannot be very good or very bad; a dog can be both better and worse; a child better and worse still; an ordinary man, still more so; a man of genius, still more so; a superhuman spirit best—or worst—of all.[2]

Lewis's assessment is entirely consistent with humanity's description in the creation account. Man is no ordinary creature. He is made in the image of God and is given the mandate to rule the earth (Gen 1:27–28). God uniquely breathes into Adam the "breath of life" (Gen 2:7) and calls him into a partnership. Human exceptionalism, even as a fallen creature, is confirmed and affirmed in Ps 8:3–6:

> When I look at your heavens, the work of your fingers, the moon and the stars that you have established; what are human beings that you are mindful of them, mortals that you care for them? Yet you have made them a little lower than God, and crowned them with glory and honor. You have given them dominion over the works of your hands; you have put all things under their feet.

Human resiliency is extraordinary. Men and women can survive and thrive in a wide range of physical environments. People and entire nations recover from devastating wars and natural disasters. If this concept is somewhat foreign to many Westerners, it's only because unearned wealth and technological ubiquity have made them a little soft, pudgy, and oversensitive. They don't realize that what they now consider to be the bare necessities

---

2. Lewis, *Mere Christianity*, 49.

of life were unattainable and unimaginable luxuries to the men and women of past generations.

God made human beings of amazingly sturdy material. The exceptional quality of what they truly are is revealed when they face extreme adversity. I never cease to be amazed at the number of people who are involved in serious accidents and manage to go on with their lives even when they come out with severe disabilities.

Lewis was right. The depth of human wickedness in no way reflects badly on God. On the contrary, it constitutes a powerful witness to humanity's resilient character.

ATONEMENT

But God's underlying project extended far beyond ensuring that humans would continue to exist in a broken state. God's plan for the species far exceeded its mere survival. His intention, originating from the depths of eternity past, was to *redeem* them.

God's plan of redemption had to address at least three problems. First and foremost, there was the issue of justice. Adam and Eve had violated a divine command. As much as some seek to ignore the legal dimension of sin, the fact remains that Adam and Eve did transgress a law. God would therefore need to resolve the issue of retribution. While it is fashionable to focus almost entirely on the so-called notion of restorative justice, there is, integral to any offense, an absolute requirement for retribution. If that were not so, then why, as Lewis rightly asks, would anyone force an offender to endure whatever restorative process might be deemed necessary to rehabilitate him?[3] While some might recommend some type of restorative justice process in the case of a man who robs a bank, no one would suggest that the man be allowed to go free as if nothing had happened. Even those who don't believe in the value of retributive justice may want to consider the possibility that some restorative justice initiatives may prove sufficiently distasteful to some offenders as to be perceived as retributive!

Old Testament law is no stranger to restorative justice. The legislator expresses implicit interest in a restorative justice process with respect to some types of offenses. While some of the motivation may well have been grounded in humanitarian concerns, it is important to note that the ancient Israelites did not, until the exilic period at least, have anything that

---

3. Lewis, *Problem of Pain*, 91–92.

resembled the sort of prison system that is found almost everywhere in the world today. Long-term incarceration was not an option available to them.[4]

When it comes to the administration of justice, two things must be kept in mind. In the case of capital crimes, the sentences are retributive in character: a life for a life, "Whoever sheds the blood of a human, by a human shall that person's blood be shed; for in his own image God made humankind" (Gen 9:6).[5] Capital punishment achieves three objectives. First, it is intended to satisfy the most basic demands of justice. If a man takes another man's life, he must forfeit his own. Second, it serves to protect the rest of society from someone who had no compunction about violating its most fundamental laws in the first place. Third, inflicting the supreme penalty also serves as deterrence to others who might be tempted to do the same.

In cases where non-capital crimes were committed, sentences entailed both retributive and restorative elements. Leviticus 6:1–3 is case in point:

> The LORD spoke to Moses, saying: When any of you sin and commit a trespass against the LORD by deceiving a neighbor in a matter of a deposit or a pledge, or by robbery, or if you have defrauded a neighbor, or have found something lost and lied about it—if you swear falsely regarding any of the various things that one may do and sin thereby . . .

According to vv. 4–5, once the wrongdoer recognized and admitted his *guilt*, he was obligated to do full restitution and add one-fifth of the principal amount as further compensation:

> When you have sinned and realize your guilt, and would restore what you took by robbery or by fraud or the deposit that was committed to you, or the lost thing that you found, or anything else about which you have sworn falsely, you shall repay the principal amount and shall add one-fifth to it. You shall pay it to its owner when you realize your guilt.[6]

The Hebrew verb translated by "realize your guilt," *asham*, has in view the notion of objective guilt following the violation of a law.[7] The legislator leaves no doubt about the nature of the punishment that results from the violation of the law. While restoration into the community is implied

---

4. Vaux, *Ancient Israel*, 1:158–60.
5. See also Exod 21:16.
6. See also Exod 22:1–4; 21:24.
7. See for instance Lev 4:13, where the author imagines a situation where the people have violated a command but are unaware of it. In such cases, they are nevertheless considered guilty.

with respect to non-capital offenses, the primary emphasis is on retribution and restitution. In the latter case, as the passage makes clear, there are sometimes provisions for a "surcharge" that is most likely intended to serve as punishment and deterrent.[8] Without retribution, there is no space for restoration.

With respect to Adam and Eve, the text describes their act of disobedience as a violation of a divine injunction. This introduces a moral and legal dimension that needs to be addressed. For God to extend forgiveness, justice must be satisfied. In this case, the difficulty lies in what could constitute adequate reparation. If stealing requires restitution accompanied by a penalty, and if murder demands the loss of the perpetrator's life, what could possibly be deemed adequate to meet the absolute requirements of justice for an offense against God himself?

It was also imperative that God's plan of redemption address the relational breakdown that resulted from the offense. Adam and Eve's transgression did not only entail a legal dimension requiring a legal response. It was an act that exhibited the highest degree of disloyalty and a total disregard for God and their relationship to him. The action was akin to spouse betraying spouse, brother betraying brother, a man betraying his country.

When a man is unfaithful to his wife, what can he possibly do to make up for the pain, the humiliation, and the feelings of betrayal that result? To ask the question is to answer it: ultimately, nothing. No amount of money or moral self-flagellation can possibly atone for such a transgression. The reason is remarkably simple and has something to do with what Hannah Arendt called "the predicament of irreversibility," an inability to undo history.[9] Commenting on the impulse to seek revenge for wrongdoings, Yale University Divinity School theologian Miroslav Volf writes, "If our deeds and their consequences could be undone, revenge would not be necessary. The undoing, if there were a will for it, would suffice. But our actions are irreversible. Even God cannot alter them. And so the urge for vengeance seems irrepressible. The only way out of the predicament of irreversibility Arendt insisted, is through *forgiveness.*"[10]

While I agree with Arendt's and Volf's contention that reconciliation hinges on forgiveness, forgiveness cannot occur in a vacuum. The hard reality is that forgiveness always exacts a price that is commensurate with the gravity of the offense. The greater the offense, the greater the cost. When the offense reaches into infinity, so does the cost of forgiveness. And the

---

8. See Vaux, *Ancient Israel*, 1:158–60.
9. Arendt, *Human Condition*, 212.
10. Volf, *Exclusion and Embrace*, 121.

cost of forgiveness always, somehow, encompasses the notion of justice.[11] If reconciliation depends on forgiveness, forgiveness is contingent on justice being done. This principle provides a critical insight into why God's plan of redemption required a provision to cover the "cost" of extending forgiveness. This now leads us to the following question: What is that provision?

The partial but anticipatory answer to this question is found in the Old Testament sacrificial system. When God established his covenant with Israel, he knew that men and women would be unable to satisfy all the demands of the law. In order to palliate for these failings, God instituted a system in which an animal's life could be substituted for a person's. While these substitutionary sacrifices had no *real* value, they symbolically signaled something about the demands of ultimate reality with respect to the satisfaction of divine justice. The author of the letter to the Hebrews clarifies the nature of the Old Testament sacrifices in ch. 10:

> Since the law has only a shadow of the good things to come and not the true form of these realities, it can never, by the same sacrifices that are continually offered year after year, make perfect those who approach. Otherwise, would they not have ceased being offered, since the worshipers, cleansed once for all, would no longer have any consciousness of sin? But in these sacrifices there is a reminder of sin year after year. For it is impossible for the blood of bulls and goats to take away sins. (Heb 10:1–4)

Finally, God's plan of redemption would need to address what humans had become as a result of the first act of disobedience. What emerged from this test was not the creature God had originally imagined. Human beings became fatally flawed creatures, characterized by an innate propensity for violence. The death sentence announced in Gen 2:17 was more than punishment; it was also intended to limit the pain and suffering any human being could inflict on others. It represented a mitigating and protective measure. Because man had mutated into a horror, God's plan of redemption would also need to address this situation. A broken humanity meant a violent humanity. There could therefore be no redemption without radical transformation.[12]

---

11. For a detailed exploration of the inescapable link between forgiveness and justice, see Rutledge, *Crucifixion*, 106–66.

12. Rutledge proposes that divine justice must include the notions of justification and "rectification." For more details, see *Crucifixion*, 571–612.

THE SACRIFICE OF CHRIST

As the first eleven chapters of Genesis demonstrate, God's grace always exceeds human sin. When, in Genesis 11, human pride appears on the brink of undoing God's project altogether, God's judgment against those who build the tower of Babel is, surprisingly, not his final word. When all seems lost, God initiates a plan to redeem humanity (Gen 12–50) through Abraham and his descendants.[13] What these first chapters outline is illustrative of God's greater redemption project.

From eternity past, God devised a way to redeem humanity, but there was only one course of action open to God (Matt 26:36–45). Only the unjust death of Christ at the hands of men would fulfill the demands of ultimate reality. God the Son would need to offer his own life in sacrifice (Mark 8:31; Luke 9:22).

The death of Christ fulfilled the demands of divine justice. An offense of infinite significance committed against a holy God required nothing less than the perpetrators' execution in retribution. The Old Testament sacrificial system taught that a substitution could be made to save the life of a transgressor. With respect to Adam and Eve's offense, a substitutionary sacrifice could in theory be made, but to fulfill the requirements of divine justice, such a sacrifice would need to be of infinite value and involve a perfectly innocent victim. Working from the perspective of Christ's sacrifice, Fleming Rutledge parses a similar idea. She writes, "The crucifixion of Jesus is of such magnitude that it must call forth a concept of sin that is large enough to match it."[14] As a perfectly innocent and infinitely valuable victim, Christ met these requirements. His unjust execution would fulfill the need for justice. By assuming the sentence pronounced against humanity, Christ provided an adequate foundation, the only possible foundation, for humanity's pardon, redemption, and restoration.

If Christ addressed the issue of divine justice by offering himself on humanity's behalf, his sacrifice also provided a mechanism to repair the broken relationship between humanity and God. That aspect of the problem is in my opinion as fundamental as the justice issue. To bring someone to justice is one thing; to aim at reconciling two estranged parties is another. Adam and Eve had not simply broken an impersonal law; they had challenged God's very integrity, and in doing so, caused nearly irreparable damage to their relationship with God. The Apostle Paul addresses this very issue in Col 1:21–22: "And you who were once estranged and hostile in mind, doing

---

13. Clines, *Pentateuch*, 76.
14. Rutledge develops this idea in more detail in *Crucifixion*, 200.

evil deeds, he has now reconciled in his fleshly body through death, so as to present you holy and blameless and irreproachable before him."

If, for all practical purposes, the precise mechanism making it possible for Christ's death to fulfill the justice requirements are opaque to human reason, the same thing is true with respect to how Christ's death enables God to entirely forgive and extend friendship to men and women. We need to remember that this is not simply about the formal satisfaction of justice; Christ's sacrificial death allows God to be fully reconciled with those who put their trust in Christ (Col 1:20). On a most fundamental level, the unmerited sufferings of Christ and his execution under Pontius Pilate provided the foundation necessary to reconcile men and women to God. We may not completely understand why Christ had to die in such a manner, but we know it was necessary.

Anyone who has ever been the victim of a crime knows that legal satisfaction doesn't necessarily entail emotional healing and reconciliation. So how do we move from the satisfaction of God's justice to a perfectly renewed relationship with God? The answer to this question is both unfathomable and yet gloriously simple. If God can welcome those who have sinned against him, it is because of his infinite love. If the requirements of justice were objectively fulfilled by the substitutionary death of Christ, God, being perfectly just, would be compelled to accept Christ's sacrifice as entirely adequate to deal with the justice issue. Once justice was dealt with, God could then extend full and complete relational reconciliation because of his love for humanity. The love of God is the key to understanding it all. It is love that motivated God to create humanity. Love was the primary impulse in providing a solution for Adam and Eve's offense in the person of Christ, and love was the imperative behind God's enthusiastic willingness to offer his friendship to all men and women. If a woman can find it in herself to forgive an adulterous husband, it is partially because he shows contrition and makes amends. But it is, essentially, I believe, because the offended party has the capacity to reach out to the unfaithful spouse by drawing on her love for that person. While only love can supply the strength and the motivation needed to overcome such betrayal, one more element needs to be considered.

Could a woman truly forgive and be reconciled to her husband if he showed no evidence of understanding the gravity of his action? Of course not. Forgiveness and reconciliation are in part contingent on one's admission of guilt and a pledge to live faithfully thereafter. Failure to commit to a life of integrity would surely doom the relationship.

In their present condition, human beings are incapable of living a sinless life. To claim otherwise is delusional (1 John 1:8). They may sincerely wish to remain sinless, but they cannot. God's forgiveness is not only based on the legal adequacy of Christ's sacrifice and his love, but on the guaranteed reality of future transformation for those who believe in Christ. In a mysterious yet real sense, we *are* in Christ and God already sees us as we will be when salvation is fully deployed (2 Cor 1:21–22; Col 3:3). While there is a historical process of transformation that begins in the life of the believer when he or she comes to the knowledge of Christ, God's promise is that it will be fully completed and realized at the resurrection (1 Cor 15:35–56; Phil 1:6). Redemption is a multi-pronged process that culminates with the actual transformation of those who accept God's forgiveness through Christ. God can already love and welcome those who are still sinners because of God's unconditional commitment to actualize his promise to make them into new creatures. Once God declares something, it is as good as done. The love of God transcends space and time.

That the Son of God had to die on humanity's behalf signals two important truths that are unfortunately often disregarded today. First, it highlights the gravity of Adam and Eve's violation. Because the choice given to these two entailed ramifications that would reach into the fabric of reality, the actual impact of the decision they would make would also reach into the core of reality. That being the case, the solution required to undo the damage occasioned by Adam and Eve would also need to reach into the very structure of reality itself. Second, the necessity of Christ's death says something about the infinite significance of the cross. While it is fashionable in some circles to describe Christ's death as a critique of empire[15] or as an example of how we should respond to violence, the reality is altogether different. Christ's death was not an unfortunate consequence of Christ "speaking truth to power." While the gospel story encompasses some of these elements, that the second person of the trinity felt compelled to take on this assignment points to an imperative that goes far beyond a political agenda.

In the long term, the New Testament offers a viable and sustainable vision for humanity's redemption. As Paul states in 1 Thessalonians, when Christ comes back, "the dead in Christ will rise first. Then we who are alive, who are left, will be caught up in the clouds together with them to meet the Lord in the air; and so we will be with the Lord forever" (1 Thess 4:16b–17). There is no doubt whatsoever about history's ultimate trajectory and end point. While there is much encouragement to be drawn from this promise, how are we to navigate the vagaries of human existence until then?

---

15. For a fresh examination and an evaluation of empire criticism, see McKnight and Modica, *Jesus Is Lord*.

LIFE IN THE SPHERE OF THE CURSE

We have seen so far that Adam and Eve's primordial act of disobedience propelled humanity into the sphere of the curse. What emerged from the aftermath is the world as we know it.

The curse is not about some judgment arbitrarily imposed by God. The curse describes the inevitable consequence of the violation of a fundamental law. Curse could in fact be used to describe the consequences of violating any moral or physical law. When we cheat, kill, or steal, consequences ensue. If we jump off a ten-story building or drive into a cement wall, we must bear the consequences of these actions as well, not because God actively intervenes to ensure that the "curse" is implemented, but because there are cause-and-effect mechanisms that are intrinsic to the physical universe. This is how reality works.

For all its perceived failings, this world may in fact be the best of all possible worlds in a universe infected by sin and under God's judgment. God designed humanity to weather the all-encompassing shadow of sin, but as signaled in Genesis 3, it would not be without some serious aggravation.

First, death is now an irreducible part of human experience. While we are not in a position to determine whether animal death was or not an outcome of the fall,[16] human death certainly is. Therein resides a great scandal. Human beings resent death. It is tragic enough in old age, but particularly despicable when it's the outcome of violence, illness, or negligence. The younger we are, the more death seems to be something that only happens to others. As much as death may be part of our daily existence, it nevertheless feels like a dreamy abstraction. As we age and begin to lose friends and loved ones, and as we ourselves experience the ever-growing limitations of old age, death becomes a silent menace, an invisible but inevitable threat that will strike, if not today, then perhaps tomorrow, but surely the day after. It's not a question of if but when. Death is the great equalizer. It is the inescapable and unavoidable sentence on all who live in this fallen world.

If the fixed boundary that death imposes may seem unbearable, especially when it threatens those we love and cherish, we must never forget that it effectively hems in the actions and influence of the wicked and violent. We may resent it, but we must believe that it is all for the best. As the biblical

---

16. While the predatory system may seem cruel to some, it's important to remember that there is nothing inherently immoral about it. It could, in theory at least, have been present in a world untainted by original sin. But based on Gen 1:30, where God is said to provide plants as food for all animals, it is more likely, if we follow the internal logic of the text, that God's original intent for the animal kingdom did not include predatory behavior. Those who would like to reflect further on the problem of animal pain can consult Lewis, *Problem of Pain*, 132–47.

story of the flood suggests, the gift of immortality to such sinful creatures as we are would likely turn out to be a poisoned gift. Genesis 6 depicts a generation of people who enjoy an exceptionally long life span. But instead of the benefits one might expect from such longevity, the text describes a civilization utterly consumed by violence: "The LORD saw that the wickedness of humankind was great in the earth, and that every inclination of the thoughts of their hearts was only evil continually" (Gen 6:5). The rationale for the limitation of the human life span mentioned in Gen 6:3 represents, within the logic of the text, a response to the exponential explosion of violence a longer-lived species could produce. The death of honorable and good people may be tragic, but can we imagine the power a megalomaniac like Hitler could gather and the suffering that would ensue if such a man could live five or six hundred years? In our present condition, death turns out to be a good thing. C. S. Lewis puts it this way:

> Again, Christianity asserts that every individual human being is going to live for ever, and this must be either true or false. Now there are a good many things which would not be worth bothering about if I were going to live only seventy years, but which I had better bother about very seriously if I am going to live for ever. Perhaps my bad temper or my jealousy are gradually getting worse—so gradually that the increase in seventy years will not be very noticeable. But it might be absolute hell in a million years: in fact, if Christianity is true, Hell is the precisely correct technical term for what it would be.[17]

Second, beside the universality of death, all human beings are vulnerable to the vicissitudes of life. Believers and nonbelievers alike experience the difficulties inherent to human existence. Pain is universal. While the actual experience may be unique to each one of us, the undeniable fact is that we all suffer. It is perhaps here that we need to pause to address, even if briefly, the reason why so many theologians advocate a simple appeal to faith as a response to the presence of evil and suffering in the world. The assumption is that there are no comprehensive answers to the problem of evil, and that the best we can do is to trust in the goodness of God and devise ways to support each other when we fall on hard times. Tim Keller's book *Walking with God through Pain and Suffering*, which otherwise makes an excellent contribution to the issue, advocates a minimalist approach with respect to trying to make sense of evil. He notes, correctly I might add, that most theologians and philosophers now tend to lean away from developing a full theodicy but choose instead to limit themselves to a *defense*.

17. Lewis, *Mere Christianity*, 74.

The distinction between the two may be lost on some, and one may in fact question whether there is a significant difference between a theodicy and a defense. Be that as it may, if we posit these two concepts on a spectrum, a theodicy would attempt to provide a comprehensive response to why a good God allows evil, whereas a defense would simply seek to demonstrate that there is no intrinsic contradiction between the reality of suffering and the existence of a good and all-powerful God.[18]

The distinction is helpful. And as Keller correctly points out, to limit ourselves to a defense has the advantage of putting the burden of proof on unbelievers rather than on Christians. There is nothing wrong, in and of itself, with trusting God when facing difficult existential issues and advocating it as a strategy to cope with suffering. The main difficulty lies in considering any sustained attempt at explaining the presence of evil as fundamentally improper or as some sort of concession to modernity. While we must recognize the limits of reason, to seek explanations does not, in itself, represent an illegitimate endeavor.

Those who, like Hauerwas, sharply oppose the search for a rational answer confuse categories. There is a fundamental difference between reflecting on all that Scripture teaches on suffering, on the one hand, and attempting, on the other hand, to explain why a given boy dies of Leukemia at the age of three. It's not because the precise cause behind a small child's death may be beyond human reason that the broader issue of gratuitous pain in the world should also be off limits. In other words, our inability to rationalize a specific instance of suffering does not necessarily delegitimize the tentative articulation of a more comprehensive response. As we have seen, Scripture does not shy away from addressing the larger issue and, in so doing, gives the reader permission to go at least as far in that direction as it does. To find refuge in trusting the goodness of God is perfectly acceptable, but to imply that there is a contradiction between trusting God and attempting to articulate an explanation, even if it's far from comprehensive, does not correctly reflect all that Scripture has to say about the subject.

A while ago, a friend of mine died after an eighteen-month fight with cancer. He was fifty-three years old. An exceptional man. A man of unshakable integrity. Loved and admired by all. I had lunch with his younger brother a few weeks after the funeral. Two urgent questions were on his mind: "Why him and why now?" The most basic reason for this good man's death is simple: we all die because of the effect of sin on the world. Death is part of the DNA of our existence. The "why now" question is obviously more

---

18. For a helpful summary of the distinction between a theodicy and a defense, see Keller, *Walking with God*, 93.

complex. Why do people die when they do? Part of the answer is buried in the interaction of a multitude of environmental factors, some of which can be readily identifiable, whereas others will forever remain opaque to us.

The case of a teenager who gets hit by a bus because he crossed the road while texting is quite different from the death of a young mother in a plane crash. The first finds its immediate cause in a moment of inattention, whereas the second was caused by factors that were entirely beyond the young woman's control. As disturbing as this may be, much of what happens to us is often the result of random causes. Whereas many Christians may find solace in the fact that God controls everything (atheists would substitute fate or destiny), it is more probable that God allows for a meaningful degree of free and undetermined interaction in nature and among humans. It is probably best to consider the tornado that strikes a small Midwestern town or the combination of genetic coding and environmental factors that trigger a terminal illness in a young girl as the outcome of random interactions.[19] To view the multitude of natural phenomena that occur on any given day as directly controlled by God effectively makes God the immediate cause of everything, and injects a moral component into all natural phenomena whether it's a tsunami that obliterates the lives of thousands or a wolf killing a fawn.

I am not at all suggesting, as some evolutionists would maintain, that the universe is the result of time and chance. The portrait that surfaces from the creation account is of an infinitely detailed engineered world in which God allows for the kind of free interaction that is required for humans to function as moral agents.

Some might conclude from this that we live in a closed system that is strictly determined by the principle of cause and effect, excluding any possibility of divine intervention altogether. The creation narrative challenges this as well. While Adam and Eve are given the authority to make a critical decision with respect to their ultimate destiny, the full consequences of their disobedience are mitigated by God, who intervenes by providing clothes and by hinting at some future deliverance.

The same applies to us. We live in a world in which chance and randomness are at play. If we have a car accident or slip and break a bone, we are confronted by the unbending reality of this principle. The alternative is a universe in which everything is divinely micromanaged and where, therefore, the most trivial event is infused with moral significance. God has, however, designed the world in such a way as to allow space for divine interventions. Such interventions are sometimes described as miracles, a term

---

19. See, for instance, *Somayaji*, "Cancer."

that is generally defined as a violation of a natural law. Perhaps that is the best way to describe such events, but we need not assume that the use of the word need be limited to large-scale divine actions. Scripture also includes examples of God as intervening in the daily flow of life.

The notion of prayer as a daily, hourly, even moment-by-moment exercise assumes a universe designed to allow God to seamlessly move in our sphere of existence in order to alter our environment and even our own selves. If prayer can affect reality, as Christians believe, then it follows that there is, inserted in the very fabric of the universe, a kind of plasticity that allows for real interaction between God and the world without necessarily involving a constant violation or suspension of the physical laws that govern it.

The biblical concept of prayer excludes, on the one hand, the notion of a closed universe entirely and solely governed by so-called natural laws and, on the other hand, a pantheistic universe that encompasses all, even the divine essence. The biblical portrait of the relationship between God and the universe is much more nuanced and complex than what is communicated by these two caricatures. As far as our experience of pain and evil is concerned, it's also significantly more unsettling.

If everything that happens to us can be viewed as the direct and unmediated result of God's action—which is one way to understand God's sovereignty—then there is no space for doubt and second-guessing; whatever happens is God's will and should be graciously and, may I add, *fatalistically* received as from the hand of God. While there is a place for recognizing both God's sovereignty and the limitations deriving from the environment and our own nature, from a biblical perspective, there is no compelling reason to believe in a deterministic universe. Let me explain further.

The world, as we know it. A world that encompasses the freedom to do good and evil, allows for the occurrence of natural disasters that entail the loss of property and human lives, and a world in which death is inevitable is indeed the result of God's sovereign design. This is the way the world must now be. On a macro level, we need to accept the way the world is as the expression of God's will for a fallen world.

On a micro level, however, the situation is more complex. Christians are subject to the same vicissitudes of life as anyone else. A spring flood does not discriminate between believers and nonbelievers. A Christian who texts while driving is as liable to having an accident as an atheist. While Christians are not exempt from the daily deployment of life's hardships, that doesn't mean that they must blindly submit to the arbitrariness of life as if every minute difficulty they encounter is willed by God.

The multitude of exhortations to pray attested in the Old Testament and the New, our Lord's teaching on prayer in Matthew 6 and Luke 11, the presence of biblical texts such as Psalms 23 and 107, which give witness to God's ability to intervene in history, signal the undeniable reality of a space in which we can appeal to God and in which, in response, God can intervene. The space is there, and it is real. Does praying before a road trip make any difference with respect to the safety of the travelers? Does asking God for his assistance for a job interview, a public presentation, or a project have any impact on the outcome of these endeavors? Skeptics would say no. Christian prayer for them is no more than a psychological crutch intended for people who are too feeble to make it on their own.

Christians, however, believe that God, as revealed in Jesus Christ, is real, good, and all-powerful, and that he has the desire and the means to be involved in our lives. God expects believers to pray for all that is of concern to them and for the advancement of the kingdom of God. To pray is the believer's responsibility; the outcome, God's. To neglect to pray is to choose to entirely subject ourselves to the vagaries of life. But if we pray, we create the conditions for God to intervene in our lives in a way that, at times, may protect us from what could otherwise befall us. How, precisely, God may manifest himself cannot be predicted, for God acts according to a set of equations and in consideration of factors that will, more often than not, remain beyond human reason, either because we do not have all the facts at our disposal or simply because of the irreducible complexity inherent to God's will.

Just consider the case of Joseph, a man who was nearly killed by his brothers and then sold into slavery (Gen 37–50). God could have delivered Joseph in the early stages of his ordeal but chose not to because Joseph would in time become the person through whom Jacob's family would be saved from famine. The same could be said of Daniel, who was taken as a prisoner of war to Babylon around 605 BC. Surely Daniel prayed for protection and deliverance, but for God's greater plan for his people to succeed, he would need a faithful man in the Babylonian court to work on behalf of the Israelites. This man was Daniel.

God is working at the fulfillment of a great plan that often requires actions whose purpose is not readily obvious or will only be understood in time. While prayer will sometimes result in a swift response, at other times, it will seem as if God is silent. This is what makes faith necessary. Even when God appears to be absent, he is never indifferent or inactive. God always works on behalf of those who call on him (Prov 3:6). Abraham is commended for his unwavering faith in the face of God's long-awaited promise (Rom 4:18–21). Like the Old Testament prophet Habakkuk, who was facing the imminent threat of war and destruction, and still chose to trust in God (Hab 3:16–19), we too must keep believing that God is good and all-powerful, and that he is at work even when circumstances do not bear this out (cf. Heb 11:6).

A student once observed that he did not feel "locked" into the so-called sphere of the curse. As far as he could tell, he had the ability to make choices that were life-giving and had experiences that could naturally be associated with the sphere of the blessing. On one level, this student's observation was correct. Even in a fallen world, human beings retain the ability to make good moral choices and to recognize and experience the good.

To address this legitimate question, we need to look closely at how the creation narrative describes the deployment of the curse. Life under the curse did not result in an existence that would be devoid of any goodness whatsoever. It entailed, rather, as specified in Genesis 3, a mutation of human nature as well as a degradation of the environment and humanity's relationship to it. On the positive side, humans are still described as being in the image of God, a characteristic that remained in effect after the fall and no doubt mitigated the impact of sin.

In Gen 2:15–17, the passage that recounts God's invitation to partner with him and stipulates the one injunction Adam and Eve are to obey, it is possible to discern two levels of reading: historical and archetypal. The historical perspective denotes Adam and Eve's unique situation. The archetypal dimension highlights the universal character of the kind of relationship God wishes to have with all human beings. While God's invitation to Adam and Eve was uniquely relevant to them, the principle that is revealed in this text is true for everyone. Men and women face the constant prospect of blessing or curse based on the daily decisions that they make. Living under the curse does not, in context, imply the total absence of good. Moreover, even as fallen creatures, humans maintain the ability to determine their destiny.

But let's be clear about one thing. The option to choose between good and evil and to experience the blessing and the curse is true only as long as humanity remains in its present condition. The capacity to indefinitely rebel against God is a direct consequence of the radical disruption occasioned by the first act of disobedience. Evil is present in the human soul in a way that would not have been true had Adam and Eve obeyed God. It is this mutation that makes the proliferation of evil possible.

While human beings are not in a position to lift the "mortgage" incurred by the fall (Rom 5:12), they are not constrained to give in to every sinful impulse the fallen nature can generate. Men and women, particularly when assisted by the Spirit of God, retain some degree of moral self-determination. If humanity had been locked into the sphere of the blessing, human beings would have been granted the latitude to exercise their free will without ever transgressing God's law or experiencing evil.

Life under the curse characterizes the broad framework of human existence, the major two characteristics being a fundamental corruption of human nature from which violence originates and the universality of death. Being locked in the sphere of the curse need not be defined as a condition that is in absolute opposition to its counterpart. If evil constitutes an inevitable and intrinsic part of our lives, it doesn't characterize the entirety of human experience. Even in a fallen world, men and women can still experience goodness and retain some capacity to choose the good.

Epilogue: Hope

THE OXFORD UNIVERSITY MATHEMATICS professor and renowned Christian apologist John Lennox often notes that most people will never get justice in this world. Injustice is rampant. The millions of unborn babies who are terminated on a yearly basis throughout the world through no fault of theirs will never see justice. The same holds true for the millions of men and women who have, throughout history, lived in primitive conditions that consistently cut down their normal life expectancy by decades. The countless millions who live under regimes that routinely violate their most basic human rights (North Korea being but one example) will never in this life be compensated for the pain, the suffering, and the indignities they have suffered.

As the author of the book of Ecclesiastes observes on several occasions, if what we see is all there is, then human life is indeed cruel, pointless, and meaningless. But as Lennox points out, what we see is not the total sum of reality. The life, sacrificial death, and resurrection of Jesus Christ are the guarantees that there is something else beyond the human horizon. The Bible teaches that God has for those who are willing to trust him an eternal future in which all will be set right (Isa 9:7; 61:8; Rev 6:9–10; 21:4).

The world is not as it ought to be! This may be the most concise expression of the problem of evil. Regardless of one's station in life, rich or poor, married or single, healthy or infirm, free or slave, I would be willing to bet that most human beings somehow *feel* and *know* that this world is not their final home. Different cultures and religions may express it differently, but I believe there is a universal recognition of this world's flawed character and a corresponding yearning for a better place.

YEARNING FOR A HOME

For C. S. Lewis, this deep yearning for a reality beyond this one was an important factor in abandoning atheism and committing his life to Christ. He writes:

> If we find ourselves with a desire that nothing in this world can satisfy, the most probable explanation is that we were made for another world. If none of my earthly pleasures satisfy it, that does not prove that the universe is a fraud. Probably earthly pleasures were never meant to satisfy it, but only to arouse it, to suggest the real thing. If that is so, I must take care, on the one hand, never to despise, or be unthankful for, these earthly blessings, and on the other, never to mistake them for the something else of which they are only a kind of copy, or echo, or mirage. I must keep alive in myself the desire for my true country, which I shall not find till after death.[1]

Our deepest and most persistent yearnings confirm what the Bible repeatedly declares about the purpose of human existence. This world is indeed not our permanent home. It gives us life and a place to live, but it in the end, it always turns out to be our grave. The New Testament repeatedly refers to another home that is not of this world. While this new residence is commonly referred to as heaven, I would rather avoid using this word here, because of the common perception of heaven as a non-corporeal, ethereal, and beatific existence that would surely bore the most devoted saint to death in less time than it takes to sing two stanzas of "Amazing Grace."

As New Testament scholar N. T. Wright points out in his book *Surprised by Hope*, our final destination as redeemed men and women is not "heaven" as such, which is more properly God's abode. As the Apostle Peter writes, God is preparing a new universe, "new heavens and a new earth" (2 Pet 3:15), that will in every way be as physical and tangible as this one. There is no hint in Scripture that human beings will spend eternity as ghost-like entities destined to forever float in some dreamy-like state. As Paul states in the great resurrection chapter in his letter to the Corinthians, every Christian will be given a new body; not some cheap knockoff but a body that will be of the same nature as the one Christ received. Bodies that will never wear out or age. Indestructible bodies and minds that will never unduly draw attention to themselves but will forever be flawlessly used in God's service and in the enjoyment of the new life we will have in Christ.

---

1. Lewis, *Mere Christianity*, 136–37.

Another thing to note about the new world is that it will really be *new*. The new earth will not be a slightly improved version of this one. The Apostle Peter could not be more explicit:

> But the day of the Lord will come like a thief, and then the heavens will pass away with a loud noise, and the elements will be dissolved with fire, and the earth and everything that is done on it will be disclosed. Since all these things are to be dissolved in this way, what sort of persons ought you to be in leading lives of holiness and godliness, waiting for and hastening the coming of the day of God, because of which the heavens will be set ablaze and dissolved, and the elements will melt with fire? But, in accordance with his promise, we wait for new heavens and a new earth, where righteousness is at home. (2 Pet 3:10–13)

The expressions used to describe the future fate of this world, "then the heavens will pass away with a loud noise,"[2] "and the elements will be dissolved with fire,"[3] "and the earth and everything that is done on it will be disclosed,"[4] are unequivocal. Like an infinitely intricate Lego model that is dismantled to build something else, the entire universe will be entirely taken apart, reduced to its most basic elements, and redesigned from the inside out. The Apostle John couches it in no less dramatic terms: "Then I saw a new heaven and a new earth; for the first heaven and the first earth had passed away, and the sea was no more" (Rev. 21:1).

While it is impossible to imagine what this new universe will be like, at the very least, we know that since it will never run down, the first and second laws of thermodynamics will no longer be in effect. The idea that God will completely take this universe apart to construct a new one is troubling for some.[5] But consider this. God paid the highest price imaginable for

---

2. *oi ouranoi roizēdon pareleusontai*, lit. "the heavens will suddenly disappear."

3. *stoicheia de kausoumena luthēsetai*, lit. "and [the] elements will be loosened by being burned up."

4. The verb translated "be disclosed" is the Greek *eurethēsetai*. In this context, the expression probably alludes to the uncovering of sin, which reminds the reader that the destruction of the universe is not merely the consequence of God's arbitrary decision but the expression of his judgment upon a sinful world. This interpretation is confirmed by Peter's exhortation to lead "lives of holiness and godliness" (v. 11, see also v. 14) and the intimate association between the new heavens and the new earth as the home of righteousness (v. 13). It should be noted that *eurethēsetai* is attested in ℵ B K P and likely represents the better reading as the more difficult variant, which accounts for the alternative readings as corrections ("will burn up," "will be dissolved," "will not be found"). For more details, see Bauckham, *Jude, 2 Peter*, 303, 316–21.

5. I'm thinking in particular of environmentalists who are persuaded there is a direct cause-and-effect relationship between the belief in this world's eschatological destruction

humanity's redemption. If the church is described as the body of Christ, it is also portrayed as his bride. That the unveiling of Christ's new bride will be a very, very big deal is a magnificent understatement. Surely Christ will want to bring this new bride into a new home, untainted by sin. A new universe for a new bride. And why not? Just like the redemption of individual men and women will require a radical transformation of their being, so it will be with the rest of the universe. As Paul intimates in Romans 8, because the present world was infected by sin, its redemption will similarly require a radical transformation from the ground up.

IMMORTALITY

Despite the hundreds of millions of dollars that annually feed it, popular culture has been remarkably inept at imagining life after death or what human immortality might look like. The afterlife is inevitably portrayed as some kind of disembodied ghostly existence. As for immortality, it's painfully obvious that the only ones to reach this highly desirable condition are the vampire who cannot stand the light of day and need human blood to survive, or the immeasurably lamer zombie who is compelled to forever feed on human brains. Hollywood's attempts at portraying the afterlife or immortality are ghastly. Even the so-called Immortals, the central protagonists of the popular *Highlander* movies and television series are pathetic. They may theoretically be immortal, but they must periodically behead each other to gain a greater portion of the power that keeps them alive.

Popular culture is unable to imagine the future without the never-ending presence of evil. In contrast, the New Testament offers an evil-free, profound, and dynamic view of a never-ending afterlife in the presence of

---

and an alleged absence of interest in ecological issues among some Christians (see, for instance, Wright, *Surprised by Hope*, 90–91). In my opinion, this perception may no longer be accurate. While there may be fringe groups that might advocate a total disregard for the planet's ecosystem based on end-times considerations, I find no widespread evidence of such thinking in Christian circles. Even if it could be demonstrated that a radical apocalyptic discourse did lead to a disregard for the planet, would that be reason enough to blacklist a doctrine simply because it may have some undesirable outcomes on how some people think? Evolutionary biologists would recoil at the mere thought of suppressing the theory of evolution because of its distasteful consequences for the belief in the sanctity of human life. Do we ever hear calls for the suppression of the laws of thermodynamics because of their implications for the future of the universe? Just like scientists insist on teaching important theories despite the possibility of unintended consequences on how some people might respond, when it comes to fundamental teachings of Scripture, Christians should not hesitate to do the same.

God beginning the moment we breathe our last and transitioning to the physical state when Jesus Christ comes back.

The notion of immortality in our present human condition is not particularly appealing. In fact, to imagine a new world where human beings would continue to indulge their destructive impulses is repulsive. The possibility that such deranged creatures, as we are, could live forever is the stuff of nightmares. Some of the difficulties inherent to envisioning a world populated with men and women untainted by the myriads of flaws that characterize human nature obviously reside in our inability to disconnect our understanding of human nature and human experience from the reality of evil. Not only is it nearly impossible to imagine a sinless human being, but one might also ask whether men and women could eternally exist with the *memory* of evil.

GOD REDEEMS PEOPLE NOT EVIL

As far as the New Testament is concerned, that redemption involves the thorough eradication of evil from human nature is not open to debate. Whether we can concretely imagine it is irrelevant. The eradication of the sin nature does not, however, imply the loss of awareness and knowledge of what evil is. For God to reengineer human consciousness in such a way as to suppress the very memory of evil would represent an unacceptable denial of reality.

I am convinced we will remember that sin and evil once ruled the world. It must be so if we are to adequately appreciate the redeeming work of Christ throughout the ages (cf. Rev 5:1–14). When the book of Revelation refers to a time when God "will wipe every tear from their eyes" (21:4), the text does not suggest that the memory of pain and suffering will be erased. The Apostle John indicates rather that God will comfort those who have suffered, and that he will ensure it will never happen again. God redeems people not evil *per se*. Redemption is not about making evil good, but about healing men and women who have been devastated by it. Evil will never cease to be evil, even when God uses it to bring about a greater good. God redeems the effects of sin but that process never transforms evil itself into good. What was truly evil in human history will always and forever deemed to have been so. It is imperative we maintain this important distinction, for when we don't, as we saw in the first chapter of this book, good and evil become interchangeable.

AN ETERNITY WITHOUT SIN? REALLY?

Few Christians blink an eye when they read that in heaven, sin will never again have a foothold. But when I argue that sin would never have entered human history in the first place, had Adam and Eve obeyed God when tempted, some express skepticism at such an idea. Surely, they say, someone would eventually have disobeyed and dragged the whole human race into the sphere of death. Such people assume that disobedience was inevitable. But what they fail to realize is that the same could be said of the new world. Surely someone will one day disobey God and usher a new age of darkness. What's good for the goose is good for the gander. While I do not wish to rehearse everything I have said on this subject in chapter 4, let me offer a few thoughts to consider.

To begin, we must keep in mind Scripture's solemn promise that all those who put their trust in Christ will not only be brought back to life in due time, but they will also be transformed. At that time, God will endow every person with a new body free of the corrupt nature inherited through Adam's sin (Rom 5:12; 1 Cor 15:21). This transformation will require the death of our earthly body and a reconstruction from the ground up that will culminate in the full deployment of the resurrected body (Rom 6:5–9; 8:11; 1 Cor 15:21–22, 42–49). This organic transformation will only apply to those who have given God permission to implement it, for perfect love cannot and will never impose itself on its object. Only those transformed by God will have the capacity to live eternally without ever experiencing the whisper of a temptation to rebel against God. I cannot comment on the exact mechanisms that will make this possible. This is, strictly speaking, a matter of faith. In the same way we believe God can rebuild us even after our bones have been ground to dust, we also accept on faith that God can restore us with the inner apparatus needed to be forever faithful to him without impinging on our free will.

Some might object to whether eternal faithfulness is compatible with free will. This is a fair question. While I cannot offer a comprehensive answer, a few elements of response are in order. First, there is no contradiction in terms between the two concepts. To make a statement that can be reduced to stating that we are free with respect to God and *not* free with respect to God would represent such a contradiction and amounts to nonsense. But to state, even if we don't understand how it can be done, that a man has the capacity to forever obey God and yet remain free with respect to him, is not a formal contradiction. The difficulty in such a statement resides in the mechanism necessary to make this possible. As long as we do not attempt to posit something that is inherently impossible, then the statement remains, in principle, valid. The challenge resides in creating a process that will produce the desired outcome. And that surely will not be a significant obstacle for an all-knowing and all-powerful God. The tension inherent to eternal faithfulness and free will is resolved in the act of conversion, which is the mechanism that grants God permission to deploy the process needed to transform us.

Second, in some limited sense it is possible to validate the possibility of eternal faithfulness and free will by evoking our own experience. Every human being has what I sometimes refer to as fault lines. Fault lines refer to those areas of our lives where we experience severe moral tensions and recurrent failings. The overall configuration of our personality, strengths and weaknesses, virtues and vices, and their respective intensity are unique to each person. Individual men and women may not have the same fault lines, and they may not be expressed in the same way, but everyone has them. It's just part and parcel of being fallen creatures.

The fact that all human beings experience these fault lines in unique ways is very important to note. For example, there are some individuals living in the inner city who are not in the least tempted to buy drugs simply because drug usage is not an issue for them. While such people may have other character fault lines, the urge to do drugs just isn't one of them. But the same people may well have fault lines in the area of money or sexuality. These individuals may in fact not be able to imagine a life without intense and overwhelming temptations in those areas. Now imagine the same men and women rebuilt from the ground up with no character fault lines whatsoever; individuals perfected in every way. Logically, it is conceivable that such individuals could live forever without ever experiencing moral failures. This is what God promises.

THE END GAME

I have suggested throughout this reflection that the fall was not inevitable. The creation narrative makes it abundantly clear that God never intended for humans to die. Suffering and death were introduced into human history as a consequence of Adam and Eve's act of disobedience. But if Adam and Eve had obeyed God and been allowed to live forever, what would have been the implications for God's long-term plan for humanity? Part of the argument put forward to support the necessity of the fall, is that it gave God the opportunity to demonstrate his grace in a way that would have been impossible otherwise. Fair enough. The primordial act of human disobedience did indeed necessitate the incarnation and the death of the Son of God to redeem humanity. In turn, this process opened the horizon on a glorified humanity. Without sin, however, there is logically no need for the incarnation, a crucified savior, and the glorification of the body. A timeline without original sin does seem to dramatically narrow the range of God's self-revelation and limit the spectrum of the future God promises to those who belong to him. While any such discussion will necessarily be speculative, the alternative scenario may not be quite as simple as it first appears.

As I point out at the end of chapter 4, there is no reason to believe that an unfallen race was destined to live forever in some sort of static condition; we should be cautious not to extrapolate unduly from humanity's present state. At the best of times, we only get but brief glimpses of the human race's full potential. For most of human history, humanity's progress has too often been halted or reversed by inadequate ideologies, cosmological and political, as well as its propensity to give in to its violent impulses. Is it even possible to imagine the endless marvels, cultural and scientific, that a species unfettered by bad ideology and wars could accomplish? To what heights could humanity rise if the members of such a species could live forever? It is fallen humanity that has proven to be radically dysfunctional and relentlessly self-destructive.

Since the creation account offers but an extremely limited horizon with respect to the alternative timeline, it is nearly impossible to imagine the course human history would have taken without the catastrophic disruption brought about by disobedience. While I recognize these limitations, there is no logical necessity to assume that human civilization would have remained perpetually frozen in some kind of static agrarian society. Such a scenario is extremely unlikely as even a fallen humanity armed with an adequate worldview will make, as the development of Western civilization demonstrates, extraordinary strides forward scientifically, technologically, and economically. I believe we can safely assume that an unfallen humanity would have experienced progress on a scale that would dwarf our greatest accomplishments. Isn't it possible that after eons of exponential growth, unhindered by a flawed nature, God might have had a plan that encompassed the two greatest exhibits of his present project for humanity, i.e., the incarnation and humanity's glorification?

As far as the incarnation is concerned, there is nothing in Scripture that requires a necessary association between the Son of God coming as a man and the plan of redemption. The crucifixion was a direct outcome of human sin. Without the primordial act of disobedience, there would have been no need for Christ's sacrificial death. In a world untainted by sin, we could therefore conceive of the incarnation, not as a precondition for the crucifixion, but as a way to reveal God to humanity, to bridge the infinite chasm between the infinite and the finite; Spirit and flesh. In Col 1:15, Paul writes, "He [Christ] is the image of the invisible God." The Apostle John is careful to highlight the revelatory function of the incarnation in the opening chapter of his gospel: "And the Word became flesh and lived among us, and we have seen his glory, the glory as of a father's only son, full of grace and truth" (1:14). In a glaring contrast to the hostility with which Jesus was received two thousand years ago, in an unfallen world, his coming would have been universally welcomed with joy, wonder, and gratitude. The incarnation of the Son of God would have served to reveal God the Father in a manner that would otherwise be impossible. "For in him all the fullness of God was pleased to dwell" (Col 1:19).

To come back to the potential for a new stage in the deployment of humanity in a sinless world, isn't it possible that at God's appointed time, he might have folded the Adamic universe (keep in mind that that universe would have likely been governed by the same laws of thermodynamics and would have therefore needed to be rebooted at some point) and rebuilt it for a new species of humans endowed with a glorified body? I realize that this is all speculation, but I'm exploring this thought simply to drive home the point that the incarnation and a glorified humanity are not necessarily contingent on the introduction of sin into the world. There is simply no necessary link between those two realities.

WORLDS INTERMINGLING

Scripture teaches that God will one day bring this universe to an abrupt end. The death of this world and the birth of a new one do not, however, imply a radical discontinuity between the two. I'm not, of course, suggesting some fundamental sameness between the two. If what Paul says about the contrast between the human body in its natural and its glorified state can be extended to the rest of the universe (1 Cor 15), it is likely that the new universe will, in the same way, be radically different from the old one.

There will, nonetheless, be some important points of continuity. First and most importantly, humanity remains. While human beings will have been transformed into blindingly glorious creatures, they will retain their distinct personalities and memories. Unlike Hinduism, which teaches that human beings are destined to be dissolved in an infinite sea of undifferentiated mass and energy, Christianity states that God intends for men and women to live forever as full-fledge individuals, perfected and glorified.

But the present and future worlds will be and are already linked in a different way as well. The two are intimately connected by our attitude toward Christ. Whether we accept or reject the Son of God will determine the basic shape (misshape?) of our eternal condition. Those who trust Christ will live; those who don't will perish (John 3:16; 1 Pet 2:4–10). The Apostle Paul goes further. Not only is our ultimate destiny determined by a decision made in the present space-time continuum, Paul states that the choices we make as Christians in this present reality will echo into the next:

> Now if anyone builds on the foundation with gold, silver, precious stones, wood, hay, straw—the work of each builder will become visible, for the Day will disclose it, because it will be revealed with fire, and the fire will test what sort of work each has done. If what has been built on the foundation survives, the builder will receive a reward. If the work is burned up, the builder will suffer loss; the builder will be saved, but only as through fire. (1 Cor 3:12–15)

Every single moment of our lives appears to be organically linked to eternity. As the French historian Pierre Chaunu wrote:

> We only live our own moments, but we live each one of those moments in the perspective of the present and of Eternity. It is for that reason that we can't afford to waste them, each one of these moments is invaluable, for each moment is linked to Eternity. I experience them in this space-time reality, for God and for Eternity.[6] God doesn't just grant us the dignity to impact this life. Our actions create ripples that will also extend into the eternal realm. What this will look like is anybody's guess. All I know is that whatever it turns out to be, it will then be of utmost importance to each one of us.[7]

There is something ominous about Chaunu's observation about the organic link that exists between this world and the next. As he notes, it implies that every moment given to us in this space-time continuum is invaluable. What does that mean for our lives right now? Since none of us have the capacity to use our time and resources in a perfectly efficient way, does that imply that we should live under a cloud of anxiety, inadequacy, and guilt? Absolutely not.

First of all, we have our Lord's encouraging assurance to those who take his yoke: "Take my yoke upon you, and learn from me; for I am gentle

---

6. "Nous ne vivons que nos instants, mais chacun de ces instants, nous les vivons, pour le temps et pour l'Éternité. Pour cette raison, nous ne pouvons pas nous permettre d'en gâcher un seul; tous les instants que nous vivons ont une valeur incommensurable puisqu'ils ont une valeur d'Éternité. Je les vis maintenant dans l'espace-temps, pour Dieu and pour l'Éternité" (Chaunu, *Le chemin des mages*, 106).

and humble in heart, and you will find rest for your souls. For my yoke is easy, and my burden is light" (Matt 11:29–30, cf. 1 John 5:3). The link that exists between this life and the kingdom is not meant to be a cause for despair. On the contrary, it is intended to be a source of joy, as it offers each one of us, regardless of our station in life, the opportunity to reach into ultimate reality simply by doing as best we can what God has entrusted us to do right now. Paul writes, "Whatever your task, put yourselves into it, as done for the Lord and not for your masters, since you know that from the Lord you will receive the inheritance as your reward; you serve the Lord Christ" (Col 3:23–24).

Second, we have the promise of the Holy Spirit, whose role is to permanently mark those who trust in Jesus Christ (2 Cor 1:22; 5:5; Gal 4:6; Eph 1:13), sanctify, shepherd, strengthen, and empower them to do what otherwise they would not be able to do (2 Thess 2:13; Eph 5:18; Rom 8:26; John 14:16–17, 26; 16:7, etc.). The promise of a "helper" (John 14:16) is extraordinary. It reminds us of a unique characteristic of the Christian faith. Christianity is the only religious ideology that both requires its adherents to adopt a rigorous lifestyle but also empowers them to do so. Christian discipleship does not in any way focus on meeting endless and ever more detailed rules to gain God's approval. His approval is already "in the bag" so to speak. It's a given. Those who believe in Jesus Christ are immediately adopted into his family. Christian discipleship is, at its core, a joyful, grateful, and open-ended response to God's grace.

Third, despite God's every effort to sustain and assist us, we will experience failures and setbacks. There will be periods during which we will experience the depths of despair and the crushing waves of discouragement. At times, the very presence of God will seem to have vanished, sending us into a free fall from which there will seem to be no recovery. On such occasions, we will ask whether all this misery is worth it. As long as the present age goes on, sin will continue to do what sin does. It is when the power of evil seems to be at its peak that we must remember and clutch to the two most fundamental truths found in Scripture: God is good, and he is all powerful.

When Christ ascended into the heavens forty days after his resurrection, the disciples were taken aback by the sudden and unexpected disappearance of their lord. In fact, it's only after "two men in white robes" urged them to get on with their lives that the disciples ended their short vigil. It's been two thousand years since Christ left. I think at this point, we may be justified in asking why it's been so long. When I pause to ponder the question, I am torn in two opposite directions.

As long as the present order continues, suffering, violence, wars, oppression, injustice, and death rule. For every day our Lord waits, thousands of little children are snuffed out before they even had a chance to take a breath or see their mother's smile. And with each passing day the wrath of God swells up like a nuclear mushroom. For every day our Lord waits, Christian men and women are brutalized, tortured, and put to death. Their only crime: their faith in Jesus Christ. And with each passing day God's wrath expands. For every day our Lord waits, people, good and bad, relentlessly die. I could think of a thousand reasons to hasten our Lord's return.

Surely, it would have been a good time to bring the curtain down when Jesus went up. Think of the headlines on the six o'clock news: "Jesus ascends! Curtain comes down! The end! Good night everybody."

But if we are going to think like this, why not back it up a little and bring the whole project to a screeching halt immediately after Adam and Eve's rebellion in the garden of Eden? That would have been a sure fire way to avoid the tsunami of misery that followed.

But that would not do. God had a project and was infinitely committed to it. God had envisioned the creation of a glorious people composed of men and women who would freely love and serve him for all eternity. That was God's ultimate intent. Everything else hinged upon this. God's commitment to this project was unconditional; his love for human beings, infinite.

While Christ's death and resurrection produced the necessary conditions for the redemption of humanity, it came at great cost. An action of infinite significance, motivated by infinite love, to meet an infinite need. It should be noted that the cost of humanity's salvation was the same for one person or one hundred billion. As Peter points out in his second epistle, that may well be at the root of the considerable hiatus between Christ's ascension and his return: "The Lord is not slow about his promise, as some think of slowness, but is patient with you, not wanting any to perish, but all to come to repentance" (2 Pet 3:9). If God is waiting to reveal the fullness of his kingdom, it is first and foremost to give more people the opportunity to come to the knowledge of Christ. The delay is a function of God's grace and mercy. I for one am grateful.

Two thousand years may seem like a long time to some, but as C. S. Lewis points out, in the big scheme of things, it's not really that significant:

> Compared with the development of man on this planet, the diffusion of Christianity over the human race seems to go like a flash of lightning—for two thousand years is almost nothing in the history of the universe. (Never forget that we are still "the early Christians." The present wicked and wasteful divisions

between us are, let us hope, a disease of infancy: we are still teething. The outer world, no doubt, thinks just the opposite. It thinks we are dying of old age. But it has thought that very often before. Again and again it has thought Christianity was dying, dying by persecutions from without and corruptions from within, by the rise of Mohammedanism, the rise of the physical sciences, the rise of great anti-Christian revolutionary movements. But every time the world was disappointed. Its first disappointment was over the crucifixion. The Man came to life again. In a sense—and I quite realise how frightfully unfair it must seem to them—that has been happening ever since. They keep on killing the thing that he started: and each time, just as they are patting down the earth on its grave, they suddenly hear that it is still alive and has even broken out in some new place. No wonder they hate us.)[7]

So perhaps Lewis is right. Maybe two thousand years isn't so bad after all. Who knows? Perhaps it will be three, perhaps four thousand years before Christ's return. I guess that's fine. While that realistically translates into seventy or eighty years for most of us before we are in *his* presence, can we realistically believe that God can endure human sinfulness for that long? If human sin were the only horizon available to God, I don't think he could, even for one instant, let alone a thousand years, allow human history to unfold. But the age of sinfulness is but one layer of reality in God's eternal perspective. Christ's sacrificial death opens an infinite horizon of grace (1 John 2:2) that allows God to frame all of human history, as hideous as it is, in the greater perspective of a justified and perfected humanity.

The death of Jesus Christ and the love of God transcend all time and space. Therein resides the ultimate resolution of the problem of evil.

---

7. Lewis, *Mere Christianity*, 221–22.

Bibliography

Aletti, Jean-Noël. "Rm. 7–25 encore une fois: Enjeux et propositions." *NTS* 48 (2002) 358–76.
Alonso-Schökel, Luis. "Sapiential and Covenant Themes in Genesis 2–3." In *Studies in Ancient Israelite Wisdom*, edited by James L. Crenshaw, 468–80. New York: Ktav, 1976.
Alter, Robert. *The Art of Biblical Narrative*. New York: Basic, 1981.
Antognazza, Maria Rosa. "Metaphysical Evil Revisited." In *New Essays on Leibniz's Theodicy*, edited by L. M. Jorgensen and Samuel Newlands, 112–34. Oxford: Oxford University Press, 2014.
Arendt, Hannah. *The Human Condition: A Study of the Central Dilemmas Facing Modern Man*. Garden City: Doubleday, 1959.
Asimov, Isaac. "Runaround." *Astounding Science Fiction*, March 1942.
Augustine. *Concerning the Nature of Good, Against the Manichaeans*. Minnesota: Lighthouse, 2018.
———. *Of True Religion*. Translated by J. H. S. Burley. South Bend, IN: Gateway, 1959.
———. *On the Holy Trinity, Doctrinal Treatises, Moral Treatises*. In vol. 3 of the *The Nicene and Post-Nicene Fathers*, series 1, edited by Philip Schaff, 1886–89. 14 vols. Repr. Peabody: Hendrickson, 1994.
Baker, John. "The Myth of Man's 'Fall': A Reappraisal." *ET* 92 (1981) 235–37.
Baker, Mark D. *Religious No More*. Downers Grove: InterVarsity, 1999.
Bastani, Hossein. "Iranians 'Least Anti-Semitic in the Mid-East.'" *BBC News*, May 16, 2014. http://www.bbc.com/news/world-middle-east-27438044.
Bauckham, Richard J. *Jude, 2 Peter*. Word Biblical Commentary. Waco, TX: Word, 1983.
Behe, Michael J. *Darwin's Black Box: The Biochemical Challenge to Evolution*. New York: Simon and Schuster, 1996.
Bibby, Reginald. *Restless Churches*. Toronto: Novalis, 2004.
Biddle, Mark E. *Missing the Mark: Sin and Its Consequences in Biblical Theology*. Nashville: Abingdon, 2005.
Blocher, Henri. *Evil and the Cross: An Analytical Look at the Problem of Pain*. Translated by David G. Preston. Grand Rapids: Kregel, 1994.
———. *In the Beginning: The Opening Chapters of Genesis*. Translated by David G. Preston. Downers Grove: InterVarsity, 1984.

———. *Original Sin: Illuminating the Riddle.* New Studies in Biblical Theology. Grand Rapids: Eerdmans, 1997.

Boersma, Hans "The Disappearance of Punishment: Metaphors, Models, and the Meaning of the Atonement." *Books & Culture,* March/April 2003. http://www.ctlibrary.com/bc/2003/marapr/16.32.html.

Bottéro, Jean. *La plus vieille religion en Mésopotamie.* Folio/histoire. Paris: Gamillard, 1998.

———. "Le Dieu de la bible." In *La plus belle histoire de Dieu: Qui est le Dieu de la bible?,* edited by Hélène Monsacré and Jean-Louis Schlegel, 15–46. Paris: Seuil, 1997.

———. *Mesopotamia.* Translated by Zainab Bahrani and Marc Van de Mieroop. Chicago: University of Chicago Press, 1992.

———. *Naissance de Dieu: La Bible et l'historien.* Paris: Gallimard, 1986.

———. *Religion in Ancient Mesopotamia.* Translated by Teresa Lavender Fagan. Chicago: University of Chicago Press, 2001.

Boyd, Gregory. *God at War.* Downers Grove: InterVarsity, 1997.

———. *Satan and the Problem of Evil.* Downers Grove: InterVarsity, 2001.

Brock, Sebastian. "Clothing Metaphors as a Means of Theological Expression in Syriac Tradition." In *Typus, Symbol, Allegorie bei den östlichen Vätern und ihren Parallelen im Mittelalter,* 11–34. Eichstätter Beiträge 4. Regensburg: Friedrich Pustet, 1981.

Brown, Francis, et al. *A Hebrew and English Lexicon of the Old Testament.* Oxford: Clarendon, 1906.

Bruce, F. F. *Romans.* Rev. ed. Tyndale New Testament Commentaries. Grand Rapids: InterVarsity, 1985.

Brueggemann, Walter. *Genesis.* Interpretation. Atlanta: John Knox, 1982.

———. *Theology of the Old Testament.* Minneapolis: Fortress, 1997.

Bullinger, E. W. *Figures of Speech Used in the Bible.* 1898. Reprint, Grand Rapids: Baker, 1968.

Campbell, Antony F., and Mark A. O'Brie. *Sources of the Pentateuch: Texts, Introductions, Annotations.* Minneapolis: Fortress, 1993.

Cassuto, Umberto. *The Documentary Hypothesis and the Composition of the Pentateuch: Eight Lectures.* Translated by Israel Abrahams. Jerusalem: Magnes, 1961.

Cenkner, William. "Hindu Understandings of Evil: From Tradition to Modern Thought." In *Evil and the Response of World Religion,* edited by William Cenkner, 130–41. St. Paul: Paragon, 1997.

Chaunu, Pierre. *Le chemin des mages: Entretiens avec Gérard Kuntz.* Paris: Presses bibliques universitaires, 1983.

———. *Le temps des réformes: La crise de la chrétienté, l'éclatement.* Paris: Fayard, 1975.

———. *Un futur sans avenir.* Histoire et population. Paris: Calmann-Lévy, 1979.

Chaunu, Pierre, and Jacques Renard. *La femme et Dieu.* Paris: Fayard, 2001.

Chesterton, G. K. *Orthodoxy.* New York: Dodd, Mead, & Company, 1908.

Clines, David J. A. "The Image of God in Man." *TB* 19 (1968) 53–103.

———. *The Theme of the Pentateuch.* JSOTS 10. Sheffield: JSOT, 1978.

Coleman, M. A. "Process Theology." In *GDT,* 709–11.

Copleston, Frederick. *A History of Philosophy.* Vol. 7. New York: Doubleday, 1963.

Curtis, Edward M. "Image of God (OT)." In *ABD,* 3:389–92.

Dalley, Stephanie. *Myths from Mesopotamia.* Oxford: Oxford University Press, 1989.

Damrosch, Leo. *Jean-Jacques Rousseau: Restless Genius*. Boston: Houghton Mifflin, 2005.
Darling, John. *Child-Centred Education and Its Critics*. London: Chapman, 1994.
Dawkins, Richard. *The God Delusion*. Boston: Houghton Mifflin, 2006.
Dennett, Daniel C. *Breaking the Spell*. New York: Viking, 2006.
Dintaman, Stephen. "The Spiritual Poverty of the Anabaptist Vision." *CGR* 10 (1992) 205–8.
D'Oro, Giuseppina, and James Connelly. "Robin George Collingwood." *The Stanford Encyclopedia of Philosophy*. First published January 2006; revised May 2010. http://plato.stanford.edu/archives/sum2010/entries/collingwood.
D'Souza, Dinesh. *God Forsaken*. Carol Stream: Tyndale House, 2012.
Dumont, Fernand. "Après le système Chrétien." In *L'incroyance au Québec*, edited by Gregory Baum, 187–92. Montreal: Fides, 1973.
Dunn, James D. G. *Romans 1–8*. Word Biblical Commentary. Dallas: Word, 1988.
Eareckson Tada, Joni. *Joni: An Unforgettable Story*. Grand Rapids: Zondervan, 2001.
———. "A Victory through Suffering." *Power to Change: Spirituality*. Available at https://sermons.faithlife.com/sermons/61184-joni-eareckson-tada.
Eliade, Mircea. *Myth and Reality*. Translated by Willard R. Trask. New York: Harper & Row, 1963.
Evans, G. R. *Augustine on Evil*. Cambridge: Cambridge University Press, 1982.
Feeney, John. "Humanity Is the Greatest Challenge." *BBC News*, November 5, 2007. http://news.bbc.co.uk/2/hi/science/nature/7078857.stm.
Fitzmyer, Joseph A. *Romans*. Anchor Bible. New York: Doubleday, 1993.
Foerster, Werner. "Diabolos." In *TDNT*, 2:75–79.
———. "Satanas." In *TDNT*, 7:152–56.
Frazer, J. G. *The Golden Bough: A Study in Magic and Religion*. 3rd ed. New York: Macmillan, 1935.
Gadamer, Hans-Georg. *Truth and Method*. 2nd ed. London: Continuum, 2004.
Garrett, Duane. *Rethinking Genesis: The Sources and Authorship of the First Book of the Pentateuch*. Grand Rapids: Baker, 1991.
Gesenius, W. *Gesenius' Hebrew Grammar*. Edited by E. Kautzsch. Translated by A. E. Cowley. 2nd ed. Oxford: Clarendon, 1960 [1910].
Gibert, Pierre. *Bible, mythes et récits de commencement*. Parole de Dieu. Paris: Seuil, 1986.
Gilbert, Pierre. "The Case of the Venus Flytrap: The Argument of Job." In *The Old Testament in the Life of God's People: Essays in Honor of Elmer A. Martens*, edited by Jon Isaak, 173–92. Winona Lake, IN: Eisenbrauns, 2009.
———. *Demons, Lies & Shadows: A Plea for a Return to Text and Reason*. Winnipeg: Kindred, 2008.
———. "Fighting Fire with Fire: Divine Nihilism in Ecclesiastes." *Direction* 40 (2011) 65–79.
———. "The Function of Imprecation in Israel's Eighth-Century Prophets." *Direction* 35 (2006) 44–58.
———. "Le motif imprécatoire chez les prophètes bibliques du 8e siècle A.C. à la lumière du Proche-Orient ancient." PhD diss., Université de Montréal, 1993.
Goldberg, David J. "Providence and the Problem of Evil in Jewish Thought." In *Evil and the Response of World Religion*, edited by William Cenkner, 32–42. St. Paul: Paragon, 1997.

Goldberg, Jeffrey. "Is It Time for the Jews to Leave Europe?" *Atlantic*, April 2015. http://www.theatlantic.com/magazine/archive/2015/04/is-it-time-for-the-jews-to-leave-europe/386279/.

Gordon, Robert P. "טוֹב (ṭwb)" In *NIDOTTE*, 2:353–57.

Grossman, Dave, and Loren W. Christensen. "On Sheep, Wolves, and Sheepdogs." In *On Combat: The Psychology and Physiology of Deadly Conflict in War and in Peace*, 181–86. Illinois: PPCT Research Publications, 2004.

Hamilton, Victor P. *The Book of Genesis Chapters 1–17*. New International Commentary on the Old Testament. Grand Rapids: Eerdmans, 1990.

Harris, Sam. *The End of Faith*. New York: Norton, 2004.

———. *Letter to a Christian Nation*. New York: Knopf, 2006.

Hartshorne, Charles. *The Divine Relativity*. New Haven: Yale University Press, 1948.

———. *A Natural Theology for Our Time*. La Salle, IL: Open Court, 1967.

Hasel, Gerhard F. "The Polemic Nature of the Genesis Cosmology." *EQ* 46 (1974) 81–102.

Hauerwas, Stanley. *Naming the Silences: God Medicine and the Problem of Suffering*. Grand Rapids: Eerdmans, 1990.

Heller, Eric. *The Importance of Nietzsche*. Chicago: University of Chicago Press, 1988.

Hick, John. *Evil and the God of Love*. New York: Harper & Row, 1966.

Hitchens, Christopher. *God Is Not Great*. New York: Twelve Hachette, 2007.

Horton, Robin. "African Traditional Thought and Western Science." *Africa* 37 (1967) 50–71, 155–87.

Jacobsen, Thorkild. *The Sumerian King List*. Assyriological Studies 11. Chicago: University of Chicago Press, 1939.

Jaki, Stanley L. *Cosmos and Creator*. Edinburgh: Scottish Academic, 1980.

Jewett, Robert. *Romans: A Commentary*. Hermeneia. Minneapolis: Fortress, 2007.

Kaplan, Stephen. "Three Levels of Evil in Advaita Vedanta and a Holographic Analogy." In *Evil and the Response of World Religion*, edited by William Cenkner, 116–29. St. Paul: Paragon, 1997.

Kaufmann, Yehezkel. *The Religion of Israel: From Its Beginnings to the Babylonian Exile*. Chicago: University of Chicago Press, 1960.

Keller, Timothy. *The Reason for God*. New York: Riverhead, 2008.

———. *Walking with God through Pain and Suffering*. New York: Dutton, 2013.

Kidner, Derek. *Genesis: An Introduction and Commentary*. Tyndale Old Testament Commentaries. London: Tyndale, 1967.

Kitchen, Kenneth A. *On the Reliability of the Old Testament*. Grand Rapids: Eerdmans, 2003.

Kushner, Harold S. *When Bad Things Happen to Good People*. New York: Schocken, 1981.

LaCocque, André. *The Trial of Innocence: Adam, Eve, and the Yahwist*. Eugene, OR: Cascade, 2006.

LaCocque, André, and Paul Ricoeur. *Thinking Biblically*. Translated by David Pellauer. Chicaco: University of Chicago Press, 1998.

Last, Jonathan V. *What to Expect When No One's Expecting*. New York: Encounter, 2014.

Leibniz, Gottfried W. *Essais de Théodicée sur la bonté de Dieu, la liberté de l'homme et l'origine du mal*. Paris: Flammarion, 1999 [1710].

Lewis, C. S. *The Abolition of Man*. New York: HarperCollins, 2001 [1944].

———. *An Experiment in Criticism*. Cambridge: Cambridge University Press, 1961.

———. "The Funeral of a Great Myth." In *Christian Reflections*, 82–93. Grand Rapids: Eerdmans, 1967.
———. *The Great Divorce*. London: Bles, 1946.
———. *Mere Christianity*. New York: HarperSanFrancisco, 2001 [1952].
———. *Perelandra*. New York: Macmillan, 1965 [1944].
———. *A Preface to Paradise Lost*. Oxford: Oxford University Press, 1942.
———. *The Problem of Pain*. New York: HarperSanFrancisco, 1996 [1940].
Maier, G. "How Did Moses Compose the Pentateuch?" *STJ* 1 (1993) 157–61.
Marshall, I. Howard. *Aspects of the Atonement: Cross and Resurrection in the Reconciling of God and Humanity*. London: Paternoster, 2007.
Martens, Elmer. *God's Design*. 4th ed. Eugene, OR: Wipf and Stock, 2015.
Martin, John, ed. *Moral Responsibility*. Ithaca: Cornell University Press, 1986.
Matthews, Victor H., and Don C. Benjamin. *Old Testament Parallels*. 2nd ed. New York: Paulist, 1997.
McKnight, Scot. *Jesus and His Death: Historiography, the Historical Jesus, and Atonement Theory*. Waco, TX: Baylor University Press, 2005.
McKnight, Scot, and Joseph B. Modica. *Jesus Is Lord: Caesar Is Not*. Downers Grove: IVP Academic, 2013.
Meyer, Stephen C. *Darwin's Doubt*. New York: HarperOne, 2013.
———. *Signature of the Cell*. New York: HarperOne, 2009.
Milton, John. *The Lost World of Genesis One*. Downers Grove: IVP Academic, 2009.
Moo, Douglas J. *The Epistle to the Romans*. New International Commentary on the New Testament. Grand Rapids: Eerdmans, 1996.
Mounce, Robert H. *Romans*. New American Commentary. Nashville: Broadman and Holman, 1995.
Murphy, Roland E. "Wisdom and Creation." *JBL* 104 (1985) 3–11.
Neiman, Susan. *Evil in Modern Thought: An Alternative History of Philosophy*. Princeton: Princeton University Press, 2002.
Newson, Carol A. "Genesis 2–3 and 1 Enoch 6–16: Two Myths of Origin and Their Ethical Implications." In *Shaking Heaven and Earth*, edited by Christine Roy Yoder et al., 7–22. Louisville: Westminster John Knox, 2005.
Nietzsche, Friedrich W. *The Will to Power*. New York: Random, 1967 [1901].
Oden, Robert A. "Myth and Mythology." In *ABD*, 4:945–56.
———. "Myth in the OT." In *ABD*, 4:956–60.
Osborne, Grant R. *The Hermeneutical Spiral*. 2nd ed. Downers Grove: InterVarsity, 2006.
———. *Romans*. IVP New Testament Commentaries. Downers Grove: IVP Academic, 2004.
Page, Sydney H. T. *Powers of Evil: A Biblical Study of Satan and Demons*. Grand Rapids: Baker, 1995.
Pasinya, L. M. "Le cadre littéraire de Genèse 1." *Biblica* 57 (1976) 225–42.
Peck, M. Scott. *People of the Lie*. New York: Simon & Shuster, 1983.
———. *The Road Less Traveled*. New York: Simon & Shuster, 1978.
Plantinga, Alvin. "Christian Philosophy at the End of the Twentieth Century." In *The Analytic Theist: An Alvin Plantinga Reader*, edited by James F. Sennett, 328–52. Grand Rapids: Eerdmans, 1998.
———. *God, Freedom, and Evil*. Grand Rapids: Eerdmans, 1989.
———. *The Nature of Necessity*. New York: Oxford University Press, 1974.

Plantinga, Cornelius. *Not the Way It's Supposed to Be: A Breviary of Sin*. Grand Rapids: Eerdmans, 1995.

Pritchard, James B. *Ancient Near Eastern Texts Relating to the Old Testament*. 3rd ed. Princeton: Princeton University Press, 1969.

Rad, Gerhard von. *Genesis: A Commentary*. Translated by John H. Marks. Rev. ed. Old Testament Library. Philadelphia: Westminster, 1972.

Ricoeur, Paul. *Le conflit des interprétations*. Paris: Seuil, 1969.

———. "'Original Sin': A Study in Meaning." In *Paul Ricoeur: The Conflict of Interpretations*, edited by Don Ihde. Evanston: Northwestern University Press, 1974.

———. *The Symbolism of Evil*. Translated by Emerson Buchanan. New York: Harper and Row, 1967.

Ritchie, Mark. *The Spirit of the Rainforest*. 2nd ed. Chicago: Island Lake, 1989.

Rodin, R. Scott. *Evil and Theodicy in the Theology of Karl Barth*. Issues in Systematic Theology 3. New York: Lang, 1997.

Rousseau, Jean-Jacques. *Emile; or, On Education*. Translated by Barbara Foxley. Aukland, NZ: Floating Press, 2009 [1762].

———. *The Social Contract and Discourses*. Translated by G. D. H. Cole. London: Dent, 1920.

Russel, Jeffrey B. *The Devil: Perceptions of Evil from Antiquity to Primitive Christianity*. Ithaca: Cornell University Press, 1977.

———. *Lucifer: The Devil in the Middle Ages*. Ithaca: Cornell University Press, 1984.

———. *Mephistopheles: The Devil in the Modern World*. Ithaca: Cornell University Press, 1986.

———. *Satan: The Early Christian Tradition*. Ithaca: Cornell University Press, 1981.

Rutledge, Fleming. *The Crucifixion: Understanding the Death of Jesus Christ*. Grand Rapids: Eerdmans, 2015.

Schleiermacher, Friedrich D. E. *The Christian Faith*. Edited by H. R. MacKintosh and J. S. Stewart. 2nd ed. Edinburgh: T. & T. Clark, 1999.

Seevers, Boyd V. "עָרוֹם (ʿārôm; ʿārōm)." In *NIDOTTE*, 3:532–33.

Seibert, Eric A. *Disturbing Divine Behavior*. Minneapolis: Fortress, 2009.

Seters, John Van. *Abraham in History and Tradition*. New Haven: Yale University Press, 1975.

———. *Prologue to History: The Yahwist as Historian in Genesis*. Louisville: Westminster John Knox, 1992.

Silva, Aldina da. *Une lecture de la théologie de genèse 37–50 à la lumière de la symbolique des vêtements et des rêves*. Montreal: Université de Montréal, 1991.

Smith, Mark S. *How Human Is God?* Collegeville: Liturgical, 2014.

Somayaji, Chitra. "Cancer Largely Due to Biological 'Bad Luck' Rather Than Behavior." *Bloomberg*, January 2, 2015. https://www.bloomberg.com/news/articles/2015-01-02/cancer-largely-due-to-biological-bad-luck-rather-than-behavior.

Speiser, E. A. *Genesis*. Anchor Bible. Garden City: Doubleday, 1964.

Stackhouse, John G. *Can God Be Trusted?* New York: Oxford University Press, 1998.

Stern, Harold S. "The Knowledge of Good and Evil." *VT* 8 (1958) 405–18.

Steyn, Mark. *After America*. Washington, DC: Regnery, 2011.

Stott, John R. W. *Romans*. The Bible Speaks Today. Downers Grove: InterVarsity, 1994.

Sweeney, Deborah, and Julia M. Asher-Greve. "On Nakedness, Nudity, and Gender in Egyptian and Mesopotamian Art." In *Images and Gender*, edited by S. Schroer, 125–76. Oriens Biblicus et Orientalis 220. Göttingen: Vandenhoeck & Ruprecht, 2006.

TenBruggencate, Jan. "'Ewa center tried in vain to help." Honoluluadvertiser.com, December 29, 2004. http://the.honoluluadvertiser.com/article/2004/Dec/29/ln/ln05p.html.

Thompson, J. A. "Genesis 1: Science? History? Theology?" *TSF Bulletin* 50 (1968) 12–23.

Thompson, Thomas L. *The Historicity of the Patriarchal Narratives: The Quest for the Historical Abraham*. Valley Forge, PA: Trinity, 2002.

Tillich, Paul. *Systematic Theology*. Vol. 1, *Reason and Revelation, Being and God*. Chicago: University of Chicago Press, 1951.

Toews, John E. *Romans*. Believers Church Bible Commentary. Scottdale, PA: Herald, 2004.

———. *The Story of Original Sin*. Eugene, OR: Pickwick, 2013.

Tooley, Michael. "The Problem of Evil." *The Stanford Encyclopedia of Philosophy*. Published September 2002; revised August 2009. http://plato.stanford.edu/archives/spr2010/entries/evil.

Tooley, Michael. "Does God Exist?" In *Knowledge of God*, 70–150. Great Debates in Philosophy. Malden, MA: Blackwell, 2008.

Tosato, Matteo, et al. "The Aging Process and Potential Interventions to Extend Life Expectancy." *Clinical Interventions in Aging* 2 (2007) 401–12.

Tylor, Edward B. *Primitive Culture*. 2 vols. New York: Harper and Row, 1958 [1871].

Vaux, Roland de. *Ancient Israel: Its Life and Institutions*. 2 vols. Translated by John McHugh. New York: McGraw-Hill, 1965.

Vajiragnana, Medagama. "A Theoretical Explanation of Evil in Theravada Buddhism." In *Evil and the Response of World Religion*, edited by William Cenkner, 99–108. St. Paul: Paragon, 1997.

Vanhoozer, Kevin J. *Is There a Meaning in This Text?* Grand Rapids: Zondervan, 1998.

Vawter, Bruce. *On Genesis: A New Reading*. Garden City: Doubleday, 1977.

Volf, Miroslav. *Exclusion and Embrace*. Nashville: Abingdon, 1996.

Weaver, J. Denny. *The Non-Violent Atonement*. 2nd ed. Grand Rapids: Eerdmans, 2011.

Wenham, Gordon. *Genesis 1–15*. Word Biblical Commentary. Waco, TX: Word, 1987.

Wenham, John. "Large Numbers in the Old Testament." *TB* 18 (1967) 2–36.

Westermann, Claus. *Genesis 1–11*. Translated by John J. Scullion. Minneapolis: Fortress, 1992.

Whitehead, Alfred North. *Process and Reality: An Essay in Cosmology*. Corrected ed. New York: Free Press, 1978.

Whitney, Barry L. *Theodicy: An Annotated Bibliography on the Problem of Evil, 1960–1991*. Bowling Green, OH: Philosophy Documentation Center, 1998.

Wilder, William N. "Illumination and Investiture: The Royal Significance of the Tree of Wisdom." *Westminster Theological Journal* 68 (2006) 51–69.

Willimon, William H. *Sighing for Eden*. Nashville: Abingdon, 1985.

Wright, N. T. *Evil and the Justice of God*. Downers Grove: InterVarsity, 2006.

———. *Surprised by Hope*. New York: HarperOne, 2008.

Yancey, Philip. "Chess Master. God Brings Victory Even from Our Bad Moves." *Christianity Today*, May 22, 2000.

———. *Where Is God When It Hurts?* Rev. ed. Grand Rapids: Zondervan, 1990 [1977].

———. "Ongoing Incarnation: Would Christmas Have Come Even If We Had Not Sinned?" *Christianity Today*, January 10, 2008. http://www.christianitytoday.com/ct/2008/january/20.72.html.

Young, Dwight. "The Incredible Regnal Spans of Kish I in the Sumerian King List." *JNES* 50 (1991) 23–35.